# WITNESS TO TRANSFORMATION
## REFUGEE INSIGHTS INTO NORTH KOREA

# WITNESS TO TRANSFORMATION
## REFUGEE INSIGHTS INTO NORTH KOREA

Stephan Haggard and Marcus Noland

PETERSON INSTITUTE FOR INTERNATIONAL ECONOMICS
Washington, DC

January 2011

**Stephan Haggard**, visiting fellow at the Peterson Institute, is the Lawrence and Sallye Krause Distinguished Professor at the Graduate School of International Relations and Pacific Studies, University of California, San Diego (UCSD). He is the author of *The Political Economy of the Asian Financial Crisis* (2000) and *Pathways from the Periphery: The Politics of Growth in the Newly Industrializing Countries* (1990) and coauthor of *The Political Economy of Democratic Transitions* (1995) and *Development, Democracy, and Welfare States* (2008) with Robert Kaufman and of *Famine in North Korea: Markets, Aid, and Reform* (2007) with Marcus Noland. He is a member of the Institute's Advisory Committee.

**Marcus Noland**, senior fellow, became deputy director of the Peterson Institute in September 2009. He has been associated with the Institute since 1985. He is concurrently a senior fellow at the East-West Center. He was a senior economist for international economics on the Council of Economic Advisers (1993–94); visiting professor at Yale University, Johns Hopkins University, the University of Southern California, Tokyo University, Saitama University (now the National Graduate Institute for Policy Studies), and the University of Ghana; and a visiting scholar at the Korea Development Institute. He is author, coauthor, or editor of *The Arab Economies in a Changing World* (2007), which was selected as Choice Outstanding Academic Title for 2007, *Famine in North Korea: Markets, Aid, and Reform* (2007), *Korea after Kim Jong-il* (2004), *Industrial Policy in an Era of Globalization: Lessons from Asia* (2003), *No More Bashing: Building a New Japan–United States Economic Relationship* (2001), *Avoiding the Apocalypse: The Future of the Two Koreas* (2000), which won the 2000–01 Ohira Memorial Award, and *Economic Integration of the Korean Peninsula* (1998).

**PETER G. PETERSON INSTITUTE
FOR INTERNATIONAL ECONOMICS**
1750 Massachusetts Avenue, NW
Washington, DC 20036-1903
(202) 328-9000   FAX: (202) 659-3225
www.piie.com

C. Fred Bergsten, *Director*
Edward A. Tureen, *Director of Publications,
Marketing, and Web Development*

*Typesetting by Susann Luetjen*
*Printing by United Book Press, Inc.*
*Cover photo: © Jean Chung*

Printed in the United States of America

13   12   11       5   4   3   2   1

**Library of Congress Cataloging-in-Publication Data**

Haggard, Stephan.
  Witness to transformation : refugee insights into North Korea / Stephan Haggard and Marcus Noland.
    p. cm.
  Includes bibliographical references and index.
  ISBN 978-0-88132-438-9
  1. Refugees—Korea (North) 2. Korea (North)—Economic conditions. 3. Korea (North)—Social conditions. 4. Korea (North)—Economic policy. 5. Korea (North) Social policy. I. Noland, Marcus, 1959– II. Title.
  HC470.2.H34 2011
  330.95193—dc22

                                    2010048990

*To our parents*

*Phyllis (1928–2009) and John Haggard*
*and*
*Mary Ann and Jess Noland*

# Contents

**Box**

# Preface

Throughout history, the Korean peninsula has been the scene of recurrent major power conflict. Korea's regrettable partition following the Second World War has created a remarkable "natural experiment" for social scientists. North and South Korea have not only pursued divergent development strategies but also pushed those strategies to extremes. South Korea adopted a capitalist system and went on to pioneer an outward-oriented development strategy, emphasizing international trade as a catalyst, as explored in a series of Institute publications including *Korea in the World Economy* (1993), *The Dynamics of Korean Economic Development* (1994), *Free Trade Between Korea and the United States?* (2001), and *Reforming Korea's Industrial Conglomerates* (2003). Over the past half century economic performance in South Korea has been nothing short of spectacular, and its political development has been as impressive, if not more so, transitioning from military authoritarianism to a fully contestable democracy in little more than a decade.

North Korea, in contrast, not only organized its economy through central planning but in doing so also created the world's most autarkic economy, a process examined in Marcus Noland's Ohira Award-winning book *Avoiding the Apocalypse: The Future of the Two Koreas* (2000) and *Korea After Kim Jong-il* (2004). During the 1990s, North Korea experienced one of the 20th century's worst famines, a catastrophe intimately linked to the nature of its political system, a totalitarian dynasty that has systematically denied its populace the most elemental human, civil, and political rights and that channels its meager resources into its military, even developing nuclear weapons.

The Korean peninsula remains a flashpoint of potentially monumental proportions. While South Korea deepens its linkages to the rest of the world, entering into free trade agreements with partners in Asia, Europe, and North America, North Korea remains remarkably closed to the world. Under such circumstances, analysts are pressed to develop innovative ways of penetrating the informational barrier. In this book, authors Stephan Haggard and Marcus Noland use two surveys of North Korean refugees, one conducted in China and the other in South Korea, both to illuminate the plight of the refugees and to explore the implications of their testimonies for North Korea's ongoing internal transformation. Haggard and Noland find that the rapid marketization of the economy over the past 15 years is better understood as a by-product of state failure rather than of conscious reform. They uncover the regime's extraordinary use of the penal system as an instrument to try to reestablish control. Their interviews suggest that the state's hostility to the market is well founded: Participants in market activities not only harbor more negative attitudes toward the regime than the general populace but also are more willing to communicate their dissenting views to others. From this analysis, Haggard and Noland develop an extensive set of policy recommendations both for economic engagement of North Korea and to address the refugee crisis itself, as well as the deeper issues of human rights abuses in North Korea.

The Peter G. Peterson Institute for International Economics is a private, nonprofit institution for the study and discussion of international economic policy. Its purpose is to analyze important issues in that area and to develop and communicate practical new approaches for dealing with them. The Institute is completely nonpartisan.

The Institute is funded by a highly diversified group of philanthropic foundations, private corporations, and interested individuals. About 35 percent of the Institute's resources in our latest fiscal year was provided by contributors outside the United States. This study was undertaken with support from the Smith Richardson Foundation, the MacArthur Foundation, and the Academy of Korean Studies.

The Institute's Board of Directors bears overall responsibilities for the Institute and gives general guidance and approval to its research program, including the identification of topics that are likely to become important over the medium run (one to three years) and that should be addressed by the Institute. The director, working closely with the staff and outside Advisory Committee, is responsible for the development of particular projects and makes the final decision to publish an individual study.

The Institute hopes that its studies and other activities will contribute to building a stronger foundation for international economic policy around the world. We invite readers of these publications to let us know how they think we can best accomplish this objective.

C. Fred Bergsten
Director
January 2011

# Acknowledgments

The core of the book consists of two large-scale surveys of North Korean refugees, the first conducted in China and the second in South Korea. The China survey was sponsored by an American nongovernmental organization (NGO), the US Committee for Human Rights in North Korea (later renamed the Committee for Human Rights in North Korea [HRNK]) while Noland was the chair of that group's research committee. Noland and others from HRNK participated in the design of the survey instrument together with Dr. Yoonok Chang of Hansei University, who was responsible for the implementation of the survey. The interviews were conducted in China by a team of volunteers trained by Dr. Chang from August 2004 to September 2005. Chang, Haggard, and Noland subsequently conducted the analysis of the survey results, which were published via HRNK as well as the academic journals cited in the references. The authors owe HRNK and Dr. Chang an enormous debt of gratitude for their essential roles in conducting this path-breaking work on which Haggard and Noland build.

The second survey of 300 refugees was conducted in South Korea in November 2008 with financial support of the Smith Richardson Foundation under the guidance of program officer Allan Song. The Smith Richardson Foundation Board originally suggested undertaking a second survey under more hospitable conditions to get at issues that were simply beyond the scope of the initial effort. Haggard and Noland designed the survey instrument, which was implemented through a South Korean organization, the Association of Supporters for Defecting North Korean Residents (ASDNKR). In particular, they would like to thank the director of ASDNKR, Mr. Chung Tae-ung, a former official at the refugee resettlement center operated by the Ministry of Unification (Hanawon), and Dr.

Daniel Pinkston, head of the International Crisis Center's Seoul office. The authors owe these two individuals an enormous debt for their steadfast efforts to see this project through to its conclusion. The subsequent analysis of these data and the writing of this book were further supported by the MacArthur Foundation's Asia Security Initiative and an Academy of Korean Studies Grant funded by the Korean Government (Ministry of Education, Science, and Technology), AKS-2007-CB-2001. Erik Weeks, Jennifer Lee, and Jiyeon Jeong provided extraordinary research assistance.

Preliminary results were presented at seminars hosted by the University of Toronto, the University of Hawaii, the Committee on Human Rights in North Korea, the Korea Development Institute, the (Japanese) National Graduate Institute for Policy Sciences (GRIPS), Princeton University, the KORUS House, and Yale University; Nicholas Eberstadt and David Hawk, in particular, provided extensive written comments on these preliminary papers. The manuscript was strengthened immensely by the commentary of participants in a study group sponsored by the Peterson Institute. Finally, Haggard and Noland appreciate the comments of Profs. Kim Byung-yeon, Andrei Lankov, Courtland Robinson, and You Jong-sung, who read the penultimate draft in its entirety. The authors bear responsibility for any remaining errors.

# North Korea

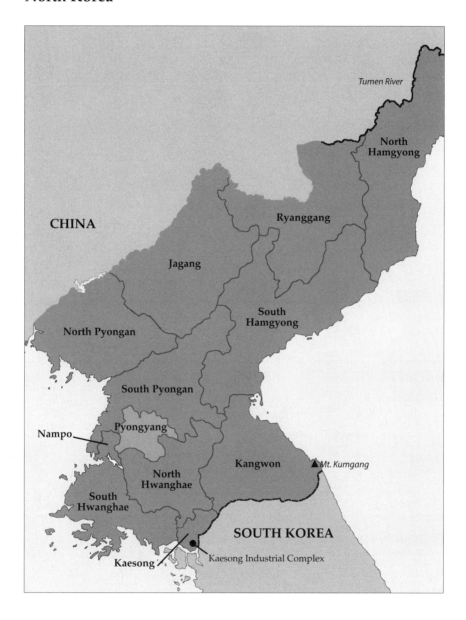

# 1

# Introduction

In the past century the Korean peninsula was conquered, colonized, partitioned, and devastated by civil war. While South Korea has emerged as an economic and political success story of the past 50 years, North Korea, repressive, truculent, and now nuclear-armed, stands as a political and economic anachronism in the midst of vibrant East Asia.

The attention showered on North Korea has focused largely on security issues. Pyongyang continues to drive high politics on the Korean peninsula and among the major powers in Northeast Asia. Much less energy has been focused on the internal economic and social changes that have occurred over the last two decades, changes with profound implications for the political future of the country, the prospects for economic reform, and the economic integration of the region. The reasons for this oversight are well known. Closed and opaque, North Korea poses profound analytic and informational as well as political and military challenges.

Yet an important resource on the changing political economy of North Korea remains relatively untapped. During the mid-1990s the country experienced one of the most destructive famines of the 20th century. As many as one million people—nearly 5 percent of the entire population—perished. One side effect of the famine, continuing food shortages, and political repression has been an ongoing exodus of refugees, primarily into China (see box 1.1). In addition to their heartbreaking stories of separation and survival, these refugees are witnesses to the deep and painful transformation of North Korea and thus a window into the country's future.

We approach the refugees using two lenses. First and foremost, they are an extraordinarily vulnerable population, and their current status and future prospects constitute a first-order humanitarian problem for the

## Box 1.1    How many refugees?

In October 2010, South Korean Minister of Unification Hyun In-taek estimated there were 100,000 North Koreans in China (Yonhap News Agency 2010). However, the precise number of North Koreans who have exited their country remains highly uncertain.

First, the number of border crossings and the number of North Koreans who have left the country are sometimes confused. The number of border crossings is by definition an overestimate of the number who have actually emigrated. In our survey conducted in China, 1 percent of the respondents preferred returning to North Korea permanently. However, many North Koreans temporarily return to North Korea, typically carrying money. Others have been forcibly deported.

Courtland Robinson (2010) has made the most systematic attempt to count North Korean refugees through a network of community contacts in the border region. He estimates that the number of refugees in China has dramatically declined since the peak of the famine and that in 2009 between 5,000 and 15,000 North Koreans were residing in the three Chinese provinces constituting the border region.

However, China does not allow North Koreans to seek asylum. As a result, North Koreans seeking to leave China do so via third countries such as Thailand, Vietnam, or Mongolia, and by definition exit the border region and drop out of this reporting network as a result. North Korean secret police and Chinese law enforcement agencies have reportedly cooperated in hunting down North Korean refugees throughout much of China, focusing on routes of escape to Indochina, as well as cities such as Guangdong, where ethnic Korean-Chinese may be hiding refugees (Asahi Shimbun 2010).

Apart from those attempting on-migration via third countries, significant numbers of North Koreans appear to be pooling in areas beyond the border region. With the Chinese economy growing robustly, Chinese attitudes toward illegal Asian migrant workers are relaxed, and North Korean counterfeiters are reportedly forging identity documents necessary to work in China (Carothers 2010, Good Friends 2010). The Committee for Human Rights in North Korea (2009) reports evidence of North Koreans in the sex industry in Shandong province, where there is a South Korean investment presence.

In principle, one could use North Korean censuses to extract an estimate of departures. But the published numbers are unreliable. In any event, substantial uncertainty surrounds how many people died in the 1990s famine, which sparked the surge in emigration.

How many refugees? Probably fewer than 100,000. But this number is nothing more than an educated guess.

international community. The Chinese government has refused to recognize those crossing the border from North Korea as refugees (terming them instead "economic migrants") and has forcibly repatriated those apprehended back into the hands of North Korean authorities. North Korea is a party to the International Covenant on Civil and Political Rights, which states unambiguously that "everyone shall be free to leave any country, including his own" (Article 12 (2)). However, North Korean law does not conform to this obligation. Those who "illegally" cross the border or help others to do so face stiff penalties on their return, ranging from incarceration in labor camps to the death penalty. Vulnerable to apprehension and incarceration by both Chinese and North Korean authorities, the refugees face the difficult choice of returning to North Korea, surviving at the margins of Chinese society, or taking on the risks of entering an emergent underground railway. These emerging networks seek to smuggle refugees across China to exit via air or sea or over land through Mongolia or Southeast Asia to permanent resettlement in South Korea or other countries.

The experiences of the refugees raise a number of important research and policy questions. Why and how exactly do the refugees leave? To what extent are they motivated by political as well as economic considerations? What are the sources of vulnerability in China, including not only fear of arrest but also the uncertainty of work and living arrangements and risks of outright abuse? Do refugees intend to remain in China, return to North Korea, or migrate to a third-country destination, and if so, where would they prefer to go?

An ongoing concern with all refugees is their ability to integrate into host countries, even when conditions are nominally hospitable. A growing literature on the acculturation of refugees in South Korea suggests that these problems are particularly profound in the case of North Koreans (Lankov 2006). Educated in a highly authoritarian and economically decaying state socialist system, North Koreans clearly have remarkable survival skills. Nonetheless, they may or may not possess the skills required to navigate an advanced industrial democracy even where the language barrier is (at least partially) neutralized, as in South Korea.

A particular problem is the psychology of the refugees; this human dimension of the refugees' plight is a recurrent theme in refugee testimony. These refugees suffer from anxiety and depression associated with the uncertainty of their circumstances and the loss of ties with North Korea. Yet we also find an enduring imprint of the traumas suffered in North Korea itself such as witnessing the starvation of family members or abuse at the hands of state authorities. These psychological problems resemble post-traumatic stress disorder in their severity and constitute an additional burden to successful assimilation.

A second reason for interest in the refugees is the more instrumental one already noted. North Korea is a notoriously closed society that not only seeks to control the flow of information into the country but exercises tight control over information flowing out as well. It is nearly impossible to conduct direct research on any aspect of North Korea. One exception—on which we and other researchers draw extensively—is data that international organizations and nongovernmental organizations (NGOs) have been allowed to collect, primarily on the food economy and to a lesser extent on public health and nutrition.[1] A second important exception consists of reports provided by South Korean NGOs, think tanks, and media that have cultivated networks of informants within North Korea.[2] These networks provide information ranging from data on market prices to local stories on current economic, social, and political conditions. These accounts are invaluable, yet they naturally suffer from the tremendous constraints placed on such information gathering and may be susceptible to other biases in coverage as well.

Memoirs, such as Kang Chol-hwan's harrowing *The Aquariums of Pyongyang*, and interviews with refugees thus provide an important window into life in North Korea, although this population is vulnerable to its own biases as we will discuss in more detail below. Such interviews may be more open-ended, including oral histories (Demick 2009, Hassig and Oh 2009, K. D. Lee et al. 2008, Lankov and Kim 2008), or take the form of structured surveys that permit statistical analysis of responses (Y. H. Lee 2007; Kim and Song 2008; K. D. Lee et al. 2008). This study takes the latter approach, drawing on two surveys, the first of 1,346 refugees living in China conducted from August 2004 to September 2005 and the second of a smaller sample of 300 refugees conducted in South Korea in November 2008.

The questions that might be asked of refugees are boundless, ranging from features of everyday life to their perceptions of the society, polity, and economy as a whole. We have necessarily taken a focused approach, looking primarily at economic and political issues. How did households adjust to the collapse of the socialist economy in the wake of the great famine? Did the massive humanitarian relief effort, primarily in the form of food aid, have effect? How did households adjust to the government's

---

1. For example, the UN Food and Agriculture Organization (FAO), at times jointly with the UN World Food Program (WFP), publishes special reports on crop and food assessment in North Korea. This was done continuously from 1995 to 2004 and most recently in late 2008. We also have access to assessments carried out by the WFP and a consortium of US NGOs in conjunction with the large-scale aid program finalized in 2008 (Anderson and Majarowitz 2008, WFP 2008). The American NGOs evaluated conditions in two provinces in the northwest, North Pyongan and Jagang, while the UN agencies were responsible for evaluating conditions in the rest of the country.

2. In particular, we and other researchers are indebted to Good Friends' Research Institute on North Korean Society, which produces *North Korea Today*, the newspaper *Daily NK*, the Network for North Korean Democracy and Human Rights' *NK In & Out*, and *Open News for North Korea*.

tentative approach to economic reform and its subsequent reversal after 2005?

Probing the nature of the political system is more complex. The authoritarian nature of the North Korean regime makes many of its core features opaque not only to outsiders but to most North Korean citizens as well. Nonetheless refugees can provide important insights into crucial issues such as attitudes toward the regime and its performance, the perceived prevalence of dissent, the strategies of the government in dealing with it, and what North Koreans think about the future of the political system, including reunification with the South.

This study is divided into four core chapters: the refugee experience itself (chapter 2); refugee insights into the economic transformation of the country, including the emergence of a de facto market sector (chapter 3); the state's increasing criminalization of this economic activity and the growing role of the country's sprawling penal system as an instrument for punishing economic crimes (chapter 4); and political attitudes and the prospects for dissent (chapter 5). In the remainder of this introduction, we outline briefly the evolution of the North Korean economic and political system in order to provide the context for the survey results we report. A second section discusses the nature of the surveys themselves as well as some of the well-known pitfalls of relying on refugee data.

## The Political Economy of North Korea, 1990–2010: A Brief Introduction

All of the refugees surveyed left North Korea after 1990. However, these 20 years mark a particularly tumultuous historical period for the country, encompassing a major famine, a leadership transition from Kim Il-sung to his son Kim Jong-il, and a period of cautious economic reform and opening from 1999 to 2002. The high point of this reform interlude was the North-South summit of 2000 between Kim Dae-jung and Kim Jong-il and the initiation of a major package of economic policy changes in 2002. These developments were quickly followed by the onset of the second nuclear crisis in 2002 and a period of "reform in reverse" beginning in 2005, punctuated by the recurrence of acute food shortages in 2008, political uncertainty associated with Kim Jong-il's health, and a disastrous currency reform at the end of 2009.

### Economic Developments I: Marketization from Below

Beginning in the mid-1980s, external shocks associated with deteriorating relations with the Soviet Union and the subsequent dissolution of the Soviet Union and the Eastern Bloc contributed to the implosion of North

Korea's industrial economy.[3] Deprived of industrial inputs, agricultural yields and output went into a secular decline. The government's response was to suppress consumption, initiating a "let's eat two meals a day" campaign in 1990 and cutting rations delivered by the public distribution system, the quantity rationing system from which urban residents, roughly two-thirds of the country, obtained their food.

It was not until the spring of 1995, with the famine already well under way, that North Korea appealed for external assistance. Aid was rapidly forthcoming, although the government impeded the normal assessment, monitoring, and evaluation functions of the relief organizations and thus no doubt undermined its effectiveness. Estimates vary widely, but the most sober academic research suggests that between 1994 and 1998, the famine killed 600,000 to 1 million people, or roughly 3 to 5 percent of the precrisis population (Goodkind and West 2001, S. Lee 2003). Certain groups and geographical areas, particularly the three northeastern provinces, were disproportionately affected and as a result probably generated the bulk of the country's refugees. Yet, although the famine had differential effects across regions and political and social strata, it was in the end a truly national trauma; virtually no segment of the population outside of the top elite completely escaped its effects. Pyongyang and the lower levels of the military and party were by no means spared from the tribulations of this so-called arduous march period.

With the state unable to play its traditional role as a provider of food, the socialist social contract broke down and households had to rely on their own efforts to secure food. As in all famine settings, our surveys show that households relied on a range of coping strategies, including increased informal work effort, compressed consumption, barter, foraging, remittances from relatives in the countryside, and purchase of food on emerging markets (chapter 3). Local institutions were also left to fend for themselves; government, party, and military entities and other work units resorted to these coping behaviors too, including barter and eventually monetized trade to secure food and other inputs.

The marketization that began with food gradually encompassed a broader range of goods and activities. Market activity built in part upon officially sanctioned farmers' markets and cottage industries, which were permitted from the mid-1980s to compensate for the shortage of consumer goods. But the market quickly encompassed forced sales of household items by liquidity-constrained households and gray-area activities by local government and party officials and enterprise managers, including the exploitation and stripping of state assets. There is evidence that the military as well as state and party functionaries were involved in this spontaneous marketization and decentralization process; indeed, precisely because of

---

3. This section draws on Haggard and Noland (2007) on the famine and its aftermath and Haggard and Noland (2008) on the evolution of the external sector.

its existing organization and resources such as trucks and fuel, the military was ideally situated to perform the role of middlemen distributors.

These crisis-driven adaptations resulted in considerable decentralization of both the agricultural and industrial sectors, with local political authorities and managers playing a more important role. The loosening of the central distribution mechanism was manifested in an increase in direct sales outlets, where these ventures sold directly to the public at noncontrolled prices, but both formal and informal markets also operated.

Given that many of the market activities that we can identify were technically illegal, corruption was also an inevitable concomitant of the process. Diversion of food aid during times of shortage yielded incredible rents, but our surveys show that corruption went far beyond the food economy to the operation of the entire market sector.

An important aspect of this "marketization from below" was an unprecedented level of internal movement. The government has long controlled internal movement as well as emigration. However, as standard distribution channels for both final goods and intermediates broke down, people and work units went on the move. The system fraying was sufficiently large that the state established an ad hoc penal system to handle the surge in criminalized coping behaviors, including internal movement for foraging and trade, as well as exit from the country (Noland 2000, Natsios 2002, Hawk 2003); we provide detailed survey evidence of this system in chapter 4.

It is difficult to quantify the scope of this marketization process over time, though one Western firm operating in North Korea during the 1990s estimated that as early as 1994 the unofficial economy was already nearly one-quarter the size of official output (Michell 1998). The one area where we can document the magnitude of the informal economy with a somewhat narrower margin of error is the food economy; this has been done in part by aggregate balance sheet exercises, such as those undertaken by us in Haggard and Noland (2007), which attempt to estimate the share of consumption that is likely to come from the market. Yet it is also partly confirmed by household focus group interviews conducted by the World Food Program (WFP) in North Korea. The general conclusion of this work is that at least for the nonprivileged classes, the market became the primary institutional mechanism for securing food in the late famine period and has continued to play that role since. Results reported in chapter 3 suggest that the public distribution system broke down rapidly in the early 1990s and that a significant number of households came to rely entirely on the market for food, with more than 40 percent of the respondents in the South Korea survey responding as such. Conversely, nearly half (46 percent) of the South Korea survey respondents indicated that all of their income was derived from market activities.

The implications of the famine spilled over into the external sector as individuals crossed the border into China, both on a more permanent basis and in order to trade. During the famine North Korea's trade with China increased, consisting of a complex mix of central government aid, more localized humanitarian efforts on the part of Korean-Chinese, and an expansion of barter and commercial trade. Famine-era exports included raw materials and foodstuffs that could be easily harvested, gathered, or fished, such as logs, mushrooms, or marine products. Imports from China came to include not only capital and intermediate goods associated with the official trade but also consumer goods and food that subsequently fed the emerging market economy. South Korea's trade also grew rapidly following the political thaw of the 2000 summit but was largely confined to a handful of enclave projects (the Mt. Kumgang tourism project and the Kaesong Industrial Complex).

The onset of the nuclear crisis in 2002 gave an unintended boost to North Korea's ties with China's booming economy. The crisis generated multilateral sanctions, an effective Japanese embargo, and US financial sanctions. In combination these developments had the unintended effect of linking North Korea more closely with China (Haggard and Noland 2010a). By 2010, North Korea's trade with China accounted for over 40 percent of the country's total trade.

## Economic Developments II: The State Responds

The North Korean regime's response to this "marketization from below" and increasing economic openness was both slow and ambivalent. During the peak of the famine and its immediate aftermath, the regime had little choice but to tolerate this new sphere of activity. It even decriminalized some of the market activities that had sprung up during the famine, for example, by permitting the growth of controlled markets.

By 1998, the economy had bottomed out and a slow process of recovery took hold. A variety of signs—including political ones that we take up below—suggested a willingness on the part of the government to tolerate the market and to undertake reforms. In July 2002, the government initiated a package of reforms that, while flawed in important respects, appeared unprecedented (Noland 2004). In the agricultural sector, the government introduced some incremental changes in the cooperative system to increase incentives for individual effort, for example, by narrowing the size of work teams so that they corresponded more closely to families and by regularizing access to private plots (Nam 2007). In the state-owned enterprise sector, managers were given somewhat greater discretion. However, as we show in chapter 3, these reforms had much less dramatic consequences on the ground than initial assessments suggested. One of the more striking findings of our surveys is just how little these purported reforms affected either the well-being of households or the operations of work units.

One objective of the reform was to change relative prices and wages in an attempt to align them with underlying scarcities. Food prices were increased sharply in an effort to reduce the extent of government subsidies and to encourage production. Certain classes of favored workers also enjoyed larger wage increases than others. But the North Korean reforms did not simply alter *relative* wages and prices; they also raised the overall price *level* by roughly 1,000 percent. Our interpretation is that this feature of the reform targeted the class of traders and black marketeers that had sprung up since the famine. Since traders maintain large cash holdings to run their businesses, the huge jump in the overall price level destroyed working capital; in this regard, the government-engineered change in the price level in 2002 foreshadowed the reversal of reform that was to follow and in retrospect bears a certain resemblance to the 2009 currency reform.

Quite apart from this one-off increase in the price level, the mishandled policy changes set off a more general inflation. North Korea experienced ongoing inflation estimated at well in excess of 100 percent a year in the three years following the July 2002 policy changes. Rapidly rising prices and deteriorating real incomes—even though the result of the design of the reform package—no doubt colored the regime's subsequent approach to economic policy.

Beginning in 2005, the government began to abandon the reforms and revert to more direct controls to revive the socialist sector, limit the sphere of private activity, and control inflation. This coincided with the elevation of Park Nam-ki to the position of economic policy director of the Korean Workers' Party, akin to finance minister, who allegedly vowed to end the "capitalist fantasy." An early indication of this new direction was the decision in August 2005 to reinstate the public distribution system and to ban private trading in grain. This was accompanied by anecdotal reports from the agricultural cooperatives of grain seizures in contravention to the existing rules over the distribution of output. At the same time the government was intervening in both the demand and supply sides of the grain market, it threatened to expel the foreign official and nongovernmental aid agencies that had maintained a presence in the country for a decade. In the end the government backed away from its expulsion threat, but the scope of operations of the relief groups was greatly curtailed, foreclosing an important source of information at a critical moment.

As in the past, the ability of the government to close markets and revive the state-administered food distribution system varied across the country, and eventually the government was forced to quietly shelve the policy. But such moves intensified again in the wake of floods in 2006 and particularly in 2007. The government increased production quotas on cooperative farmers, including through exactions earmarked for the military, cracked down on "embezzlement" and "corruption" on the part of cooperative managers, and placed new restrictions on private plots and cooperative leasing of land to redirect effort back into cooperative work.

Besides the weather and global price increases, this reversion to state controls no doubt played some role in the rapid inflation in food prices in 2008 and the most serious shortages since the famine of the mid-1990s (Haggard and Noland 2009a).

The postreform effort to reassert control over the market has not been limited to the food economy but has included a wider assault on market activity. The antimarket campaigns began with the imposition of escalating age restrictions on market traders in the fall of 2007, ultimately banning women under 40 from trading in general markets. From mid-January 2008 the government stepped up inspections on the general markets, or *jangmadang*, in an effort to control the range of goods offered and in late 2008 signaled that these markets would be allowed to open only once every ten days. In 2009, it revised the laws on economic planning, overturning reforms introduced in 2001 and 2002 and codifying top-down planning (IFES 2010). The reactionary tenor of government policy was probably most vividly represented by a revival of the 1950s Stalinist "Chollima" movement of Stakhanovite exhortation and the initiation of "speed-battle" mobilization campaigns.[4]

On November 30, 2009, the government introduced a surprise confiscatory currency reform aimed at crushing market activity and reviving orthodox socialism (Haggard and Noland 2010b). The regime was not coy about its intent to undercut the market and reconstitute the state socialist sector; these policy changes bear no resemblance to reform socialism. Earlier in August, North Korean leader Kim Jong-il's sister, Kim Kyong-hui, telegraphed the move in an essay extolling the superiority of central planning over the market and, consistent with the changes in the planning laws, even trashing the notion of giving enterprise managers greater autonomy in the context of a socialist economy. This basic motive—to crush the market and strengthen direct state control—was confirmed by central bank statements immediately after the reform.

The move set off chaos, precipitating civil disobedience and sporadic protests. These actions appear to have been relatively small and uncoordinated, but they led to haphazard backtracking on the part of the regime. An important party directive issued in May 2010 acknowledged that the government could not solve the food problem and that officials should allow retail markets to reopen, citizens to hold foreign exchange, and firms engaged in cross-border trade to operate more freely.

Park, the policy's reputed architect, and Premier Kim Yong-il even delivered a historically unparalleled apology to state officials and party cadre in February 2010.[5] While the signal of greater accountability could be

---

4. Not all the news was bad: One of the most obviously positive developments was the establishment of limited cell phone service via investment by an Egyptian firm, Orascom (Noland 2009a).

5. Kim subsequently resigned his position. Park's fate is less clear: According to various

welcomed, the subsequent scapegoating of Kim and Park may have been related less to the particulars of the currency conversion than to its self-inflicted nature. The "reform" was nakedly inconsistent with the regime's ascription of economic difficulties to foreign "hostile forces." Moreover, the currency conversion had potentially damaging implications for the hereditary succession because of the putative identification of the policy with Kim Jong-il's third son, Kim Jong-un. Yet to underscore the oddity of the situation, despite the fact that the reform was the year's single biggest economic event, it went unmentioned in the 2010 New Year's Day joint editorial of official publications, traditionally the cornerstone announcement of government policy, something akin to the State of the Union address.

The regime's recent resort to controls has also extended to cross-border trade, which poses profound challenges to the North Korean leadership. When economic circumstances deteriorate, the incentives rise to move into China either permanently or in search of business opportunities and food. Informal trade channels became important means of earning foreign exchange and financing much-needed imports. This movement and trade eroded the government's monopoly on information about the outside world. Cross-border trade has also come to include an array of communications and cultural products that directly undermine the government's monopoly on information: from small televisions capable of receiving Chinese broadcasts in border areas to South Korean videos and DVDs and even mobile phones. In chapter 5, we show that the availability of foreign sources of information, at least to refugees, was quite high and even tight controls did not completely deter it. In response to these developments, the government appears to be attempting to execute a highly controlled opening in which North Korean state organs would engage in cross-border commerce with China, but activities not controlled by the state would be quashed.

The most dramatic signal sent by the regime was the 2008 public execution of 15 people on charges of trafficking. But sentences have also been increased; single border crossings not related to South Korea or having political overtones that were previously overlooked now carry sentences of three years, with those found guilty of multiple crossings— even if not political—receiving sentences of up to ten years. More generally, we show in chapter 4 that the government stepped up punishments across the board for market-related activities, including but by no means limited to border crossing.

Government meddling and controls have even extended to two important showcase projects with South Korea. In 2009, the Mt. Kumgang tourism project was shut down after a North Korean guard killed a South Korean tourist. After negotiations failed to assure the South Korean

---

reports he is rumored to have been sent to a reeducation camp (along with his family), died while being interrogated, or been publicly executed.

government that such incidents would not recur, North Korea simply announced that it was seizing South Korean assets at Mt. Kumgang. Beginning in the fall of 2008, the regime also initiated a series of confrontations over the Kaesong Industrial Complex, including efforts to unilaterally adjust existing contracts and what amounted to a hostage-taking episode involving a South Korean manager.

In sum, the arc of economic development in North Korea over the last two decades begins with the external shocks of the early 1990s and the famine of mid-decade. These developments unleashed a vibrant process of marketization, which the regime initially accommodated to some extent. However, the government's support of these changes proved tentative and cautious, probably because of concerns about loss of economic and social control. After 2005, we find evidence of a gradual turn away from reform toward reestablishing the state socialist sector, albeit with limited success.

## Political Developments: The Dynamics of Authoritarian Rule in North Korea

The course of these economic developments is quite closely linked to features of North Korea's political system. The authoritarian nature of the North Korean political system has been well documented, and much of its standard characterization reflects important truths.[6] In 1955, founding leader Kim Il-sung proclaimed *Juche*, the national ideology. Typically translated as "self-reliance," North Korean ideology in fact combines a number of elements—extreme nationalism, Stalinism, Confucian dynasticism, even myths of racial purity—into a complex mix. The political order has also exhibited a high degree of personalism. Kim Il-sung was deified as the Great Leader and similar efforts have been made to canonize his son, Kim Jong-il (Dear Leader), who assumed the reins of political power when his father died in 1994.

Personalism was combined with an extreme, even caste-like social regimentation. The government classified the population—and kept dossiers on them—according to perceived political loyalty ("reliable," "wavering," "hostile") and even the political and social standing of parents and grandparents, as discussed further in chapter 2. The share of the citizenry deemed reliable is relatively small, on the order of one-quarter of the population, with a core political and military elite of perhaps 200,000, or roughly 1 percent of the population. As our surveys show, these political classifications continue to have implications for life chances.

The country is characterized by a complete absence of standard political freedoms or civil liberties. Independent political or social organiza-

6. Recent accounts from different perspectives include Hassig and Oh (2000), Cumings (2003), Lintner (2005), and Myers (2010).

tions are not weak in North Korea; they are virtually nonexistent. Any sign of political deviance, from listening to foreign radio broadcasts to singing South Korean songs to inadvertently sitting on a newspaper containing the photograph of the leader, can be subject to punishment. An unfortunate finding of our surveys is that the repressive apparatus, buttressed by a sprawling penal system, has in fact been quite effective at holding collective action, and even private expressions of discontent, at bay (chapter 4).

The regime maintains a network of political prison camps estimated to hold anywhere from 100,000 to 200,000 or more political prisoners. Death rates in these camps are high, and torture is practiced. Survivors' testimony suggests an extraordinarily high incidence of public executions, torture, and other forms of abuse, most notably deprivation of food and basic medical care. Yet as we show in some detail in chapter 4, the extent of the penal system is by no means exhausted by the infamous concentration camps. Given the authoritarian and state socialist nature of the system, the concept of crime—including economic crimes—is quite expansive. In addition to penitentiaries and jails designed to incarcerate criminals, a second network of smaller extrajudicial detention centers developed as an ad hoc response to coping behavior at the height of the famine, including unauthorized internal movement and crossing into China. Over time this system has become institutionalized, and refugees detained by it reported levels of abuse that appear similar to those experienced in the political prison camps.

Personalism does not imply the absence of functioning institutions, as is the case in some autocracies. Personal rule was historically supported by the Korean Workers' Party. From the late 1990s, however, the regime has relied more heavily on the military, the military-industrial complex, and the internal security apparatus. Extreme militarization has become an increasingly distinctive feature of both the political and economic systems, a particular feature of North Korean communism that has resulted from both external and internal developments.

Viewed with the benefit of hindsight, the division of the peninsula has proven surprisingly stable; the disaster of full-scale war has been avoided. Yet underneath this apparent stability is a history of sustained military competition, arms buildups, and recurrent crises. By standard statistical measures such as the share of the population under arms or the share of national income devoted to the military, North Korea is the world's most militarized society (Noland 2004, Bechtol 2007). The bulk of its million-strong army is forward-deployed along the demilitarized zone separating it from South Korea, a highly destabilizing military configuration.

In addition, the regime has periodically pursued a nuclear option and has sustained a well-developed missile program. These efforts have had the predictable effect of generating tension between North Korea, its neighbors, and particularly the United States, which in turn has complex domestic political ramifications in North Korea. Following a nuclear crisis in 1992–94, North Korea reached an agreement—the Agreed Framework—

that stabilized the country's external relations. The advent of the Kim Dae-jung government in South Korea also provided the foundations of détente on the peninsula. These developments, which overlapped with the onset and immediate aftermath of the famine, provided the external political foundations for the tentative reforms of the late 1990s and early 2000s.

Yet in 2002, American intelligence revealed that North Korea had sought to enrich uranium, setting in train an escalating conflict over the country's nuclear ambitions that remains unresolved to this day. Despite the creation of a multilateral process, the so-called Six Party Talks, North Korea effectively "broke out" of the nonproliferation regime by testing nuclear weapons in 2006 and again in 2009.

As external pressure on North Korea intensified under the George W. Bush administration, it triggered intense debates over economic priorities as well. Should the reforms be pushed forward or did the hostile external environment require a greater focus on building up the military-industrial complex (Carlin and Wit 2006)? These debates appear to have intensified following the imposition of sanctions beginning in 2005 and to ultimately have been resolved in favor of hardliners.

Yet the increasing role of the military and security apparatus in North Korean politics is not simply a result of self-imposed external constraints; it also reflects important internal dynamics that pre-date the second nuclear crisis. Partly as a result of his efforts to consolidate political control following the death of his father, Kim Jong-il naturally turned to the military as a key base of support. In 1998, he unveiled a new ideological doctrine of *Songun* or "military-first" politics that looked to the military not only as a central political institution but as a model of political and social discipline as well (Koh 2005). The perceived need to maintain internal security during the famine and the effective collapse of the state socialist sector no doubt also played a role. Our surveys reveal widespread perceptions that the military is favored, for example, in the distribution of food.

Beneath this picture of surprisingly durable authoritarian rule are important political subcurrents that we seek to explore through our surveys. Evidence of outright dissent is limited, and our surveys confirm the perception that such activities are limited and extraordinarily costly (chapter 5). Yet we can document increasing cynicism about the regime, particularly in the form of information on how North Koreans seek to get ahead through market-related activity. We are particularly interested in the de facto decentralization of the political economy: the extent to which work units, their managers, and workers are decoupled from the fraying central planning process and thus left increasingly on their own. Even though this process of decentralization does not constitute a frontal polit-ical challenge to the regime, it has unexplored consequences for the ability of the regime to continue on the state socialist path, for example, in the possible emergence of an independent "space" surrounding illicit market activity. The antireformist backlash of the post-2005 period is by no means the last chapter in North Korea's evolving political economy.

## Using Refugee Surveys: Sample Characteristics and Caveats

This study is based largely on two refugee surveys, although we have supplemented them with consideration of a number of others conducted by other researchers. The two surveys, while providing considerable information about both the refugees and life in North Korea, have some obvious limitations.[7]

Given that the two surveys are samples of convenience, they pose particular problems of inference. They do not constitute a random sample with respect to the refugee population. Neither we nor anyone else knows the underlying characteristics of that group in China, and while the South Korean government maintains data on the refugees, little are made public. Each sample might have been subject to idiosyncratic forms of bias as well. The characteristics of those who were able to get to South Korea might have been somewhat different from those who remained in China, for example, in having more developed networks, placing a higher value on political freedom, or having more marketable skills.

More generally, those who did not respond to our questions may be different from those who did. Nor do we have any way to control for the veracity of responses. For example, our collaborators in South Korea noted that North Korean refugees are prone to exaggerate their education, the jobs they held in the North, and their *songbun* or "official social status." Some respondents might also have misrepresented their ages since older defectors are known to face employment discrimination.

A second and arguably more important problem of inference has to do with our ability to draw any conclusions from refugee surveys about the wider North Korean population. If the refugees are unrepresentative, why do we believe that they can be used as a source of evidence for what is going on in North Korea? In one important sense, this criticism is unavoidably true; refugees are distinctive. However, there are techniques for controlling for at least some sources of this variation by comparing the distribution of known characteristics of the sample with the distribution of those characteristics in the North Korean population as a whole. We can even use these independent sources of information on the North Korean population to generate counterfactual projections of results from the refugee sample for the remaining resident population based on estimated statistical models.

No matter how careful we are in seeking to control for various demo-

---

7. More detail on the surveys and underlying methodology is provided in appendix A.

graphic characteristics of the population, however, there are undoubtedly some unobservable ways in which refugees are different from their compatriots. Some of these characteristics almost certainly introduce bias, or what social scientists call a selection problem. First, the refugees are characterized by a particular level of disaffection with the regime. Refugees are not typically a good barometer of political attitudes in their home countries; their views of politics are usually colored by resentments associated with the loss of power, status, and wealth. These factors are particularly potent with respect to exiled elites, as refugee communities from the White Russians in Paris to the Miami Cubans have demonstrated.

Even this problem is not altogether intractable, however. For example, we can control for possible sources of disaffection ex post just as we control for demographic and other markers by drawing on experiential factors on which we have evidence from the surveys, such as refugees' experiences during the famine or at the hands of political authorities. Nonetheless, it is difficult if not impossible to completely overcome the selection problem and associated sources of bias, such as the tendency to project their views onto others. For example, it is almost certainly the case that the refugees are characterized by some unobservable characteristics that set them apart from their compatriots, such as the willingness to take risks or some particular source of disaffection with the regime.

A final methodological problem we should note has to do with the history we have elaborated above. All survey research is plagued by the volatility of human opinion. We would expect this to be particularly the case where individuals are exposed to withering shocks: famine, food shortages, abrupt changes in policy, detention, and arrest.

To some extent, however, we actually benefit from the fact that major shocks, such as the famine, had very widespread effects, and we can control for others by asking questions about personal experiences. For example, we have divided the sample in various ways by time of departure. In analyzing the 2008 South Korea survey, we consider differences between pre- and post-reform subsamples, with those leaving in 2003 and after as the "postreform" group. For other purposes, we have divided the pre- and post-reform groups into two groups each, generating a total of four subperiods based on time of departure from North Korea: the famine era (those who left in 1998 or before, 25 percent of the sample), the immediate postfamine period (1999–2002, 25 percent of the sample), the reform period (2003–05, 35 percent of the sample), and a retrenchment group (2006 and after, 15 percent of the sample), during which some of the earlier reforms appear to have been reversed. These differences in time period cannot be treated as the equivalent of a "treatment effect" with respect to the events outlined. Nonetheless, the differences do provide some interesting insights into both continuity and change in the North Korean political economy.

In short, caveat lector! There is a long tradition of using refugee surveys to get information on closed societies, most notably with respect to the Soviet Union and China.[8] Those doing such work are probably more aware of the limitations of this work than its consumers. Nonetheless, we believe strongly that with appropriate caveats, we can learn interesting things by listening to the refugees. Testimony in the form of memoirs and unstructured interviews is much more elegant than what we present here, but structured surveys can also add value, particularly since they do allow us to control for at least some possible sources of bias.

---

8. Large-scale refugee interviews on the Soviet Union began with Bauer, Indeles, and Kluck-hohn (1956). See also Gregory Grossman's work on the "second economy" in the Soviet Union, including efforts to measure incomes from it (Grossman 1977, 1988), Gur Ofer and Joyce Pickersgill's use of emigrant families to analyze Soviet household economics (Ofer and Pickersgill 1980), and the large number of papers released under the auspices of a Berkeley-Duke program on the Second Economy in the USSR between 1985 and 1993. Jerome Cohen (1968) explored the early judicial process in postrevolutionary China through refugee interviews. For a review of other early survey efforts with respect to China, see Wong (1968).

# 2

# Perils of Refugee Life

As we argued in the introduction, our interest in the North Korean refugees is twofold: We are concerned about their material and psychological well-being—their experiences as refugees—as well as interested in the insights they might provide with respect to life in North Korea itself. This chapter takes up the first question, drawing primarily on the results of the China survey of 2004–05.

We first consider the reasons why refugees left North Korea and their living conditions in China. Despite the precariousness of their status and their preference for a decent life in North Korea, few plan on returning. Most envision themselves as temporarily residing in China before moving on to a third country. Yet there is evidence of considerable movement back and forth across the border, mostly people carrying money and food back to their extended family members in North Korea.

The refugee community in China is exposed to multiple sources of vulnerability, including not only fear of arrest but also the uncertainty of their work circumstances. We highlight the particular vulnerability of women to forms of abuse such as trafficking, which has recently received increasing attention (Hawk 2003, K. Lee 2006, Sheridan 2006, Committee for Human Rights in North Korea 2009, National Human Rights Commission of Korea 2010).

In the third section we extend this analysis of objective conditions to a consideration of the psychology of the refugees. A key finding, confirmed by more detailed clinical work in South Korea (Jeon 2000, Y. Lee et al. 2001), is that many North Korean refugees suffer severe psychological stress akin to post-traumatic stress disorder (PTSD). This distress is caused in part by the pressures of refugee life in China. As with refugees in other environments, the inhospitable nature of the initial host country is no doubt an important cause of the psychological problems we document.

In the fourth section we document how the refugees' distress not only is caused by their treatment in China but is also a result of the long shadow cast by the North Korean famine and abuses suffered at the hands of North Korean authorities, including with respect to the distribution of food. These traumas, in turn, affect the ability of the refugees to hold jobs in China and accumulate resources for on-migration. We also find some evidence that women are more vulnerable to psychological distress than men.

## Who Are the Refugees? A Demographic Profile

Before turning to the substantive questions of interest, it is important to consider the demographic profile of the refugees we interviewed. Except for a few notable differences between them, particularly with respect to the share of women respondents, the characteristics of the two survey samples are broadly similar. They also roughly mirror what we think we know about the North Korean adult population as a whole with the exception of the two differences described in appendix A: Members of lower-income classes and residents of the northeast provinces were both overrepresented, as has been the case with previous surveys conducted in both China and South Korea.[1]

Most of the respondents were prime age adults; the median age of the respondents was 38 years in the China survey and 43 in the South Korea survey, compared with 45 in the most recent census data released by the North Korean authorities (United Nations Statistics Division 2009).[2] In the China survey, females slightly outnumbered males, 52 to 48 percent. This is a bit unusual insofar as females account for more than three-quarters of North Koreans entering South Korea, and 63 percent of the respondents in the South Korea survey were female. According to the North Korean

---

1. A smaller survey conducted in South Korea (Y. H. Lee 2007) is an exception; the socioeconomic profile of respondents is decidedly more upscale. The Lee sample may be unrepresentative (as might be inferred by comparison to a larger survey conducted by Chon et al. 2007), or it might reflect the fact that North Koreans from more advantaged backgrounds have the resources and connections (either on their own or through family connections in South Korea) to get to South Korea more expeditiously. The South Korean–based respondents in B. Y. Kim (2010) similarly do not perceive themselves as poor. Under this second interpretation, the socioeconomic profile of our China sample may reflect a sample selection issue: More advantaged refugees spend less time in China and thus escape counting in our survey. However, this would not be the case for the South Korea survey, which also asks the amount of time spent in China before on-migrating. See Harden (2007). Interestingly, the northeastern provinces are less overrepresented in our surveys than in Y. H. Lee (2007).

2. The veracity of North Korean official statistics, including demographic data, is questionable. See Eberstadt (2007, chapter 2) for discussion.

**Table 2.1 Educational attainment of survey respondents and North Korean population** (percent)

| Level | China survey | South Korea survey | UN Census 2009 |
|---|---|---|---|
| Elementary | 43.9 | 1.1 | 5.3 |
| Secondary | 52.9 | 61.7 | 73.4 |
| Technical school (3 years or less) | 1.2 | 15.3 | 3.6 |
| Tertiary or higher | 1.2 | 21.6 | 17.7 |
| Other | 0.9 | 0.4 | n.a. |
| Total (ages 15–64) | 100 | 100 | 100 |

n.a. = not applicable

census, males make up 48 percent of the adult population and females account for 52 percent.

There are a number of possible explanations for this pattern. The conventional wisdom is that most refugees leaving North Korea in recent years have been female, reflected in the figures for those arriving in South Korea.[3] The comparatively higher share of males in the China survey may also reflect that it is the older of the two surveys and the conventional wisdom is that the female share has risen over the years, but given patterns of refugee settlement in South Korea it could be aberrant. However, it may also be that the patterns of exit, experiences in China, and on-migration via third countries are different for males and females. For example, if males tend to stay in China (and third countries) working and accumulating money, which is then transferred to their families or villages in North Korea, then even if the numbers of males and females leaving North Korea were equal, those entering South Korea would be disproportionately female.

North Korea's mandatory education includes a year of kindergarten, four years of primary school, and a six-year middle school; at that point (age 15–16), students come to the end of mandatory education and either exit the education system or are channeled into technical school (two to three years), college (four years) or university (four to six years), and from the latter on to postgraduate studies. The responses are self-reported, and if anything, the respondents would be expected to exaggerate their credentials. The China survey results appear to belie the regime's claims regarding the achievement of universal education goals (table 2.1). In the China survey, a slight majority of the sample reported high school education (53 percent), but 44 percent reported having only elementary

---

3. The average female share of defectors between 2000 and 2009 was 66 percent; the share has risen steadily from 43 percent in 2000 to 69 percent in 2005 to 77 percent in 2009 (see South Korean Ministry of Unification website, www.unikorea.go.kr [accessed on October 12, 2010]).

education (which would encompass junior high school in the US system). Educational attainment is somewhat higher in the South Korea survey, yet 62 percent reported having only a middle school education, approximately equivalent to graduating from high school in the United States. Another 15 percent reported that they had technical school training, with 22 percent having college training.[4] The higher rates of educational attainment among the South Korea–based survey respondents may reflect some selection bias. Those with higher education may either have access to more resources in North Korea or more efficiently accumulate resources in China, facilitating successful on-migration to South Korea.

In terms of occupation, most respondents in the China survey were laborers (56 percent), with farmers (35 percent) the next largest occupational group (table 2.2). Other reported occupations included student, trader, professional or technician, administrator, soldier, party official, and government official, although some of these were quite small in number. In the South Korea survey, the occupational status of the respondents is complicated somewhat by the large number of women in the sample; 17 percent of respondents reported that they were housewives. Looking only at those in the economically active population—excluding housewives, students, and retirees (in combination, just under one-quarter of the sample)—the largest category among those in the workforce was laborers (40 percent), followed by government workers (19 percent), merchants (8 percent, with nearly two-thirds of these women), and professionals, farmers, office workers, soldiers, and others (each between 5 and 7 percent).[5]

In both surveys, the pattern of responses is highly correlated with those to a question about the respondents' fathers' occupation, suggesting little occupational mobility between generations. In the China survey, there is some intergenerational mobility into the "technical" class, yet the class structure is remarkably stable: More than 90 percent of those surveyed who were laborers also had laborers as parents. Virtually all farmers had farmers

---

4. In the South Korea survey, a question about the education of the respondents' fathers suggests at least some increase in educational attainment over time: 17 percent reported that their fathers had only an elementary education compared with fewer than 2 percent of the respondents in the sample.

5. The small share of farmers in the sample is unusual compared with past surveys. However, 14 percent responded that their work unit was a state farm or cooperative, and in an answer to a different question, 133 respondents—fully 44 percent of the full sample—answered that they worked on a state farm or collective. A closer inspection of this group reveals that 54 of them, just over 40 percent, self-identify as "laborers." For our purposes, it is useful to separate out this entire group as "state farm or collective employees," even though they reflect a variety of different occupational categories (in addition to farmers and workers, this group includes 34 housewives, 11 administrative staff [professional, government, office worker/teacher], 6 merchants, 6 students, 2 soldiers, and 2 "other"). Because of their involvement in state farms and collectives and their probable rural location, we would expect them to constitute a distinct group.

**Table 2.2  Occupational profile of survey respondents and (economically active) North Korean population** (percent)

| China survey | | South Korea survey | | UN Census 2009 | |
|---|---|---|---|---|---|
| Professional | 1.6 | Professional | 7.1 | Professionals, technicians, and associate professionals | 11.3 |
| Farmer | 34.9 | Farmer | 7.1 | Market gardeners and crop growers | 28.1 |
| Trader/merchant | 1.7 | Trader/merchant | 7.9 | n.a. | n.a. |
| Laborer | 56.1 | Laborer | 40.1 | Craft and related trades workers, machine operators and assemblers, workers in elementary occupations, forestry and fisheries | 46.5 |
| Politician | 0.2 | Office worker/government | 18.9 | Senior officials and managers | 1.5 |
| Administrative worker | 1.4 | Teacher | 5.3 | Clerks, service, and sales workers | 7.1 |
| Soldier | 0.7 | Soldier | 5.7 | Military | 5.5 |
| Occupation not specified | 3.4 | Occupation not specified | 7.9 | Occupation not specified | 0.1 |
| Total | 100 | Total | 100 | All occupation groups | 100 |

n.a. = not applicable (no category comparable to "trader/merchant" category)

Note: Categories "student" (3.4 percent of the China survey and 7 percent of the South Korea survey) and "housewife" (17.3 percent of the South Korea survey) are excluded since only the working population is considered here. Some categories are not comparable due to differences in classification.

**Table 2.3    Provincial distribution of survey respondents and North Korean population** (percent)

| Province | China survey | South Korea survey | UN Census 2009 |
|---|---|---|---|
| North Hamgyong | 57.1 | 50.0 | 10.0 |
| South Hamgyong | 18.8 | 14.7 | 13.1 |
| Pyongyang | 2.3 | 7.0 | 13.9 |
| North Pyongan | 6.3 | 6.7 | 11.7 |
| South Pyongan | 0.6 | 4.0 | 17.4 |
| North Hwanghae | 1.1 | 2.7 | 9.1 |
| South Hwanghae | 0.7 | 3.3 | 9.9 |
| Ryanggang | 4.9 | 5.0 | 3.1 |
| Kangwon | 0.8 | 4.3 | 6.3 |
| Jagang | 7.2 | 2.3 | 5.6 |
| Other | 0.3 | n.a. | n.a. |
| Total | 100 | 100 | 100 |

n.a. = not applicable

Note: The figure of North Korean population includes only the civilian population.

as parents. The number of farmers or laborers whose parents did not come from these classes was trivial. Similarly, in the South Korea survey, the two dominant categories with respect to father's employment were those whose fathers were laborers (41 percent) or government-employed (22 percent); we see little intergenerational movement from these categories either. Apart from policies to limit certain types of mobility, this stability could also be implicit evidence of the low rate of economic growth and a relatively stagnant composition of output in North Korea.

Residents of the northeast provinces were overrepresented in both surveys, as has been the case with most previous surveys conducted in both China and South Korea (table 2.3). There are two main reasons for this bias. The more obvious is proximity (see map at front of the book). The eastern end of the Tumen River is relatively narrow at points and freezes during the winter. It has become the main route for egress. Travel within North Korea has historically required approval, subjecting those engaged in unauthorized travel to punishment. Those living near the border are less likely to be apprehended and punished while escaping.[6]

The second reason for the overrepresentation of refugees from the

---

6. One implication of this is that there may be a certain sample selection bias at work in the results: Since it is comparatively easier to exit from the northeast than from other parts of the country, refugees from this region may have relatively distinct attitudes or life experiences. This possibility is explored in the subsequent chapters.

northeast is that these provinces were the worst affected during the famine period and have remained economically depressed since. These provinces include mountainous, traditionally food-deprived areas, which are more lightly populated, but also highly urbanized industrial population centers on the east coast. North Korea is surprisingly industrialized and urbanized for a country at its level of development. At the outset of China's reforms in 1978, about 15 percent of the workforce was in industry. Vietnam had 12 percent of the workforce in industry when the government initiated reforms in that country in 1989. Just prior to the famine in 1993, by contrast, fully 37 percent of North Korea's labor force was in industry (Noland 2000, table 3.7), the result in part of Japanese industrial investments, predominantly in the northern part of the peninsula during the colonial era, and in part of a Stalinist development strategy that placed particular emphasis on heavy industry.

As food shortages became apparent in the early 1990s, the working classes of the industrial cities in the northeast were particularly vulnerable to the declining ability of the public distribution system to provide adequate rations (Smith 2005; Haggard and Noland 2007, chapter 2). These traditionally food-deprived provinces were highly dependent on the public distribution system, and famine appears to have started there well before it hit the rice-growing western provinces. During 1994, the North Korean government reportedly stopped sending food shipments to North and South Hamgyong and Ryanggang altogether.

It is important to underscore, however, that while this overweighting of the northeast limits the conclusions that can be drawn from the sample with respect to the North Korean population as a whole, it does not necessarily present a problem for drawing inferences about the North Korean refugee diaspora, which almost certainly is similarly skewed. In addition, multivariate regression techniques can be used to control for region to some extent since all provinces in the country, as well as the privileged capital city of Pyongyang, were represented among the respondents.

The North Korean regime has conducted a succession of classification exercises, and family background is a key determinant of life in North Korea (Hunter 1999).[7] The regime has divided the population into categories of reliable supporters, the basic masses, and the "impure class"; these are commonly called the "core" (*haek-sim-gye-cheung*), "wavering" (*dong-yo-gye-cheung*), and "hostile" (*juk-dae-gye-cheung*) classes.[8] In our sample,

---

7. "Core" supporters of the government, including party members, enjoy educational and employment preferences, are allowed to live in better-off areas, and have greater access to food and other material goods. Those with a "hostile" or disloyal profile, such as relatives of people who collaborated with the Japanese during the Japanese occupation, of those who went south during the Korean War, or of landowners, are subjected to a number of disadvantages, assigned to the worst schools, jobs, and localities, and sometimes sent to labor camps.

8. The North Korean classes are generally known to consist of "core group" or "core class"

the bulk of respondents were categorized as "wavering" (62 percent), with 11 percent "hostile" and 14 percent reporting that they did not know. Nonetheless, 14 percent reported being in the "core" group, suggesting that even privileged political status did not provide benefits adequate to deter migration. There is some evidence of a cross-generational downward drift in status, though the classification of respondents is statistically indistinguishable from that of their fathers. Taken as a whole, these indicators depict a relatively stagnant society. It is possible, however, that the relatively low education levels and lack of occupational or political mobility reflect the stunted opportunities for those who took the risk to migrate, including as a result of their political status.

A final set of demographic variables of importance are the date when respondents left North Korea, how much time they spent abroad before coming to South Korea, and how much time they have spent in South Korea. As noted in chapter 1, the date of exit is crucial in methodological terms, because it determines the relevant time frame for all of our retrospective questions, which are about conditions at the time they left North Korea. For some purposes it is useful to consider what we will call the pre- and post-reform subsamples, with those who left in 2003 and after being the postreform group; in both surveys these groups are of roughly equal size. In the case of the more recently conducted South Korea survey, we use a "four era" periodization: a "famine era" group (those who left in 1998 or before, roughly 25 percent of the sample), a "postfamine" group (1999–2002, again 25 percent), a "reform era" group (those who left between 2003 and 2005, 35 percent of the sample), and a "retrenchment era" group (2006 and after, 15 percent).

Duration outside North Korea, particularly time in South Korea, may also be important in shaping attitudes and perceptions. Those with the perspective of a long-time refugee in a third country or as a resident of South Korea may view North Korea very differently because of the tribulations of being a refugee (particularly in China) or socialization to alternative views of the country (particularly in South Korea). In the case of the China survey, the median length of time in China was two to three years, with nearly one-third of the sample having resided in China for more than

---

(*haek-sim-gun-jung* or *haek-sim-gye-cheung*), "basic group" or "wavering class" (*gibon-gun-jung* or *dong-yo-gye-cheung*), and "complex group" or "hostile class" (*bok-jab-gun-jung* or *juk-dae-gye-cheung*). Important to note is that these classifications are not communicated directly to citizens, although the most favored and disfavored classes are aware of their classifications by the treatment they receive. It has also been reported that the official terminologies used by the local police are different from the ones above; these terminologies are "basic group" (*gibon-gun-jung*), "complex group" (*bok-jab-han-gun-jung*), and "the remaining elements of the hostile class" (*juk-dae-gye-geup-jan-yeo-bun*). For the purpose of our analysis, we used in our survey the terminologies that are colloquially used and understood among the North Korean people: "core" (*haek-sim-gun-jung*), "basic" (*gibon-gye-cheung*), and "people needing reeducation" (*gyo-yang-dae-sang*).

three years. In the South Korea survey, the median time spent in China or other third countries before reaching South Korea was three years, and the median time spent in South Korea was four years and outside North Korea was six years. It is possible that the responses of those who have been outside North Korea for an extended period are less reliable due to faulty memories. However, our attempts to explore whether time outside North Korea or in South Korea had a significant impact on the pattern of responses, at least with respect to fact-based questions (as distinct from normative opinions), did not uncover systematic memory bias.

## Leaving North Korea, Coming to China

The decision to escape North Korea is not a trivial one, particularly given the harsh penalties on both sides of the border. Refugees consider leaving their homeland for diverse reasons, some having to do with inclination ("push" factors), others with information on opportunities in the target country ("pull" factors). But even if there are good reasons to cross the border, migration requires resources and planning and is rarely done without some kind of support, be it from friends, family, or experienced traffickers motivated by financial gain, religious conviction, or political fervor. Such networks and connections enable refugees to leave in the first place and provide them with at least some hope of sustaining themselves on the other side of the border.

### Legal Risks

Before turning to the push and pull factors that are generating this flow of refugees, it is important to understand the legal risks North Korean refugees face. Those who "illegally" cross the border or help others to do so face stiff penalties on their return. However, the severity of punishment has oscillated over time. Periods of greater accommodation—and milder punishment—have been followed by harsh crackdowns and increased punishment, including the death penalty.

Historically, unauthorized departure was regarded as an "act of treason" and put defectors at risk of capital punishment. Of necessity, these draconian measures were relaxed during the famine as the movement of refugees accelerated rapidly. Prior to changes in the North Korean penal code in 2004, a person who illegally crossed "a frontier of the Republic" nonetheless typically faced a sentence of up to three years in a *kwan-li-so*, the notorious political penal-labor camps where conditions are abysmal, torture is practiced, and death rates are high (Hawk 2003).

Several factors influenced the severity of the actual punishment meted out to North Koreans repatriated from China, however. These included the number of times the person had been to China, their background, and whether their movement into China had a political motivation. Those who did not appear politically dangerous were sent to newly established labor training camps, where they would spend between three months and three years in forced labor (see chapter 4).

Those detained who are classified as "political offenders" face more severe penalties. The law criminalizes defection and attempted defection, including the attempt to gain entry to a foreign diplomatic facility for the purpose of seeking political asylum. Individuals who cross the border with the purpose of defecting or seeking asylum in a third country are subject to a minimum of five years of "labor correction." In "serious" cases, defectors or asylum seekers are sentenced to indefinite terms of imprisonment and forced labor, confiscation of property, or death. Because of the regime's emphasis on racial purity (Myers 2010), miscegenation is also treated brutally. Women who are suspected of having become pregnant in China are subject to forced abortions, and in other cases, infanticide is practiced.

Facilitating exit is also a crime. Under Article 118 of the criminal code, an official with the "frontier administration" who helps "someone to violate a frontier" faces sentences of between two and seven years in one of the country's political prison camps. Private "traffickers" also meet harsh fates, including summary execution.

These risks are compounded because of the stance of the Chinese government (Kurlantzick and Mason 2006). According to the South Korean Ministry of Unification, a secret agreement was signed between China and North Korea in the early 1960s governing security in the border area. In 1986, another bilateral agreement was signed calling for the return of North Koreans and laying out security protocols. As a result, North Koreans in China are denied their right to seek and enjoy asylum from persecution. Although China is a party to the 1951 Convention Relating to the Status of Refugees (the 1951 Refugee Convention, for short), it is virtually impossible for North Koreans to access refugee determination procedures through the United Nations High Commissioner for Refugees (UNHCR) or be afforded protection as a group. According to several reports Amnesty International has received from nongovernmental organizations (NGOs) and contacts in Japan, South Korea, and the United States, China regularly returns North Koreans to their country of origin without giving them the opportunity to claim asylum and without even the pretense of an objective determination with respect to their fate once returned. Moreover, there are credible reports of torture in the Chinese detention facilities (Amnesty International 2000, 2001, 2004; K. Lee 2006, 53; Muico 2007). The Chinese government has also arrested and imprisoned NGO activists—most of whom are South Koreans or Japanese nationals—and others who have helped North Koreans seeking to leave China and reach South Korea or other final destinations.

The 2004 penal code appears to have codified the differential treatment between economic refugees and those deemed political, who are still vulnerable to charges of treason (S. A. Kim 2006). A defector who is sent back to North Korea is subject to interrogation and investigation by the city- or country-level representative of the National Security Agency (NSA). If the NSA concludes that the defector crossed the border for economic reasons, the new code stipulates sentences of up to two years of "labor correction." The government even signaled the promise of a pardon under the 2004 penal code, and several NGOs operating in the region confirmed that punishments became less severe than in the past. Changes in the legal code relaxed treatment for pregnant women, though in practice these protocols are breached, and forced abortions continue to be reported (K. Lee 2006).

Although coming after the date of exit of most of the refugees in our sample, the government began much tighter surveillance of the border beginning in 2008, conducting a number of sweeps and localized campaigns to identify traffickers and those involved in illicit cross-border trade. The most dramatic signal in this regard was the public execution of 15 people, 13 of them women, in Onsung on February 20, 2008 on charges of trafficking. But sentences have also been increased; single border crossings not related to South Korea or having political overtones that were previously overlooked now carry sentences of three years. Those found guilty of multiple crossings—even if not political—receive sentences of up to ten years. These efforts only accelerated following the currency reform of November 30, 2009, which wreaked economic havoc and once again increased incentives to emigrate, trade, and gain access to foreign exchange (Demick 2010).

Unfortunately, Chinese authorities appear to have cooperated in these recent efforts to limit border crossing, no doubt from their own concerns about how deteriorating economic and political conditions in North Korea would influence the influx of refugees. Chinese authorities have recently built border patrol stations and cooperated with North Korean authorities in tracking down refugees who have moved beyond the border areas, including through monitoring of cell phone usage (Y. K. Kim 2010).

## Push Factors

Over the years, the predominant motivation for North Koreans deciding to cross the border into China has fluctuated somewhat. Early interviews with refugees from the famine period and immediately after found not surprisingly that hunger and the search for food was a major push factor (Good Friends 1999, 14). By 2002, however, a Human Rights Watch report found that hunger was just one of the motives for flight; others included loss of status, frustration over lack of opportunities, political persecution due to family history, and the wish to live in similar conditions as North Koreans living outside North Korea (Human Rights Watch 2002).

**Table 2.4   Main motive behind leaving North Korea**
           (percent)

| Motive | China survey | South Korea survey |
|---|---|---|
| Economic conditions | 94.7 | 56.7 |
| Political freedom | 1.8 | 27.0 |
| Religious freedom | 0.2 | 1.0 |
| Fear (afraid of doing anything wrong) | 1.8 | 8.0 |
| Other | 1.6 | 7.3 |
| Total | 100 | 100 |

Following others who had already left was yet another motive cited by refugees debriefed in South Korea (K. Lee 2006, table 1).

The refugees in our China survey were asked whether they left for economic, political, religious, or "other" reasons (table 2.4). For them, the economy was the overwhelming reason for leaving North Korea (95 percent). Political reasons were a distant second (less than 2 percent), with only 0.2 percent citing religion. This pattern of responses would appear to confirm the Chinese government's claim that the North Koreans are "economic migrants" rather than refugees fearing persecution. However, as economic circumstances in a state socialist regime such as North Korea are closely tied to political characteristics of the regime and restrictions on private activity, we should be cautious in drawing a sharp line between "economic" and "political" motives. Indeed, nearly 10 percent of the respondents reported having been incarcerated, and as we show in chapter 4, there is a correlation between participation in the market and arrest and confinement. Moreover, the fact that the regime penalizes exit and incarcerates returnees raises the question of whether North Koreans in China have a prima facie case for refugee status; we take up this important legal issue in chapter 6.

The question about motivations was one of the few common questions in our surveys that generated quite disparate responses between the two samples. In the South Korea survey, economic conditions still dominated as a motive, with over 57 percent reporting that as the dominant factor in their decision to leave, but 27 percent of respondents cited political motives and another 8 percent listed fear, which no doubt encompasses concerns about the risks of repression (table 2.4).

What might account for these differences between the two surveys? One explanation may be differences across the two surveys in the respondents' dates of departure. A larger share of the respondents in the earlier China-based survey left during the famine period and its immediate aftermath, when economic conditions were quite naturally a dominant consideration. This interpretation is consistent with the South Korea–based survey, in which the share citing political motives rose monotonically across the four eras of departure: lowest in the famine era and spiking in the most recent retrenchment phase.

Sample selection effects represent another possible explanation. The South Korea survey had a higher share of respondents from relatively elite backgrounds, and such respondents may have been more likely to both cite political as opposed to economic motivations and have the wherewithal to actually make it to South Korea or other democracies. Those staying in China, by contrast, may have been more motivated by economic than political or religious concerns (religious motivations did not figure prominently in either sample).

A third possibility is that the location of the refugees may have influenced their responses. Those living in South Korea may have retrospectively put marginally more weight on political calculations because they came to have an enhanced appreciation for how badly their rights were suppressed in North Korea, because such political motives are regarded as more "politically correct" in their new environment, or because citing such a motive could be regarded as a face-saving way to avoid admitting their poverty in North Korea. Those who remained in China, by contrast, remained economically vulnerable as we will see and may therefore put more weight on those factors. Ultimately, the two responses may not be entirely distinct if bad governance causes economic decay.

These questions about motives for departure cannot be resolved definitively, in part because the overwhelming share of those citing economic motives in the China sample makes it difficult to model responses in that survey. The South Korea sample, however, shows more variance and thus allows us to model the propensity to cite political motives as a function of other factors. In Haggard and Noland (2010b) we reported multivariate probit regressions that show that apart from those classified as politically hostile or having been detained by the political police (*bo-wi-bu*), respondents identifying political reasons for departure are disproportionately college educated and from Pyongyang—in short, members of the elite. (We return to the issue of elite disaffection in chapter 5.) Statistically, the evidence is mixed about whether time spent outside North Korea or in South Korea matters; the influence of "socialization" appears modest at best. If another survey of refugees were now conducted in China, the results might indicate a greater propensity to cite political motives.

## Pull Factors

How did North Koreans hear about opportunities and conditions in China? Historically North Koreans have suffered under near total state control of information flows and suppression of information either about or from the outside world, although as we show in chapter 5 this informational barrier is eroding. The tuners in domestically produced radios and televisions are set to receive only officially sanctioned frequencies, although a lively black market exists in retrofitting these with new, more flexible tuners. Refugee testimonies indicated that North Koreans who own radios or television sets are often monitored to ensure that they do not listen to South Korean or Chinese radio broadcasts or see "illegal" foreign television programs. News stories in the official radio and television broadcasts obviously reflect official positions and propaganda efforts and no doubt limit any information that might encourage emigration, such as images of foreign prosperity.

We asked the refugees in the China survey what their source of information was about China prior to departure: word of mouth, media, books and videos, or simply that they didn't have information. It is not surprising that for a vast majority of the refugees (89 percent) "word of mouth" was their primary source of information, no doubt including a mix of actual experiences, rumor, and myth.[9] Remarkably, 5 percent admitted that they had little information on China before launching on such a life-changing exodus.

### The Mechanics of Escape

How, precisely, do people get out of North Korea? In the China survey, respondents were asked whether they received help getting out of the country, and three-quarters said they did. Of these, slightly more than half (52 percent) reported that they had paid for assistance—suggesting that bribery of officials and/or the emergence of a group of brokers or "coyotes" plays a large role in escape. The presence of corruption and of an underground engaged in such politically risky business is suggestive of broader changes in the North Korean political economy, as we show in more detail in chapter 3, although the recent crackdown has made these activities much more risky.

The second most frequent response for sources of help was "other" (46 percent), presumably family or friends who assisted in the escape. Although it is often thought that missionaries and NGOs are playing a major role in the underground railway getting out of North Korea, only 2 percent—a total of 17 respondents—reported that these groups helped them directly in getting out of North Korea. But once in China these groups play a larger role in the refugees' lives as demonstrated below.

## Vulnerability

An important question is the stability of the North Korean community in China and their intentions with respect to staying, moving to third countries, or going back to North Korea. Nearly one-third of respondents in

---

9. According to K. Lee (2006) some refugees from Pyongyang and Hamheung debriefed in South Korea reported watching South Korean television via satellite dishes installed on top of high-rise apartment buildings. These cases would appear relatively atypical, however.

**Table 2.5   Length of time in China** (percent)

| Period | China survey (at time of survey) | South Korea survey (total time in China, approximate) |
|---|---|---|
| Less than 6 months | 5.2 | 20.3 |
| 6 to 12 months | 11.5 | |
| 1 to 2 years | 15.4 | 25.0 |
| 2 to 3 years | 35.9 | 10.0 |
| More than 3 years | 32.0 | 44.7 |
| Total | 100 | 100 |

the China survey had been there for three years or more (table 2.5). Here interpretation of the data is complicated by the fact that the demographics of the migrants (and perhaps their motivations, capacities, and expectations) have changed over time. For most migrants, residence in the border region, where our China survey was conducted, is not their ultimate goal: It is a temporary residence until they can accumulate the resources to continue on to some preferred location for permanent settlement.

Yet while most migrants do not want to reside permanently in China, their "transitional" stay prior to on-migration may be protracted. Refugees who have been in China for a long period may simply have integrated successfully, or they may have dependents such as small children or disabilities that have impeded their on-migration out of the border region. These considerations underscore the complexity of the migration process.

When asked whether they were holding a job, only 22 percent of the refugees in China said that they were. Low levels of employment reported by the refugees may stem from a multiplicity of factors, including lack of skills and language. But the low level of employment and exploitative conditions among those who are employed are related to the vulnerability of the refugees with respect to the public authorities. To be able to work in China, one needs a *hukou* (residence permit) or a *shenfenzheng* (ID card), which North Koreans do not have. The lack of papers and vulnerability to arrest and deportation place the North Koreans at the mercy of employers willing, for whatever reasons, to employ them illegally. In addition to the risk of arrest during regular "cleanups" by the police or denunciation by unhappy neighbors, refugees are also vulnerable to private exploitation. The refugees' vulnerable status has pushed them into low-wage "dirty, difficult, and dangerous" work, a common circumstance for refugees (Lankov 2004, K. Lee 2006). There is some evidence that women on average receive higher wages than men, but this may be due to involvement in the sex industry and there is ample evidence of trafficking (K. Lee 2006, 40).

Not surprisingly, it has been reported that North Korean counter-feiters now forge these Chinese identity papers.[10] Our surveys asked whether the respondent was receiving a fair wage, and only 13 percent said they were; 78 percent reported receiving meager wages and 9 percent reported receiving none. (A well-known example of the last case is farm workers, who are denied wages after being promised that they would be paid after the harvest.) Admittedly, fairness is a subjective concept. Nevertheless given that real wages and their purchasing power are unquestionably higher in China than in North Korea, the finding that 7 out of 8 respondents believed that they were being treated unfairly is a strong suggestion that vulnerability invites exploitation.

At the same time, we have evidence that refugees also received assistance from Chinese nationals. The survey asked whether people received help from Korean-Chinese, missionaries, non-Korean Chinese, or others. The overwhelming majority (88 percent) reported receiving help from the Korean-Chinese community directly, and three-quarters reported living with Korean-Chinese. The second most frequently cited places of residence were shelter provided by missionaries and mountain hideouts.[11] This pattern probably reflects the posture of Chinese authorities. Missionaries face the most severe punishments and fines because their activity is seen as having a political character. Punishments meted out to missionaries harboring refugees include beating, long-term sentences, and deportation. Korean-Chinese by contrast are given lighter sentences, and refugees have greater opportunity to simply blend into that community.

It is interesting to note, however, that the share reporting residing with missionaries (5 percent) is multiples of the percentage citing assistance by missionaries in leaving North Korea. Missionaries play a much larger role in China sheltering refugees after their escape than in assisting with egress. This may simply reflect the greater social "space" for religion in China than in North Korea.[12] Among the "word of mouth" North Korean refugee lore is the advice that once in China one should approach buildings displaying a cross to receive assistance.

In other settings, including across the US-Mexican border, a number of migrants choose not to emigrate permanently but rather to move back and forth. Is North Korean migration intended to be permanent or temporary? Do migrants plan to return to North Korea or move on to third countries? On the issue of whether North Koreans living in China intended to

---

10. "After Two Years, Professional Counterfeiters in Pyongsung Finally Arrested," *North Korea Today* 348, July 2010.

11. Seventy-six percent reported living with Korean-Chinese, 5 percent with missionaries, 5 percent in the mountains, and 1 percent on the streets, with 13 percent reporting "other."

12. In May 2010, 23 missionaries dispatched from China were arrested in North Korea. Three were reportedly executed (W. W. Lee 2010).

return to their homeland permanently, the answer was a decisive "no": More than 97 percent expressed no intention of returning to North Korea. This reluctance to return is particularly striking since an overwhelming majority of respondents—more than 90 percent—reported still having family in North Korea. The North Koreans' well-founded fear of persecution appears to be a fundamental impediment to return. This simple fact is extremely important. It contradicts Chinese claims of purely economic motives and thus constitutes prima facie evidence to support their status as *refugees sur place* entitled to protection under the 1951 Refugee Convention.

Yet many do go back—at least temporarily, in some cases on multiple occasions. Among our respondents, one-fifth had returned temporarily of their own volition. But the slightly more common pattern is forced repatriation; more than a quarter of the sample had been repatriated. Of those repatriated, 26 percent (86) had been repatriated twice and another 15 percent (49) had been repatriated three or more times. In these cases, even imprisonment did not deter them from trying to escape again upon release. This pattern is consistent with a substantial minority of respondents reporting multiple border crossings in a previous survey (Y. Lee et al. 2001, table 1).

As for their motivations for returning, nine out of ten respondents crossing the border reported playing the role of couriers bearing food and/or money. Comparatively smaller shares returned to do business (5 percent) or because they found prospects in China bleak (2 percent).

## Trafficking of Women

A disturbing finding of our China survey is the particular insecurity among women refugees. Following the onset of acute food shortages and the decline of the public distribution system, women found it increasingly difficult to find daily necessities for their families, and many left their homes in search of food or work, including to China. Almost from the moment they cross the border—and sometimes when they are still in North Korea—refugee women are tapped by marriage brokers and pimps involved in human trafficking. Marriage brokers provide North Korean women as wives, particularly in the rural areas of China, where the historical preference for male babies and the exodus of younger women to employment opportunities in cities has led over time to an acute shortage of marriage-age Chinese women. Having a Chinese husband, however, does not guarantee a North Korean woman's safety, as she is still subject to repatriation. Moreover, women sold into Chinese families where they suffer physical, sexual, mental, and emotional abuse have very little recourse because of their status. Many women resort to prostitution as a source of income (Human Rights Watch 2002, 12–15; Amnesty International 2004, 28; Muico 2005; K. Lee 2006; Committee for Human Rights in North Korea 2009; National Human Rights Commission of Korea 2010). In addition, North

Korean women also suffer abuse from Chinese guards along the border and North Korean officials upon repatriation (Faiola 2004).

We asked respondents if they knew of women being trafficked in China and a majority responded affirmatively. Prices vary depending on the age of the woman and whether she is encumbered by dependents, with young, single women fetching the highest prices. These findings are strong testament to both the desperation of refugees and the multiple insecurities they face in the Chinese environment. However, the crackdown on both sides of the border and growing fears of repatriation, together with better information on the dire situation of women trafficked in China, have begun to attenuate the numbers of North Korean women willing to go to China. Anecdotal reports suggest that the price for women has risen in response to dwindling supply (Kato 2006, T. H. Lee 2010).

## Psychological Condition of Refugees: Prevalence of Distress[13]

A growing clinical literature has established that the particular difficulties faced by North Korean refugees have been associated with major psychiatric disorders, including PTSD (Jeon 2000, Y. Lee et al. 2001). Controlled clinical studies by doctors working with North Korean refugees in South Korea found few of their patients to be free of psychological disorders, with rates of PTSD ranging from 30 percent (Jeon et al. 2005) to 48 percent (Baubet et al. 2003) to 51 percent partial PTSD and 26 percent full PTSD (Kim, Yoon, and Han 2007).

Table 2.6 provides an overview of the responses to questions about psychological state derived from the China survey, grouped into three clusters of questions: those dealing with anxiety and fear; those dealing with other psychological issues, particularly anger and capacity to concentrate; and those related to refugees' perception of the future. Table 2.7 displays the mean responses[14] to these questions and the standard deviation.

The responses indicate that a majority of survey respondents exhibit significant psychological distress, findings consistent with those obtained by Lee et al. (2001) for a smaller group of subjects. Among the questions asked, mean scores are highest for those relating to the anxiety of their status: "usually anxious," "bad things will happen," and "fear for family." The descriptive statistics also suggest differences between men and women on this cluster of questions, with women showing greater incidence of fear and anxiety.

---

13. The following draws on Chang, Haggard, and Noland (2009a).

14. The responses to these questions were on a 1-5 scale, where 1=strongly disagree, 2=disagree, 3=neutral, 4=agree, and 5=strongly agree. The mean value is an arithmetic mean of these responses.

**Table 2.6  Indicators of psychological distress: China survey** (percent)

| Indicator of distress | Males | | Females | | Total | |
|---|---|---|---|---|---|---|
| | Agree | Strongly agree | Agree | Strongly agree | Agree | Strongly agree |
| Fear and anxiety | | | | | | |
| Usually anxious | 45.0 | 22.6 | 48.0 | 35.0 | 46.6 | 29.1 |
| Bad things will happen to me | 68.9 | 27.0 | 58.9 | 39.0 | 63.7 | 33.3 |
| Fear for my family | 70.6 | 26.2 | 54.9 | 42.8 | 62.5 | 34.9 |
| Always in fear | 56.6 | 21.0 | 52.7 | 35.2 | 54.7 | 28.4 |
| Other psychological problems | | | | | | |
| Get angry easily | 28.5 | 12.3 | 40.2 | 15.7 | 34.8 | 14.0 |
| Hard to concentrate | 57.1 | 13.5 | 53.1 | 18.6 | 55.1 | 16.2 |
| Hope for the future | | | | | | |
| Not sure of future | 29.3 | 10.3 | 36.6 | 12.2 | 33.1 | 11.2 |
| Not able to reach goals | 34.3 | 10.1 | 39.9 | 12.4 | 37.3 | 11.2 |
| Current situation is hopeless | 25.7 | 11.5 | 32.1 | 14.1 | 29.0 | 12.9 |

**Table 2.7　Mean scores of responses on psychological state: China survey**

| Psychological state | Males | | Females | | Total | |
|---|---|---|---|---|---|---|
| | Mean | Standard deviation | Mean | Standard deviation | Mean | Standard deviation |
| Fear and anxiety | | | | | | |
| Usually anxious | 3.9 | 0.79 | 4.2 | 0.73 | 4.0 | 0.77 |
| Bad things will happen to me | 4.2 | 0.56 | 4.4 | 0.54 | 4.3 | 0.56 |
| Fear for my family | 4.2 | 0.53 | 4.4 | 0.56 | 4.3 | 0.55 |
| Always in fear | 4.0 | 0.74 | 4.2 | 0.70 | 4.1 | 0.73 |
| Other psychological problems | | | | | | |
| Get angry easily | 3.3 | 1.01 | 3.5 | 1.04 | 3.4 | 1.03 |
| Hard to concentrate | 3.7 | 0.89 | 3.8 | 0.93 | 3.7 | 0.91 |
| Hope for the future | | | | | | |
| Not sure of future | 3.3 | 0.92 | 3.4 | 0.95 | 3.4 | 0.93 |
| Not able to reach goals | 3.4 | 0.88 | 3.5 | 0.97 | 3.4 | 0.93 |
| Current situation is hopeless | 3.3 | 0.92 | 3.4 | 1.04 | 3.3 | 0.99 |

**Table 2.8    Reported reasons for anxiety: China survey** (percent)

| Reason | Males | Females | Total |
|---|---|---|---|
| Arrest | 57.1 | 77.2 | 67.1 |
| Hunger | 1.5 | 0.3 | 0.9 |
| Home | 21.5 | 9.5 | 15.5 |
| Family in North Korea | 19.7 | 12.6 | 16.2 |
| Others | 0.3 | 0.3 | 0.3 |
| Total | 100 | 100 | 100 |

Clearly, the sources of this anxiety are multiple and encompass events in North Korea that pushed refugees across the border, the stresses associated with the trip itself, as well as conditions in China once refugees arrived. To get at the immediate causes of stress, the respondents were asked the main reason for their anxiety; the answers are reported in table 2.8. The regugees' lack of status in China was an overwhelming source of anxiety. Approximately 67 percent identified fear of arrest and repatriation as their biggest concern, while another 16 percent identified the related concern over uncertainty about their residence ("home"). The second most reported reason for their anxiety was for their family in North Korea (16 percent).

There is some evidence of differential responses according to gender. Almost from the moment they cross the border—and sometimes when they are still in North Korea—refugee women are subject to multiple sources of trauma. Respondents in one survey of 100 female refugees in China conducted between August 2001 and October 2003 reported experiences including arrest (44 percent), extradition (34 percent), human trafficking (24 percent), rape (20 percent), and prostitution (9 percent) (C. Kang 2006). Indeed, as shown in table 2.8, women are more likely to trace their anxiety to fear of arrest than men, who showed more concern than women with respect to their residence. While our surveys did not probe directly into whether women had been involved in trafficking or prostitution, respondents were asked if they knew of women being trafficked in China, and 53 percent answered affirmatively. Interestingly, hunger was not a widely reported source of contemporaneous concern, at least among North Koreans who had made it to China.

However, it cannot be assumed that the sources of psychological distress are related only to the immediate experiences of refugee life in China. The respondents were also asked a battery of questions about their experiences in North Korea, including whether they lost family members to the famine, whether relatives were arrested, about separation from their families, whether they had been incarcerated, and about their experiences while in prison.

**Table 2.9    Family members arrested or whereabouts unknown: China survey** (percent)

| Have any family members been missing or arrested? | | |
|---|---|---|
| Yes | 22.8 | |
| No | 77.3 | |

| If yes, what are the reasons? | Share of those who replied affirmatively | Share of all respondents |
|---|---|---|
| Speaking against the regime | 2.2 | 0.5 |
| Traveling without permission | 13.7 | 3.1 |
| Crossing the border to China | 54.7 | 12.4 |
| Stealing food | 1.8 | 0.4 |
| Don't know | 20.1 | 4.6 |
| Unspecified | 7.6 | 1.7 |
| Total | 100 | 22.7 |

These experiences are harrowing. More than 23 percent of men and 37 percent of women reported having had family members die of hunger. More than 40 percent of the respondents were unaware of the international food aid distribution effort; of those who were aware of it, less than 4 percent believed that they were beneficiaries. When asked about the distribution of the aid in a question allowing multiple responses, 90 percent believed that the aid went to the military and 27 percent believed party and government officials were beneficiaries.

Twenty-three percent of the respondents reported separation from adult family members. In 55 percent of these cases, the disappearance was associated with family members crossing the border into China; the second most cited reason was disappearance after traveling without permission (table 2.9). Disappearance for speaking out against the regime was relatively rare (2 percent). Seventy-nine percent of the sample reported separation from children. In 66 percent of these cases, the children were left behind in North Korea; in nearly 19 percent of the cases, however, children had died due to hunger or illness.

More than one-quarter of the sample reported having been arrested, and nearly 10 percent of the respondents reported having been incarcerated in political detention facilities. While there were no statistically significant differences in self-reported arrest rates across genders, males were significantly more likely than females to report incarceration in political detention facilities. Among those incarcerated in political detention facilities, 90 percent reported witnessing forced starvation, 60 percent reported witnessing deaths due to beating or torture, and 27 percent reported witnessing executions. Pregnant women thought to be carrying children of Chinese paternity have allegedly been subject to forced abortions or infanticide; 5 percent of the respondents indicated that they had witnessed these practices.[15]

## Modeling Psychological Distress

Further insight into the sources of psychological distress can be gained by modeling the survey responses as a function of the respondents' demographic characteristics and self-reported personal experiences. Chang, Haggard, and Noland (2009a) report multivariate regressions on the indicators of psychological distress shown in table 2.6; we discuss only those findings that meet standard tests of statistical significance. A number of demographic markers are statistically correlated with the responses to the psychological questions. But their impact is dwarfed by correlates relating to personal experiences in North Korea, including knowing of food aid but believing that one was not a beneficiary; incarceration in a political detention facility, which also captures in part the previously discussed experiences in the prison system; arrest; knowledge of human trafficking; and death of a family member due to hunger. Refugees' stresses appear related not only to their refugee status but also to the underlying experiences in North Korea that no doubt pushed them to migrate in the first place.

The most basic demographic variable, age, is negatively correlated with psychological health/status in most of the regressions. This is particularly true with respect to the questions dealing with orientation toward the future; not surprisingly, advancing age is correlated with a greater sense of hopelessness and despair about reaching life objectives.

Education tended to be associated with increased fear and anxiety but did not have effects on other psychological problems noted nor on orientation toward the future. Occupational status (trader, student, farmer, other job) is frequently correlated with psychological state. Traders showed a significantly higher level of psychological distress, and across all questions, than workers (the reference point or benchmark occupational category against which the responses of the other occupations are measured). Farmers—perhaps because of their lack of other skills—did show a more despairing outlook toward the future.

The experiences of the relatively small number of traders may reflect more idiosyncratic, specific, and personal experiences. Trading is often illicit and thus highly vulnerable in North Korea and is subject to a variety of idiosyncratic risks in China as well. Stories of deals gone bad are not uncommon. A typical scenario involves an individual North Korean trader cheated by his or her Chinese counterparty and left in limbo, unwilling

---

15. It has also been claimed that North Korea conducts medical experiments on prisoners (Demick 2004, Cooper 2005); 55 percent of the respondents believed (but did not necessarily witness) that this had occurred at the facilities in which they were incarcerated.

or unable to return to North Korea to face retribution from creditors. In contrast, one can imagine that farmers' migration was driven by broadly deteriorating conditions and that they might have tapped more effectively into networks of similarly situated rural refugees. Conversely, students had the most hopeful future orientation, even controlling for their youth.

Despite apparent differences in the responses of men and women, once other correlates are taken into account, gender is statistically significant in only a minority of the regressions. Women experienced significantly higher anxiety and fear for family members than men, again reflecting their particular vulnerabilities.

An important finding, however, is that experiential variables dwarf the impact of demographic ones. Death of a family member due to hunger and knowing of the food aid program but believing that one was not a beneficiary are strongly correlated with all seven adverse psychological states. Incarceration in political detention facilities and knowledge of trafficking in women—an experiential variable that captures knowledge of a particular risk—are statistically significant with respect to six of the seven psychological state variables. Arrest is significant in four of seven cases, including both questions relating to future orientation.

But perhaps the most compelling finding is the magnitude of the psychological effect of famine-related experiences in North Korea and exposure to the North Korean penal system. In all seven models of psychological state, the experiential variables with the strongest impact are famine-related. In six of the seven cases, the belief that one was not a beneficiary of food aid has the strongest estimated effect of any of the experiential variables (though not always by a statistically significant margin), consistently larger in magnitude, for example, than the effects of being incarcerated in a political detention facility. The only case in which beliefs about food aid are not the most significant factor is the model of the ability to concentrate, in which the largest effect comes from having family members die due to hunger. The famine and the government's mismanagement of it continue to reverberate through North Korean society and appear to remain important determinants of psychological distress long after the famine had passed and the individuals in question had left the country.

## Moving On: Experiences in China

The vast majority of North Korean refugees in China do not want to return to their country of origin. This reluctance to return to North Korea is particularly striking given the fact that the overwhelming majority of respondents—90 percent—reported still having family there and that many have returned, in some cases on multiple occasions. Among our respondents, 20 percent had returned to North Korea of their own volition, and more than a quarter of the sample had been repatriated.

When asked if they planned future returns, the only group with a markedly higher propensity to return was students (31 percent), although "student" may be a proxy for age and physical condition. As noted above, the dominant reason for returning to North Korea was to bring money (80 percent) or food (11 percent) back to North Korea. At least among this sample of refugees, the phenomenon of return appears to be largely limited to short-term visits by young people bearing remittances.

Most refugees in China do not seek to reside there permanently (only 14 percent do). It should be observed that all these responses are based on existing conditions in China. If the Chinese government were willing to regularize this population in some way, the share of North Koreans willing to permanently reside in the border region and integrate into the Chinese-Korean community could be much higher. But under current Chinese policy—one of refusal to enable asylum claims and of forced repatriations—the refugees must make arduous journeys through third countries to achieve permanent legal resettlement elsewhere.

For many this means seeking employment in China to accumulate resources for on-migration, yet as we have seen, only 22 percent of the refugees reported being employed. One would like to understand what determines the ability to secure employment in China, and, implicitly, the ability to subsequently accumulate resources and on-migrate. The problem immediately arises that anxiety, inability to concentrate, and despair all potentially hinder the ability to secure and maintain employment, yet lack of employment may itself cause psychological distress—which in turn is exacerbated by the refugees' lack of legal status in China.[16]

The modeling work reported in Chang, Haggard, and Noland (2009a) indicates that psychological distress strongly impedes employment in China. Indeed, it is one of only a handful of variables strongly correlated with employment. Although difficult to tease out in a statistical sense, the data are certainly consistent with the interpretation that adverse circumstances in China and psychological state are mutually reinforcing. Vulnerability creates psychological problems, which in turn magnify the problems refugees face in coping with their difficult environment. These findings in turn have important implications for the refugees' adjustment challenges in their new environment, as well as the prospective costs of Korean unification.

Interestingly, length of time in China is negatively associated with

---

16. Statistically, this means that right-hand-side regressors may be determined endogenously or that the regression is subject to reverse causation. In principle, this can be addressed through the use of instrumental variables—namely variables that are highly correlated with the regressor in question but that cannot independently causally explain the left-hand-side variable, often because they are chronologically predetermined. In the case of the jobs regression, we use events in North Korea (knowing of food aid but believing that one had not received it and separation from family members, which cannot influence one's employment in China except through psychological impact) as instruments for the average psychological score derived from the seven indicators reported in table 2.6. This two-stage probit regression is reported in Chang, Haggard, and Noland (2009a).

employment. There are at least two possible interpretations. One is that we are sampling from a subpopulation that for whatever reason (unrecorded physical disability, for example) has essentially become stuck in the border region, unable to hold down a job, accumulate resources, and move on. (Or conversely, those with better education, skills, and networks have already moved on.) The other interpretation is that this group has become integrated into the Korean-Chinese community and does not need employment to survive, perhaps in part because of marriage. The two hypotheses are not mutually exclusive. In contrast, having child dependents encourages employment, presumably because of greater need for income.

## Conclusion

The two surveys document that refugees face a particular set of vulnerabilities that range from their insecure legal and personal status, risks of deportation, to difficulties in securing livelihoods. The survey conducted in China also provides evidence that refugees—and particularly women—are additionally vulnerable to predatory behavior and trafficking.

That these vulnerabilities would have a pronounced effect on the mental health of refugees is not surprising; an overwhelming number of those interviewed struggled with anxiety and fear. However, the multivariate regressions indicate that the psychological problems facing refugees are not simply a result, or even primarily a function, of their vulnerability in China. Rather they point to the significance of their experiences in North Korea prior to exit and treatment by North Korean authorities. These include, first and foremost, perceptions of unfairness with respect to the distribution of food aid, death of family members during the famine, and incarceration in the North Korean prison system. Before returning to these questions in more detail in chapters 4 and 5, we explore refugee insights into the changing North Korean economy in the next chapter.

# 3

# Marketization, Reform, and Retrenchment

The surveys not only shed light on the plight of the refugees but also constitute a useful source of information on conditions within North Korea. In this chapter we focus on two core questions. First, we seek to document the process we call "marketization from below." How, exactly, does the informal economy in North Korea work and what is its extent? Second, we are interested in the effects of government policy and the path of economic reform—and retrenchment. Are government policy actions having effect, either in providing incentives for private initiative or in forestalling it? How have the reforms influenced the operations of state-owned enterprises (SOEs) and cooperatives? What are the social consequences of the reforms?

As we argued in the introduction, the process of marketization in North Korea was a result of the secular decline of the state socialist economy that began in the late 1980s, accelerated by the breakup of the Soviet Union and the dissolution of the Eastern Bloc and the onset of famine. With the state unable to provide food through the socialist public distribution system (PDS), small-scale social units—households, work units, local party organs, government offices, and even military units—initiated entrepreneurial coping behavior, much of it technically illegal, to secure food.

These adaptations consisted in part of innovative uses of existing institutions and practices. One example would be the exploitation of provisions under the August 3 [1984] Movement, a campaign originally intended to mobilize marginal participants in the labor force to employ waste materials for the local production of consumer goods. The August 3 provisions were used by both individuals and enterprises in complex ways, for example, to establish satellite enterprises that could productively employ idle workers. Some firms also allowed workers to pay a fee to be classified as August 3 workers and thereby shift into alternative, higher-efficiency activities in the emergent market sector. Thus the program was associated with marketization, in the form of both involuntary "necessity entrepreneurship" by redundant workers, including particularly women, and voluntary "opportunity entrepreneurship." In addition to the exploitation of the existing statute, incremental reforms—for example, in the expansion of farmers' markets—contributed to the marketization process.

However, "market creep" was by no means confined to institutions or activities permitted by statute (S. C. Kim 2006, chapter 6; Yang and Shepard 2009; B. Y. Kim 2010). Managers, entrepreneurs, and workers drifted into market activities well beyond what was permitted, either with the acquiescence of authorities, in the context of bribe payments, or through evasion. More direct forms of official corruption also played a role, for example, as food aid was diverted into the market.

Following the peak famine years of roughly 1994–97, the state had to choose between reasserting control over the fraying state socialist system and ratifying the process of marketization from below through complementary changes in institutions and policy. After some minor adjustments starting in 1998, the government launched a poorly designed reform program in July 2002. Despite their limitations, the reforms decriminalized some of the coping behaviors that had arisen in the previous decade; among the more significant measures were an overhaul of administered prices and wages and the limited introduction of material incentives in both the industrial and agricultural sectors.

Yet it is important not to assume that reforms have their intended effects; one of our purposes is to contribute to an understanding of how economic reform actually takes place in fraying socialist systems.

Models of the political economy of reform typically are top down; they begin with some bargaining process among elites or special interests over policy (Drazen 2000, Roland 2000). Such bargaining may delay reform (Alesina and Drazen 1991) or be resolved in ways that lead to Pareto-improving changes in government policy: stabilization, liberalization, or other structural and institutional reforms such as improved protection of property rights.

However, early analysts of the transition in the Soviet Union and Eastern Europe noted that "reform" was not simply a result of top-down changes in policy. Rather, the transition to the market was also a result of independent changes in the behavior of economic agents and the emergence of grey and black markets and even "spontaneous privatization" (Fischer and Gelb 1991). Similar processes of "reform from below" have also been observed in cases of state failure, such as Somalia, where the collapse of a highly predatory state may have actually generated an increase in welfare (Leeson 2007; Powell, Ford, and Nowrateh 2008).

By exploiting differences in the time when refugees left North Korea, we can gain at least some insight into the question of whether reform had any effect on either work units or the private behavior of market participants. The China survey approached these issues through the lens of the food economy. Previous research has had some success in establishing that the collapse of the PDS and the quest for food were important drivers of the broader marketization process. The China survey also included questions about the distribution of aid, which provide insight into the actual operation of the PDS and government control over both information and the allocation of food.

The South Korea survey included a more nuanced examination of these issues, addressing not only de facto marketization but also the effects of the reforms of 2002 and their gradual reversal from 2005. One of the critical findings of the South Korea survey is how little impact either the reforms or the subsequent retrenchment appear to have had for some significant swath of the population. The economy rapidly marketized under duress with the onset of the famine; neither the 2002 reforms nor the turn toward greater controls beginning in 2005 fundamentally altered household behavior. There is some evidence that the reform increased market-oriented activities of cooperatives, SOEs, and even government offices not associated with production, but these increases were not as marked as one might expect. Work units were already engaged in these activities prior to the reforms. In sum, significant shifts in economic policy appear to have had surprisingly little impact, in part because large swaths of the populace were already detached from the state socialist sector.

The findings on behavior are mirrored in respondents' perceptions of the state socialist system. The South Korea survey reveals a secular trend in views about access to power, status, and wealth. Respondents saw officialdom as highly privileged, but increasing numbers regarded the market and corrupt and illegal activities as the dominant ways of getting ahead in North Korea. These findings suggest a changing political economy in which some state, party, and military officials not only enjoy their traditional prerogatives and benefits but also exploit office for material gain, creating an uneasy symbiosis between state and market.

## The Food Economy: Role of the Market in Household Consumption

The food economy is a microcosm of the broader institutional and behavioral changes that swept through North Korea in the 1990s. In principle, urban residents, about two-thirds of the population, were fed via the PDS, the state-run quantity rationing system. The PDS in North Korea is a very extensive system through which subsidized rations are distributed, in principle, on a gram per day per person basis, according to occupation. Farmers on the cooperatives were given rations at the time of the harvest, which were allocated to them through highly perverse incentives. When supplies were scarce, the government extracted as much as possible from the countryside, partly on the mistaken assumption that farmers would be able to make up the difference by cultivating on private plots. In fact, when farmers anticipated a bad harvest and high levels of extraction, they had strong incentives to preharvest, hoard, and divert both work effort and grain into private consumption and the market (Natsios 2002).

For those outside of the rural sector, access to state food supplies was effectively determined by status; this was true not only of domestic supplies but also of commercial imports and most aid supplies, which were also distributed through the PDS. Priority was given to government and ruling party officials, important military units, and urban populations, in particular residents of the capital Pyongyang. Before the famine, the PDS reportedly supplied over 700 grams per person per day to over 60 percent of the population. But the famine resulted in a collapse of domestic food supplies and the PDS.

Figure 3.1 traces what we know about the government allocation of food over time. The figure shows estimates of farmers' daily rations as well as the daily rations distributed through the PDS, including averages for each period and high and low rations reflecting variation across the country and over the period in question. These estimates are compared with a common estimate of minimum human need of about 450 grams per day. Rations during the famine and postfamine periods declined sharply, with some parts of the country distributing effectively no food through this channel at various points in time.

The South Korea survey confirms how rapidly the system collapsed: Pooling all urban respondents regardless of time of departure, 28 percent of the South Korea sample indicated that they *never* received food through this channel. Among those who indicated that they had received food from the PDS, more than 20 percent said it had ceased to be the primary source of food by 1993 (figure 3.2). Within two years, less than half of the respondents were obtaining food primarily through the PDS. These results hold not only for the full sample but also for the postfamine and postreform subsamples, demonstrating that they are not simply an artifact of sample truncation or censoring associated with early leavers providing relatively early-dated responses to the question.

As the PDS broke down, people were forced to turn to foraging and the nascent markets for sustenance. Such coping responses included rearing livestock, growing kitchen gardens, and collecting wild foods like edible grasses, acorns, tree bark, and sea algae. Yet, figure 3.1 strikingly reveals that the PDS never really revived. Rather, the market became a permanent feature of the food economy, but one highly vulnerable to shifts in government policy and changes in market prices. In 2003, heightened political tensions with key donor countries and general donor fatigue threatened the flow of desperately needed food and fuel aid. Black market prices

# Figure 3.1 Estimates of daily per capita PDS rations, November 1995 to October 2008

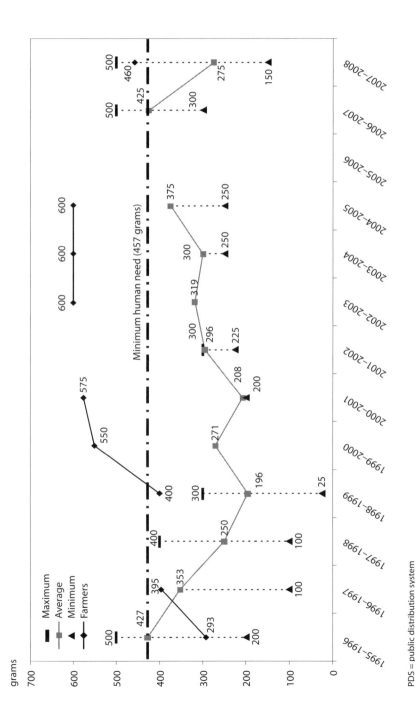

grams

PDS = public distribution system

Note: In most cases averages are taken directly from the source. Otherwise, they are calculated as the simple average of the estimates for different cohorts throughout the marketing year. FAO/WFP resumed publication in 2008 since the halt in 2004, so there are missing years during which the food situation was seen to have improved. The data do not cover the entire year for certain marketing years, and therefore the average value may be biased by seasonality or certain external conditions.

Sources: Food and Agriculture Organization/World Food Program (FAO/WFP), various publications; Natsios (2002).

**Figure 3.2 The last year respondent relied primarily on the PDS: South Korea survey** (share of those who had received food from the PDS)

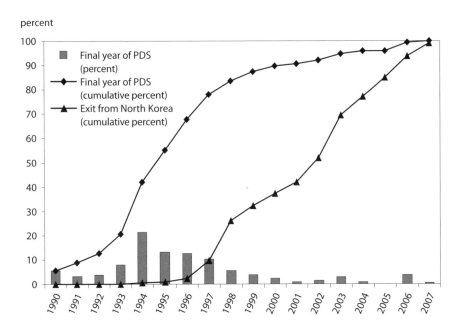

percent

PDS = public distribution system

continued to rise following the increase in official prices and wages in the summer of 2002, leaving some vulnerable groups, such as the elderly and unemployed, less able to buy goods. The regime subsequently relaxed restrictions on farmers' markets in spring 2003, which led to an expansion of market activity.

This liberalization was reversed beginning in 2005 as the authorities imposed greater restrictions on the operations of markets. These restrictions, as well as floods and rising world food prices, led to an acute deterioration in public supply in 2008, reflected in falling rations and greater dispersion in them than at any time since the famine (Haggard and Noland 2009a). Although it comes after our surveys, the 2009 currency reform also delivered a huge shock to the system, temporarily interrupting supply across the country and resulting in spiraling food prices.

## Household Access to Food

In the China survey, 62 percent reported the market as their primary source of food, 18 percent relied primarily on their own individual efforts,

3 percent reported the PDS as the primary supplier, and 16 percent relied on other channels such as friends and family. Interestingly, the group reporting that they relied on their own efforts and "other" channels corresponds almost precisely to the share of farmers in the survey. If one interprets the remaining responses to be largely of refugees from urban areas, the survey would suggest that only about 5 percent of the nonfarm respondents obtained their food primarily through the PDS, while 95 percent got it through the market. The responses are also consistent with the results of an earlier study in which only 2 percent of the refugees surveyed reported government rations as their primary source of food even after the famine had passed (Robinson et al. 2001b, table 1).

The South Korea survey further confirms reliance on the market and self-production. Urban respondents were asked about their primary source of food at the time of their departure. In all periods, "the market" was the dominant response, followed fairly closely by self-production (figure 3.3). The fact that so many reported growing their own food is particularly revealing given the low share of farmers in the sample, suggesting that resort to self-reliance was pursued even by nonagricultural households.

For those leaving in the immediate postfamine period (1999–2002), reliance on the public sector fell even further: Not a single respondent of these 74 said that he or she relied primarily on the PDS and only two reported they relied primarily on their workplace. The number of respondents relying primarily on the PDS or their workplace increased marginally among those leaving in the retrenchment period (2006–present). But in both the reform (2003–05) and retrenchment subsamples, the dominant answers remained reliance on the market and growing food on one's own.

A more refined sense of the reliance on the market for food can be obtained from responses to a question about the *share* of total household consumption that is purchased in the market; we focus here on the urban sample of the South Korea survey (figure 3.4). What is striking is both the high level of reliance on the market and the persistence of such reliance over time. Pooling across all time periods, nearly 40 percent of urban residents reported having purchased all their food in the market at the time of their departure, and more than 60 percent reported purchasing at least 75 percent. Only in the final, retrenchment subsample did the share not purchasing any food in the market rise above 10 percent, but fully half of the respondents who left during this period also reported receiving all their food through the market, the highest share of any cohort.

The overrepresentation of respondents from northeastern provinces affects the ability to draw inferences from the responses of refugees about the food economy in North Korea as a whole. It is widely believed that the breakdown of the PDS occurred earliest and most completely in these areas (Smith 2005, Haggard and Noland 2007; see, however, Smith 2009 on more recent developments). The shift toward the market for food

**Figure 3.3 Primary source of food at the time respondent left North Korea: South Korea survey** (urban sample, n=167)

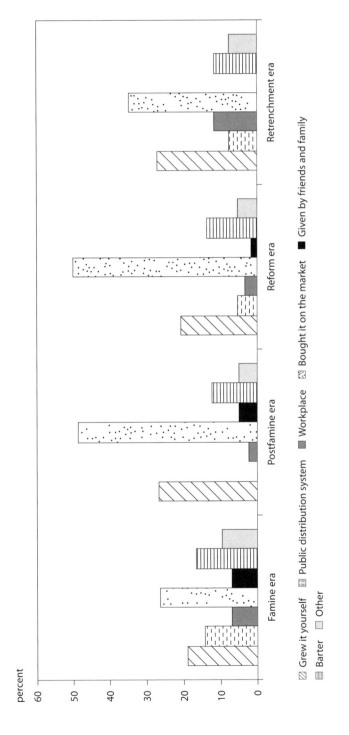

percent

Famine era   Postfamine era   Reform era   Retrenchment era

◨ Grew it yourself   ▦ Public distribution system   ▥ Workplace   ⬚ Bought it on the market
▦ Barter   ▨ Other   ■ Given by friends and family

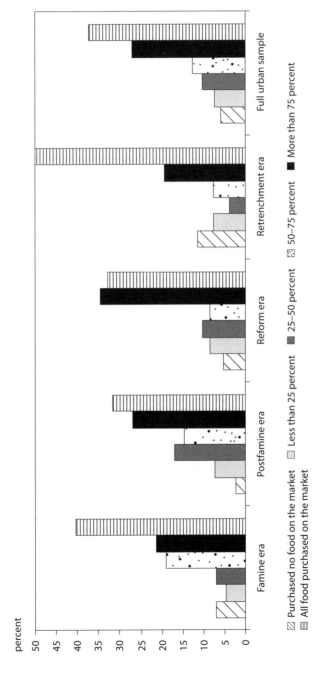

**Figure 3.4   Share of family's consumption of food purchased on the market: South Korea survey**

(urban sample, n=167)

percent

| | | | | | |
|---|---|---|---|---|---|
| | Famine era | Postfamine era | Reform era | Retrenchment era | Full urban sample |

☒ Purchased no food on the market   ☐ Less than 25 percent   ▨ 25–50 percent
▨ All food purchased on the market   ☷ 50–75 percent   ■ More than 75 percent

may have advanced the farthest precisely in those areas hit hardest by the famine.

We address this issue directly in Haggard and Noland (2010c), which reports statistical modeling of the pattern of responses displayed in figure 3.4. Underscoring the uniformity of these developments across North Korean society, the list of correlates that are *not* robustly correlated with marketization of consumption is long. Age, year or "era" of departure from North Korea, time in South Korea or a third country, educational attainment, geographic markers—such as residence in the northeastern provinces—or political classification do not matter in this regard. Farmers were less likely to buy food in the market, presumably because they had access both to rations at the time of the harvest and to self-grown food. Workers in SOEs were also less likely to get all their food from the market. Yet despite these expected differences, the more striking finding is that the centrality of the market on the consumption side mirrors the central role of the market with respect to income reported in the next section. The failure of any of the "era" variables to be significantly correlated with the share of food obtained in the market (controlling for demographic characteristics) provides additional evidence that the government never really succeeded in reconstituting the PDS. Rather, the multivariate regressions demonstrate the consistency of involvement in the market.[1]

The question naturally arises as to how meaningful these results derived from a refugee survey are for the remaining resident population. It is possible that the raw results on household expenditure patterns may reflect the overweighting of some demographic groups relative to the underlying population. To address this possibility, in Haggard and Noland (2010c) we report a counterfactual experiment: The coefficients estimated from the statistical models are combined with national-level demographic data to derive projected values, conditional on the fact that these models have been estimated from a sample of refugees whose experiences may not mirror those of the society as a whole. So, for example, if North Hamgyong province accounts for 10 percent of the national population, it was given this weight, not the 50 percent it represents in the survey sample. As seen in figure 3.5 there is a small, statistically insignificant tendency for the projected national values to exhibit less market orientation than the raw survey figures. Adjusting for all variables that can plausibly be compared with the North Korean population as a whole, it appears that our refugee findings have wider implications and that

---

1. Gender is the only robust correlate with marketization of consumption: Women reported purchasing a higher share of their consumption in the market and were more likely to get all their food in the market. This result may reflect the fact that as a matter of state policy, women were more likely to be shed from SOEs and men were more likely to remain employed. However, this pattern might also be an artifact of the household division of labor. If women were responsible for shopping, their answers may more accurately reflect real household consumption patterns. If so, the significance of the gender variable would be misleading.

**Figure 3.5  Share of family's consumption of food purchased on the market: Sample (South Korea survey) versus national projection**

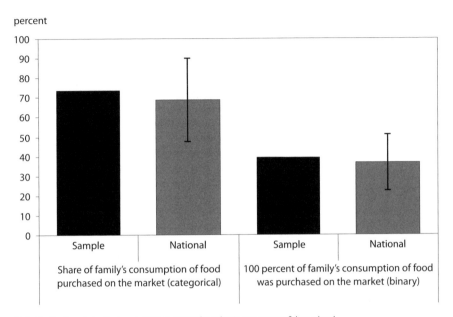

percent

| | | | |
|---|---|---|---|
| Sample | National | Sample | National |
| Share of family's consumption of food purchased on the market (categorical) | | 100 percent of family's consumption of food was purchased on the market (binary) | |

Note: Vertical brackets display confidence intervals at the 95 percent confidence level.

marketization of food and other items of basic household consumption is very far advanced in North Korea.[2]

## Role of Food Aid

Aid from the United Nations World Food Program and other Western donors began arriving in North Korea in 1995 and at its peak in 1997–2004 was in principle feeding more than one-third of the population (Haggard and Noland 2007). Although volumes have ebbed and flowed, North Korea has received aid from official and private sources continuously since 1995, most recently in a large-scale program in 2008–09, which falls after our surveys.[3] However, enormous controversy has surrounded this

---

2. For recent evidence confirming this point, see two assessments done by NGOs and the World Food Program in 2008 (Anderson and Majarowitz 2008, WFP 2008).

3. In Haggard and Noland (2007, chapters 4 to 6) we provide a detailed analysis of the multilateral food aid effort through 2005. Because of the timing of the survey, the results in this section do not address the large US Agency for International Development (USAID) food program (500,000 metric tons) of 2008–09, which was terminated in March 2009 by

### Table 3.1 Perceptions of food aid to North Korea (percent)

| Response | China survey | South Korea survey |
|---|---|---|
| **Knowledge of food aid to North Korea** | | |
| Yes | 56.5 | 43.6 |
| No | 43.5 | 56.4 |
| Total | 100 | 100 |
| **Have you received any food aid? (of those who knew of food aid)** | | |
| Yes | 3.5 | 33.1 |
| No | 96.5 | 66.9 |
| Total | 100 | 100 |
| **Have you received any food aid? (urban subsample, of those who knew of food aid)** | | |
| Yes | 2.7 | 14.4 |
| No | 97.3 | 85.6 |
| Total | 100 | 100 |

effort, and it is fair to say that despite the efforts of the humanitarian community, neither multilateral nor bilateral assistance to North Korea has ever achieved normal standards of transparency, access, and monitoring.

In both the China and South Korea–based surveys, an astonishing share of respondents, roughly half of those surveyed, revealed that they were unaware of the long-standing, large-scale food aid program (table 3.1). Moreover, among respondents who indicated knowledge of the effort, 33 percent of the South Korea survey respondents and only 4 percent of the China survey respondents believed that they had been recipients. Looking only at urban residents (those on the agricultural cooperatives would have been less likely to receive aid), only 3 percent in the China survey and 14 percent of the later, South Korea survey believed they were recipients.

These answers do not establish whether the respondents did in fact receive assistance or not. The aid effort has been in place for more than a decade and at its peak, aid was flowing in amounts designed to feed roughly one-third of the entire population of the country. Aid on that scale, even if diverted from its intended recipients, does not just vanish into the ether.

---

North Korean authorities, leaving approximately half of the committed aid undelivered. This program had monitoring and delivery protocols more in line with international humanitarian norms but by no means fully meeting them.

**Table 3.2   Perceived food aid recipients** (percent of those who knew of food aid)

| China survey | | South Korea survey | |
|---|---|---|---|
| Army | 89.4 | Army | 67.4 |
| Government officials | 27.2 | High-level government and party officials | 27.1 |
| | | Local government or party officials | 1.6 |
| Citizens | 0.7 | General public | 1.6 |
| Laborers | 1.1 | | |
| Don't know | 7.0 | Don't know | 2.3 |
| Total | 125.4 | Total | 100 |

Note: The question was asked differently between the two surveys: In the China survey, people were asked who they thought the recipients of the food aid were, and the answer choices were not mutually exclusive nor collectively exhaustive. For the South Korea survey, the answer choices were mutually exclusive and collectively exhaustive and the question was who they thought received most of the food aid, not just any of the food aid.

There are a number of possible explanations for this lack of awareness of the foreign aid effort:

- Aid in bulk form was distributed through the PDS or through other institutional channels, such as hospitals, schools, and orphanages, and the refugees received it but did not know that what they had received was aid. This is the most benign interpretation.

- Aid was diverted into the market and the respondents purchased it there, in which case they might not have known the source of supply, or if they did, they did not consider it "aid" since they were paying for it.

- Respondents did not receive any aid, perhaps because it had been diverted to groups such as the military.

In assessing the implications of these results, the overrepresentation of northeastern provinces may again be a factor since some have argued that these regions were discriminated against in initial relief efforts (Natsios 2002; see, however, S. Lee 2003). These findings may, therefore, accurately depict the experiences of the refugee community but may not be representative of the country as a whole.

The refugees overwhelmingly believed that the aid went primarily to the military (table 3.2). The question and possible responses were posed slightly differently in the two surveys, but the results are consistent. When asked who received food aid, and allowing multiple responses, 89 percent of the refugees in China who were aware of the program believed that it went to the military and 27 percent said that it went to government officials; less than 3 percent said it went to common citizens or others. When asked in the South Korea survey who the primary recipients of aid were—not allowing multiple responses—67 percent said the military, 27 percent said high-level government or party officials, 2 percent said local government or party officials, and 2 percent said the general public.

Again, these responses do not prove that the aid was diverted to the military and officials. But at a minimum, the responses attest both to the perceived power and centrality of the military in North Korean life and to the regime's control over information and resources. In the context of a massive, decade-long multinational humanitarian aid program, North Korean refugees exhibit a significant lack of awareness of the overall aid effort. Their overwhelming impression is that the primary beneficiaries of the aid effort were the military. These findings ought to give significant pause when designing a relief program for North Korea or arguing for the "soft power" benefits of supplying aid. Aid almost certainly has had positive effects for North Korea: by hitting some targeted beneficiaries, by raising aggregate supply, and by lowering prices. But many North Koreans in our surveys didn't know about the aid effort and those who did appear to believe that aid was largely diverted to the military. The refugees' responses call into question the effectiveness of past aid programs in reaching intended targets and particularly the ability of those programs to generate goodwill, especially when the regime depicts the foreign aid donations as a kind of political tribute.

## The Emerging Market Economy: Household Earnings

If citizens are primarily obtaining food and other goods in the market, then they need money to pay for them.[4] Historically money and prices played little role in North Korea's planned economy. Urban residents received monthly rations for household goods distributed at minimal prices; workers on agricultural cooperatives and state farms retained annual in-kind allotments of food and received a basket of consumer goods in return for agricultural output sold to the state at a trivial procurement price. A closer examination of the revenue, as well as expenditure, side of the household balance sheet in the South Korea–based survey finds the market playing an important role in income as well.

The most common work unit classification among the respondents was state-owned enterprise, both for the respondents themselves (23 percent) and for spouses (31 percent). In addition, a significant share of respondents (10 percent of the sample) worked for the August 3 unit of an SOE. State farms or cooperatives accounted for 14 percent of respondents

---

4. The results reported in this section draw on Haggard and Noland (2010c).

**Table 3.3    Engagement in private activities: South Korea survey** (percent share of those who answered "yes")

| In addition to your work duties, did you ever engage in the following activities? | Respondent | Respondent's spouse |
|---|---|---|
| Private trading | 70.9 | 60.2 |
| Provision of private services | 8.9 | 10.4 |
| Other private business activities | 18.9 | 20.1 |
| August 3 unit | 14.9 | 18.1 |

and 10 percent of spouses, although as we have seen this underestimates the share of the rural population in the survey. Government and party officers accounted for 9 and 2 percent for self and spouse, respectively; the army was also represented among the refugees at around 5 percent of the sample.

Engagement in private activities, particularly trading, is ubiquitous (table 3.3).[5] More than 70 percent of respondents and more than 60 percent of their spouses reported that they engaged in trading, magnitudes consistent with earlier surveys (Kim and Song 2008, K. D. Lee et al. 2008). Fairly common also was participation in other private business activities (19 percent of respondents and 20 percent of spouses) and in August 3 units (15 percent of respondents and 18 percent of spouses), even though only 10 percent of the sample and less than 3 percent of the spouses reported the latter as their primary work unit.

The respondents were asked what share of household income came from private business activities at the time they left North Korea, a more accurate indicator of dependence on the market than simple engagement in a given activity. The results are staggering (figure 3.6). Nearly half the sample, the modal response, reported that *all* of their income came from private business activities at the time they left North Korea. More than two-thirds of the respondents—69 percent—reported that half or more of their income came from such activities. Only a handful of respondents—4 percent—reported that none of their income came from the market. Moreover, there appears to be little difference across the famine, postfamine, reform, and retrenchment periods; dependence on market income was high in all periods, although by the reform and retrenchment periods

---

5. The question was, "In addition to your regular work, did you ever engage in the following activities: private trading, providing private services (e.g., hairdresser, bicycle repair), other private business activity, or August 3 unit?" which allowed them to list all that applied. The inclusion of August 3 unit using this phrasing of the question was designed to catch activities outside of regular employ, i.e., the possibility that the respondent would formally be working for an SOE and list it as the primary work unit but in fact be working in an August 3 unit. However, we cannot rule out the possibility of double counting since the questionnaire included August 3 units in the main question concerning work unit.

**Figure 3.6    Share of total household income from private business activities: South Korea survey**

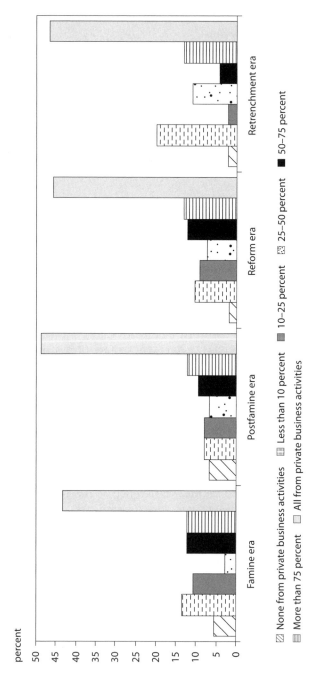

percent

Famine era    Postfamine era    Reform era    Retrenchment era

⊠ None from private business activities    ▥ Less than 10 percent    ▨ 10–25 percent    ▦ 25–50 percent    ■ 50–75 percent
▥ More than 75 percent    ☐ All from private business activities

virtually every household received at least some income from the market.[6] Such magnitudes are consistent with results from another refugee survey where respondents reported receiving more than 70 percent of their income through nonofficial channels (B. Y. Kim 2010).

As in the case of food expenditure, what is striking about the extent of engagement in the market is its uniformity across the sample and along multiple dimensions. As with the consumption side of the ledger, the list of variables *not* robustly correlated with the market component of family income is long: Respondents' sex, age, year or "era" of departure from North Korea, time in South Korea or a third country, educational attainment, residence in the capital city, Pyongyang, or in the northeastern provinces of the country, political classification, and occupation had no effect on their propensity to engage in market activity.

The two variables that were robustly correlated with the market as a source of income were work unit and residence in a province bordering China.[7] Not surprisingly, workers in August 3 units were more likely to receive income from the market than other groups (regular SOE workers, government or party employees, and soldiers). Given the very nature of these enterprises, this finding is not surprising. At first glance, it is surprising that those living near the border were less likely to earn income from the market. This possibly reflects the sample selection issue flagged earlier: Proximity to the border means that it is relatively easy to emigrate (at least in the North Korean context). Those from the border regions may be less entrepreneurially inclined than those from more remote locations, who have navigated a more challenging (and costly) path to exit the country.

As with household expenditure, it is possible to perform a similar counterfactual projection exercise with respect to income: Data on the refugees in the multivariate regressions were replaced by national-level averages derived from the UN census and other sources, and the statistical models rerun to generate projections for the national population.

The sample and projected national means, along with their 95 percent confidence intervals, are displayed in figure 3.7. There is little difference between the sample values and the projected nationwide results. The latter, with respect to total income that came from private activities, are a bit lower (indicating that our sample overrepresents the most marketized

---

6. The apparent lack of trend is consistent with an earlier survey done largely on refugees who had left North Korea before either the 2002 reform or the 2005 retrenchment (Kim and Song 2008, K. D. Lee et al. 2008).

7. Although one might expect that marketization had proceeded the furthest in the areas bordering China, the results are consistent with those we obtained in Haggard and Noland (2009a) that grain prices in the border region were not distinctly lower than in other parts of the country. They are also consistent with a sample selection issue in which people close to the border are able to exit more easily than others from locations farther away, and hence may display characteristics that otherwise might not mark them as likely to emigrate.

**Figure 3.7    Share of total household income from private business activities: Sample (South Korea survey) versus national projection**

percent

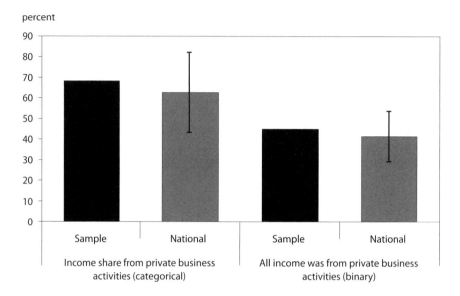

Income share from private business activities (categorical)

All income was from private business activities (binary)

Note: Vertical brackets display confidence intervals at the 95 percent confidence level.

demographic groups). But for both specifications the results fall easily within the 95 percent statistical confidence limits. We cannot reject the hypothesis that the refugee samples are providing information about the role of the market in household income as well as consumption in the lives of the remaining resident populace.

## The Political Economy of the 2002 Reforms

In July 2002, the government initiated a major policy reform with four components: microeconomic policy changes, including alteration of administered prices and wages; macroeconomic policy changes, including the introduction of direct taxes; establishment of special economic zones; and aid seeking.[8] The government subsequently reversed course starting

8. Three analytically distinct price changes occurred, each with their own political economy implications: changes in relative prices and wages, which could be interpreted as an attempt to increase the role of material incentives; a tenfold increase in the price level, which could be interpreted as an attempt to deal with monetary overhang; and ongoing inflation (perhaps 130 to 140 percent annually between 2002 and 2005), which was the product of the collapse of

in 2005, including a failed attempt to reinstitute the PDS and new controls on both domestic markets and cross-border exchanges, culminating in the botched currency reform of 2009.

What happened? A close examination of the main components of the reform suggests that in each case the ratification of market activities was coupled with parallel efforts to reassert state control. As a result, the turn away from reform may be somewhat less marked than is thought, foreshadowed in important ways in the reforms themselves. This fact has important implications for how we think about the role of the external environment, and the onset of the nuclear crisis, in the reform process.

As a component of the 2002 reforms, North Korean enterprises were instructed that they were responsible for covering their own costs, and managers were nominally given more autonomy, including the ability to sell some output in the market. At the same time, however, the state administratively raised wage levels, with certain favored groups such as military personnel, party officials, scientists, and coal miners receiving supernormal increases. The government also maintained an administered price structure, which tended to badly lag the inflation in market prices. In the absence of any formal bankruptcy or other "exit" mechanism, there was no prescribed method for enterprises squeezed between these conflicting constraints to cease operations. Some enterprises remained in operation at extremely low levels of capacity utilization supported by fiscal subsidies or central bank loans. But another tack was for SOEs to engage in entrepreneurial activity, either by establishing "funding" and "foreign exchange earning" squads within the SOE or by effectively outsourcing entrepreneurship via August 3 activities and other more informal variants of it (S. C. Kim 2006, Yang and Shepard 2009).

In the agricultural sector, the government implemented a policy of both raising the procurement prices of grain to increase the volume of food entering the PDS and dramatically raising PDS prices to consumers. The price of grain distributed through the quantity rationing system, which had been trivial historically, rose roughly 40,000 percent or more in the six months following the reform. However, procurement prices did not keep pace with rising market prices, and anecdotal accounts suggest that the policy was not successful in coaxing local supply back into PDS procurement channels.

At the same time that the government was undertaking microeconomic reforms, its inability to secure resources from the fraying SOEs and cooperative sectors forced it to undertake a fundamental fiscal and financial reform. Accounting systems in North Korea were always weak, with a nominal "independent accounting system" historically trumped by the state's demand for any firm profits (Yang and Shepard 2009).

---

fiscal revenue, exacerbated by the maintenance of a bloated military—over 1 million troops in a country of 23–24 million people.

With the central plan crumbling, the government was no longer able to raise significant revenue through a "transactions tax" levied through the central plan.[9]

Unable to tax effectively, the government initiated a campaign to sell People's Life Bonds in March 2003, an instrument more closely resembling a lottery ticket than a bond as conventionally understood.[10] The government then attempted to address its underlying fiscal crisis by moving from the "transactions tax" system to direct taxation of enterprise profits, as in a market economy.[11] This reform proved highly problematic. The enterprises did not have the accounting systems to make this shift feasible nor for that matter did the state. For 50 years the economy had run on the basis of centrally orchestrated quantity planning, not financial accounting of profits and losses. Not until March 2003 was accounting legislation enacted, and not until September 2003 was the tax collection agency even organized![12] Amid this chaos, one tack was to push responsibility for tax collection down to local governments, which were then supposed to share collections with the center. Not surprisingly, it appears that the local authorities were unwilling and/or unable to carry out these responsibilities.

In sum, rather than "leading" the transition, the reforms were responses to the de facto marketization we have described. Raising controlled prices was a response to the emergence of market prices, which

9. Lim (2005, 7) quotes a purported internal North Korean document from October 2001 in which Kim Jong-il, who took power following his father Kim Il-sung's death in 1994, bemoans the loss of state control over the economy and concludes, "Frankly the state has no money, but individuals have two years' budget worth."

10. North Korea has a history of resorting to lottery-like instruments to deal with monetary overhang problems. The People's Life Bonds had a 10-year maturity, with principal to be repaid in annual installments beginning in year five. However, there did not appear to be any provision for interest payments and no money for such payments was budgeted. Rather, for the first two years of the program the government would hold semiannual drawings (annually thereafter), with winners to receive their principal plus prizes. Moreover, there is evidence that purchase of the bonds was not altogether voluntary, as committees were established in every province, city, county, institute, factory, village, and town to promote their sale as a "patriotic deed." In the event, there were some winners whose luck was broadcast on national television, though no information was provided on the expected odds or prize values.

11. The North Korean propaganda machine promulgates the myth that North Koreans are not taxed and even celebrates the anniversary of a 1974 law "completely abolishing taxes." However, the enterprise "transaction income money" (guh-rae-soo-ip-geum) was similar to a value-added tax (VAT), and its replacement, the "national enterprise profit money" (guk-ga-gi-up-i-deuk-geum), is a corporate income tax by any other name. Citizens are furthermore subject to a variety of levies and fees, including through mobilization campaigns in which they are called on to "donate" additional work effort. For an overview of some of these levies, see Yoo (2010).

12. It's called the jip-geum-so—literally, "a place to collect money." Remember, there are no "taxes" in North Korea!

more accurately reflected real scarcities. The granting of some managerial autonomy to SOEs and price incentives to farmers were efforts to coax economic activity from the market back into state-controlled entities and channels. And the tax and financial reforms clearly reflected the declining ability of the state to access resources through the planning process. "Reforms" were motivated in part by efforts to reestablish state control. As marketization continued apace, it is not surprising that the state subsequently lost confidence in the reform effort and reverted to more direct forms of economic control.

This interpretation of the reform process has important implications for understanding the role the external environment has played in the political economy of North Korea's reform. It is often argued, including by the North Koreans themselves, that external military and political pressures limited the ability of the government to pursue opening and reform (for example, Moon and Bae 2003, Moon 2008). Under this interpretation, the changed policy environment at the end of the Bill Clinton administration and the 2000 North-South summit set the stage for the 2002 policy changes, which launched North Korea on a reform path. However, this outcome was derailed by the onset of the nuclear crisis and the hardline policies of the George W. Bush administration. We certainly cannot rule out the fact that the crisis favored hardliners (Carlin and Wit 2006), even if the crisis itself was partly of North Korea's own making. But there is also evidence, including in the design of the reforms themselves, that the process of marketization created substantial discomfort and that the government's posture toward the reform process was highly ambivalent. As a result, the reforms were partial and poorly designed in important respects, which in turn contributed to the weak response to them.

## Did Reform Matter? Effects on Market Behavior and Satisfaction

Despite the government's reluctance, the 2002 policy changes did initiate some changes in the operation of SOEs and other work units and decriminalized some entrepreneurial coping activities. To what extent did the reforms matter? And to what extent did the gradual reversal of reforms after 2005 have effect? Prior surveys of North Korean refugees have reported a decline in "criminal" activity in the postreform period, but they do not document an increase in marketization, which as we have shown from our surveys continued at a high level (Y. H. Lee 2007; Chang, Haggard, and Noland 2009a). However, a crucial question is whether marketization continued apace as a result of the reforms or in spite of them.

In the China-based survey, respondents who had spent at least one year in North Korea since the introduction of the 2002 reforms were asked

**Figure 3.8    China survey response to "Food availability has improved in North Korea"** (percent)

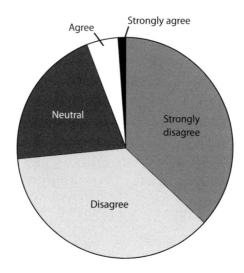

if the availability of food had increased. The results are striking: Despite the postfamine recovery, almost three-quarters of the respondents indicated that they disagreed or disagreed strongly that food availability had increased in the period since the reforms were introduced, suggesting that the reforms had not generated a significant supply response (figure 3.8). Ninety percent of the respondents agreed or agreed strongly that North Koreans were voicing concerns about food shortages; obviously, the deprivation associated with chronic shortages is likely to remain a political flashpoint for the regime as will be examined in more detail in chapter 5.

The South Korea survey undertook a more nuanced examination of these issues. Figures 3.9 and 3.10 show responses to questions about the business environment from all respondents who engaged in private business or market activities, grouped by time of departure. In each case, respondents were asked to rate their opinion or belief on a scale of 1 to 5, where 1 indicates strong disagreement and 5 indicates strong agreement. We report here the combined share of respondents who answered "totally agree" and "agree."

Figure 3.9 shows the answer to a general question about the ease of engaging in private trading. The results do show an increase in those reporting that it was easier to engage in private trading in the reform era cohort, although this trend was already well in evidence in the postfamine group. Two other trends are noteworthy, however. First, there is little difference between the reform and retrenchment groups in the answer to this question; despite increased restrictions, individuals continued to

**Figure 3.9    Ease of engaging in private trading in North Korea: South Korea survey**

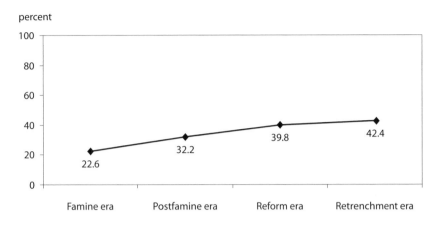

Note: The line tracks share of respondents "totally agreeing" or "agreeing" that it has become easier to engage in private trading.

**Figure 3.10    Perceptions of the business environment for market and private activities: South Korea survey** (share of respondents replying "totally agree" or "agree")

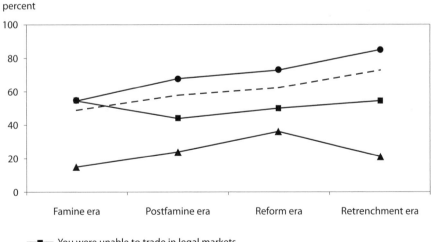

engage in trade. And second, figure 3.10 confirms a general increase in those citing restrictions on their ability to conduct business across departure cohorts. The share reporting that they were unable to trade in legal markets falls in the postfamine group but then rises again in the reform and retrenchment cohorts. Those answering that the government was able to control the prices of things sold also increases in the reform era cohort, before falling in the retrenchment period, probably reflecting a shift back toward illicit forms of trade like "alley markets" outside of official scrutiny. And most noteworthy is the steady increase in the share answering that the government frequently changed the rules governing market activities, and particularly those reporting they had to pay bribes to engage in private activity.[13] Those reporting that the need to bribe rose even during the reform and jumped sharply in the retrenchment period as the state once again tightened controls. These responses are consistent with those in another, smaller survey in which the most frequently cited motivation for paying bribes was "to continue to work as a vendor" (B. Y. Kim 2010, table 2).[14]

The foregoing questions looked at the effects of reform and retrenchment on market activity. The survey also asked questions on the perceived consequences of the reforms on particular economic activities and on different work units. Table 3.4 reports responses to a set of questions posed to respondents employed in the agricultural sector about practices at the time of their departure relative to the situation ten years earlier. Comparison of the responses provided by those leaving before and after the reforms does suggest a modest increase in the ability to sell products on the market (42 and 53 percent, respectively), an attenuation of disagreement with a statement about autonomy in decision making and an increase in the frequency of rule changing (which could be good or bad).[15]

However, most respondents in the agricultural sector replied negatively to the bottom line question—"Did you become better off?"—as did the respondents in the China survey (figure 3.11). In the postreform subsample, fewer thought that their situation had deteriorated and at least some thought that it had improved. However, this is not necessarily good news; one possible explanation is the shift in the terms of trade in favor of agriculture as shortages once again became apparent and prices rose.

---

13. The high reported response to changing market rules parallels a similar result we obtained in a survey of 300 Chinese firms doing business in North Korea, where 79 percent of the respondents cited arbitrary changes in rules and regulations as a barrier to doing business in North Korea and 52 percent reported that bribery was needed to do business in North Korea.

14. These households reported spending nearly 9 percent of household income on bribes, which B. Y. Kim (2010) estimates is equivalent to 6 to 7 percent of North Korean GDP or a figure higher than that of the Soviet Union on the eve of its collapse.

15. The number of "retrenchment era" leavers is relatively small at the sectoral level and is not reported separately.

**Table 3.4　Pre- and post-reform perceptions of agricultural policies: South Korea survey** (percent)

| Relative to conditions 10 years earlier, at the time of your departure: | Prereform (before 2002) | | | | Postreform (2003 and after) | | | |
|---|---|---|---|---|---|---|---|---|
| | Totally agree/agree | Neutral | Totally disagree/disagree | Unclear/don't know | Totally agree/agree | Neutral | Totally disagree/disagree | Unclear/don't know |
| The cooperative or farm had more control over planting decisions | 18.5 | 21.5 | 46.2 | 13.9 | 29.4 | 17.7 | 42.7 | 10.3 |
| There was greater availability of inputs such as fertilizer | 6.2 | 35.4 | 52.3 | 6.2 | 11.8 | 26.5 | 54.4 | 7.4 |
| The government or cooperative managers seemed to take more and more grain from the cooperative each year | 52.3 | 26.2 | 12.3 | 9.2 | 61.8 | 25.0 | 11.8 | 1.5 |
| You had more access to land to grow what you wanted | 18.5 | 26.2 | 49.2 | 6.2 | 29.4 | 16.2 | 50 | 4.4 |
| You had more opportunity to trade farm products on the market | 41.5 | 29.2 | 27.7 | 1.5 | 52.9 | 27.9 | 17.7 | 1.5 |
| The government changed the rules more often | 40 | 21.5 | 9.2 | 29.2 | 64.7 | 22.1 | 2.9 | 10.3 |
| You became better off | 4.7 | 20.3 | 71.9 | 3.1 | 17.7 | 16.2 | 66.2 | 0 |

**Figure 3.11  China survey response to "Did you become better off?"**
(percent)

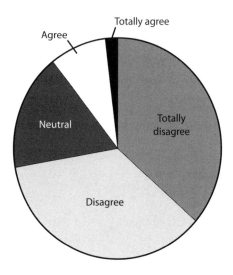

A similar set of questions asked to respondents employed in SOEs elicited a similar pattern of responses: documentation of increased marketization, though not much evidence of an acceleration of marketization in the postreform subsample (table 3.5). In contrast to the farmers, whose terms of trade may have improved following the reforms, even fewer of the previously privileged urban proletariat thought that their situation had improved, and indeed there was some increase in negative responses in the postreform subsample; nearly four out of five workers disagreed with the statement that they had become better off.

A somewhat similar set of questions was posed to those working in a government or party office (table 3.6). The responses reveal that marketization reached into the state itself. Seventy percent of the respondents reported their units spending more time on money-making activities outside their traditional duties, and only 8 percent disagreed with this characterization. Even larger margins (82 percent affirmative, 4 percent negative) supported the notion that over time public officials became more corrupt, an issue to which we return in the next section. A majority of the respondents agreed with the statement that over time more effort was devoted to ideological indoctrination in their offices, as authorities responded to eroding discipline with ideological campaigns. Finally, on the bottom line "You became better off" question, the majority disagreed, but the share (58 percent) was much lower than in the rural (66 percent) or SOE (79 percent) sectors, again reinforcing the notion of the state's relatively privileged position.

A third cut at the question of whether and how the reforms mattered

**Table 3.5  Pre- and post-reform perceptions of state-owned enterprise reforms: South Korea survey** (percent)

| Relative to conditions 10 years earlier, at the time of your departure: | Prereform (before 2002) | | | | Postreform (2003 and after) | | | |
|---|---|---|---|---|---|---|---|---|
| | Totally agree/agree | Neutral | Totally disagree/disagree | Unclear/don't know | Totally agree/agree | Neutral | Totally disagree/disagree | Unclear/don't know |
| More of your enterprise's output was sold on the market | 58.7 | 6.5 | 30.4 | 4.4 | 43.8 | 25 | 25 | 6.3 |
| More of your work was done outside the enterprise | 69.6 | 10.9 | 15.2 | 4.4 | 72.9 | 10.4 | 14.6 | 2.1 |
| People did not seem to work as hard for the work unit as in the past | 73.9 | 17.4 | 8.7 | 0 | 77.1 | 10.4 | 10.4 | 2.1 |
| Your factory was involved in market activities outside the plan | 58.7 | 15.2 | 21.7 | 4.4 | 47.9 | 31.3 | 12.5 | 8.3 |
| The quality of social services at your work unit declined | 76.1 | 13 | 6.5 | 4.4 | 87.5 | 10.4 | 2.1 | 0 |
| The government changed the rules more often | 65.2 | 8.7 | 6.5 | 19.6 | 58.3 | 27.1 | 0 | 14.6 |
| You became better off | 2.2 | 17.4 | 76.1 | 4.4 | 8.3 | 10.4 | 79.2 | 2.1 |

**Table 3.6 Government and party officers' perceptions of reform trends: South Korea survey** (percent)

| Relative to conditions 10 years earlier, at the time of your departure: | Prereform (before 2002) | | | | Postreform (2003 and after) | | | |
|---|---|---|---|---|---|---|---|---|
| | Totally agree/agree | Neutral | Totally disagree/ disagree | Unclear/ don't know | Totally agree/agree | Neutral | Totally disagree/ disagree | Unclear/ don't know |
| Over time, more effort was spent on ideological and propaganda work in your office | 54.2 | 16.7 | 25.0 | 4.2 | 50.0 | 30.8 | 7.7 | 11.5 |
| Over time, corruption among public officials and high-ranking officers increased | 87.5 | 8.3 | 4.2 | 0 | 76.9 | 7.7 | 3.9 | 11.5 |
| Over time, your office/unit devoted more time to money-making activities not directly related to your official or traditional responsibilities | 66.7 | 12.5 | 12.5 | 8.3 | 73.1 | 15.4 | 3.9 | 7.7 |
| Your office competed against other government/party/military organizations in money-making activities | 45.8 | 29.2 | 12.5 | 12.5 | 26.9 | 42.3 | 15.4 | 15.4 |
| The government changed the rules more often | 41.7 | 25.0 | 12.5 | 20.8 | 53.9 | 34.6 | 3.9 | 7.7 |
| You became better off | 16.7 | 12.5 | 62.5 | 8.3 | 19.2 | 23.1 | 53.9 | 3.9 |

is to look at the evaluation of the effects across the sample on the basis of various demographic factors. The list of variables that were *not* robustly correlated with the responses in figure 3.11 is long: sex, age, year of departure from North Korea, time in South Korea or a third country, educational attainment, and residence in the capital city Pyongyang or in a border province.[16]

There were several robust correlates, however, beginning with departure from North Korea in the retrenchment era (2006 or after), which was associated with positive self-assessments. Employment in an SOE was negatively correlated; state-sector workers did not believe that they had fared well under the new order. This is mirrored in the findings with respect to occupation. Status as a professional or merchant was positively correlated with self-assessment of being better off, and status as a worker was negatively correlated, corresponding with the SOE results reported above. Involvement in the August 3 program, and, to a lesser extent, in unspecified private activities was negatively correlated with self-assessment of being better off.[17] And not surprisingly membership in the core class and (less strongly) in the wavering class were both positively correlated with self-assessment of improved well-being.[18]

Tables 3.4 to 3.6 depict pervasive disappointment with developments in North Korea. We asked respondents to compare their situation at the

---

16. Unlike the previously reported results pertaining to a factual question—i.e., "What share of your income was earned in the market?"—the assessment of whether one is better off is inherently more subjective. As a consequence a number of "experiential variables" were also tried: whether the respondents' family members died in the famine, whether the respondents knew about the aid program but believed that they had not received aid, whether they had been arrested or incarcerated, as well as a number of others. These variables were not robustly correlated with the evaluation of whether one had been made better off. Due to the stratification of North Korean society, to a certain extent these experiences are bundled, and collinearity across responses meant that one could generate significant coefficients on some regressors in particular specifications. For example, in Haggard and Noland (2010c) we report that if work in a party office was excluded from the specification, the coefficient on death of a family member was sometimes significant.

17. This could be regarded as a surprising result—involvement in the market was associated with lower self-assessment of well-being—except that it is important to recall that involvement in the market reflects a mix of both "opportunity entrepreneurship," which would presumably reflect improved well-being, and "necessity self-employment" by women, for example, involuntarily shed from SOE employment. This is consistent with the predictably negative relationship between formal-sector wages and informal activity obtained in an earlier survey focusing on refugees who departed during the prereform period (Kim and Song 2008).

18. It is theoretically possible that rather than the demographic characteristics contributing to the respondents' views, causality runs the other direction—i.e., class and occupation are endogenous to the self-assessment of whether one is better off. In Haggard and Noland (2010c) we report that when the regressions were reestimated using the respondent's father's political classification, occupation, and educational attainment, political class no longer is correlated with the assessment of well-being.

time of their departure to conditions ten years earlier. Regression results show that members of the more politically favored classes, professionals, and merchants—i.e., precisely those best positioned to exploit emerging opportunities be they legal or not—are less unhappy than most, particularly in comparison to the industrial proletariat. The August 3 workers were the most marketized group but partly due to involuntary separation from SOEs, particularly in the case of women. Apparently the only thing worse than being an SOE employee is being a redundant SOE employee in a society without any real social safety net. It is also striking that in none of the reported regressions—on household income, expenditure, or satisfaction—was educational attainment directly correlated with outcomes. Rather, the importance of political class and sector suggests a society in which position is paramount, and returns to human capital may be quite low.

There is one potential silver lining to the process of crisis-induced marketization. Residence in North or South Hamgyong, provinces in the northeast that constitute the North Korean rust-belt and by consensus were the areas worst hit by the famine, was positively associated with self-assessment of improved well-being. People from the worst affected regions and those who were comparing recent experiences with the famine era a decade earlier had marginally more positive assessments. While conditions are bad, the emergence of markets has acted as a kind of safety valve most acutely felt in the worst conditions. Obviously, well-functioning markets supported by appropriate state institutions would be preferable to marketization in the absence of institutions, but even irregular markets appear to have an ameliorative effect. But this finding is also potentially of deeper significance, mirroring results from China's Great Leap famine (Yang 1996, Thaxton 2008). Those areas that were hardest hit by the famine also may have experienced the most robust marketization and thus be poised over the longer run to be centers of more dynamic growth and de facto reform.

Again, we need to ask whether the findings with respect to the reforms among the sample reflect the views of the underlying population. With the caveats already noted, counterfactual projections of national values can be estimated, converting the mean responses, originally scored on a 1 to 5 metric, to a 0 to 100 scale to generate an "approval rating"(figure 3.12).[19]

---

19. Sample approval ratings are simply the scaled mean score of each response variable. To calculate approval ratings, we predict the probability of observing each response conditional on estimated national values of each explanatory variable. The predicted probabilities sum to one. To estimate the mean response we sum the products of each score and its predicted probability, giving us a probability weighted mean response. We then convert this value to a 0 to 100 scale. The same procedure is applied to calculating minimum and maximum predicted probabilities of each outcome, which are estimated at the 95 percent confidence level and used to establish confidence intervals for each response estimate. See Haggard and Noland (2010c).

**Figure 3.12   Response to "You became better off ": Sample
(South Korea survey) versus national projection**

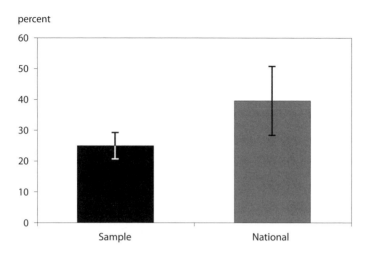

percent

Note: Vertical brackets display confidence intervals at the 95 percent confidence level.

Unlike the previous counterfactual projections on household income and expenditure, there are in fact noticeable differences in attitudes derived from the raw survey data and projected national responses. The survey sample does marginally overweight demographic groups with less favorable assessments of the regime, with the central projected values implying approximately 15 percentage points more positive assessments by the national population. This is to be expected given the likely disaffection of the refugee sample and in fact gives us some confidence in our wider findings. That said, the projected "approval rating" by the national population is still less than 40 percent in all specifications. Moreover, it is again not possible to categorically state that the projected national values are different from the reported values derived from the sample once the 95 percent confidence intervals are taken into account.

## The Market, Corruption, and the Changing Social Order

Finally, the respondents were asked a series of questions designed to get at changing perceptions of the most effective pathway to both increased status and income (figures 3.13 and 3.14). When asked the best way to get ahead in North Korea, officialdom (including both government and party) trumped both the military and engaging in business, with more than 70 percent of the respondents citing it in all sample periods. But "engaging in business" more than doubled from 8 percent among

**Figure 3.13    Best way to get ahead in North Korea: South Korea survey**

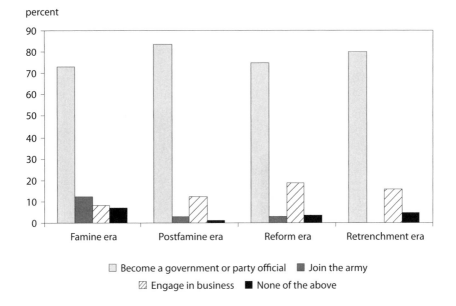

percent

Become a government or party official    Join the army

Engage in business    None of the above

**Figure 3.14    Easiest way to make money in North Korea: South Korea survey**

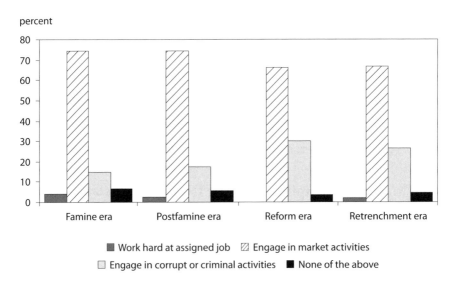

percent

Work hard at assigned job    Engage in market activities

Engage in corrupt or criminal activities    None of the above

respondents departing in the famine era to 18 percent for those leaving after the 2002 reforms.[20]

A more striking set of social changes is apparent from the question, "What is the easiest way to make money in North Korea: work hard at assigned job, engage in market activities, engage in corrupt or criminal activities, or none of the above?" (figure 3.14). Although securing a government or party position is highly desirable (figure 3.13), there is no sense that merit is rewarded; only a small—and falling—share reported that working hard at your assigned job yields fruit (figure 3.14).[21] The most frequent response in all three periods—consistently over 65 percent—was that engaging in market activities is the easiest way to make money, but a steadily increasing share—approaching 30 percent in the reform period cohort—saw corruption and criminality as the most lucrative career path.

Read in conjunction, the answers to the two questions—together with the direct testimony of rising corruption among those employed in government and party offices—suggest strongly that an official position is valuable not because hard work and merit are rewarded. Rather, public office constitutes an entitlement and increasingly provides a platform for engaging in business or corrupt or criminal rent extraction, a notion explored in further detail in the following chapter.

The views of those who were aware of the reforms confirm these findings. Among those who left North Korea after 2002, 82 percent reported awareness of the reforms, which is not surprising given the dramatic changes in both nominal and relative prices that accompanied them. Of these respondents, most believed that the reforms supported marketization (table 3.7). However, by even larger margins, they associated the policy changes with a growth in materialism (92 percent), corruption (89 percent), and inequality (84 percent).

## Conclusion

Economists often think of the state as playing a potentially enabling role for economic development, providing public goods such as the legal protection of property rights. The political economy of reform is conceived in terms of bargaining over such policies among elites or special interest groups, resulting in policies that are more or less conducive to growth.

---

20. Interestingly, despite the proclamation of "military-first" politics, the army's appeal declined as an avenue to get ahead: While institutionally the military may have experienced rising influence, from an individual standpoint, the largely conscript army was not seen as a channel of advancement, with not a single respondent in the most recent subsample citing it as the way to get ahead.

21. Indeed, in the reform period only a single respondent believed hard work at one's assigned job was the way to succeed.

**Table 3.7   Perceptions of the reforms: South Korea survey** (percent; postreform subsample n=122)

| Perception | Reform era (2003–05) | | | | Retrenchment era (2006 and after) | | | |
|---|---|---|---|---|---|---|---|---|
| | Totally agree/agree | Neutral | Totally disagree/ disagree | Unclear/ don't know | Totally agree/agree | Neutral | Totally disagree/ disagree | Unclear/ don't know |
| The reforms allowed more people to trade in the market | 55.4 | 28.9 | 15.7 | 0 | 51.3 | 25.6 | 12.8 | 10.3 |
| The reforms increased the amount of goods in the market | 57.8 | 21.7 | 18.1 | 2.4 | 59.0 | 15.4 | 15.4 | 10.3 |
| The reforms increased the amount of food in the market | 48.2 | 28.9 | 18.1 | 4.8 | 53.9 | 15.4 | 20.5 | 10.3 |
| After the reforms, people started to care only about money | 89.2 | 7.2 | 2.4 | 1.2 | 97.4 | 0 | 0 | 2.6 |
| After the reforms, corruption increased | 91.6 | 4.8 | 2.4 | 1.2 | 84.6 | 7.7 | 2.6 | 5.1 |
| As a result of the reforms, society became more unequal | 84.3 | 8.4 | 4.8 | 2.4 | 84.6 | 7.7 | 5.1 | 2.6 |

The North Korean case turns this perspective on its head. Efficiency-enhancing institutional and behavioral changes in highly distorted economies may arise not out of a conscious, top-down program of reform, but rather as an unintended (and in some respects, unwanted) "bottom-up" response to state failure.

Responses from both surveys demonstrate that the economy marketized in response to state failure with the onset of famine in the 1990s, and subsequent reforms and retrenchments appear to have had remarkably little impact on at least some significant share of the population. There is strong evidence, however, of powerful social changes, including increasing inequality, corruption, and changed attitudes about the most effective pathways to higher social status and income. These assessments appear to be remarkably consistent across demographic groups. The survey samples do marginally overweight demographic groups with less favorable assessments of the regime. But counterfactually recalibrating the samples to match the underlying resident population suggests widespread dissatisfaction with the North Korean regime, its capabilities, and accomplishments.

Moreover, there is evidence that the regime was highly insecure with respect to the potential political implications of marketization. One piece of evidence in this regard is the design of the reforms themselves, which suggests persistent efforts to maintain economic control. In the next chapter, we provide further evidence of this concern by looking at the criminalization of economic activity and an increased reliance on an expanded penal system as a tool of both political intimidation and economic predation. In chapter 5 we address frontally the internal political implications of these developments.

# 4

# The Penal System and Criminalization of Economic Activity

The previous chapter documented the grassroots marketization of the North Korean economy born of state failure and famine. This unplanned and unwanted development emerged from the coping strategies of citizens and was not overtly political. But marketization also eroded the state's control of the economy and therefore its control over pathways to wealth, prestige, and ultimately power as well; the emergence of the market even raised the specter of an independent civil society around unregulated market relations. As we saw in the last chapter, the regime's response to this process was ambivalent, sometimes tolerating market activity, sometimes seeking to control it and sustain the state sector. An important component of these control efforts has been the growing criminalization of economic activity. As a result of this process of criminalization, the penal system has played a surprisingly central role in the government's response to economic and social change.

In the last decade, a variety of sources have allowed analysts to piece together a picture of North Korea's penal system. Satellite imagery, including images secured through providers such as DigitalGlobe and Google Earth, have permitted a precise mapping of the country's major prisons. Refugee memoirs, unstructured interviews, and databases of human rights violations[1] have focused particular attention on the political prison camp system, a sprawling, Soviet-style gulag characterized by arbitrary arrest and widespread abuse, including extreme deprivation of food and medical treatment, torture, and public executions.

---

1. See C. H. Kang (2002), Hawk (2003), Muico (2007), KINU (2009), Database Center for North Korean Human Rights (2008), and Y. Kim (2009).

The penal system is by no means limited to the political prison camps, however. As is true of all authoritarian systems, North Korea has a complex and differentiated set of penal institutions, which cannot be understood without reference to the economic and social changes of the past two decades. During the famine, the regime established an extensive system of low-level labor training facilities that were used to incarcerate those caught crossing the border into China or repatriated by Chinese authorities, movements that increased in the wake of the famine. However, labor training facilities were also used to punish the unprecedented level of internal movement and market activity as heavily affected segments of the population wandered the countryside in search of food (Noland 2000).

The 2004 reforms of the criminal code and procedures regularized these facilities and specified "labor training" for up to two years as punishment for a growing number of economic and social crimes (Han 2006, Yoon 2009).[2] A further set of amendments to the criminal code in 2007 lengthened the list of these crimes and increased punishments for them.

In this chapter, the two refugee surveys are used to elucidate these developments. The respondents portray a judicial and penal system characterized by high rates of arbitrary detention and release, processing large numbers of people engaged in illicit activities for relatively short periods. In the China survey, roughly one-quarter of respondents reported having been arrested in China and repatriated to North Korea and nearly 10 percent reported incarceration in political and correctional detention facilities. Incarceration exposes prisoners to terrible abuses. Among the group reporting incarceration, 90 percent witnessed forced starvation, 60 percent deaths due to beating or torture, and 27 percent executions.

The South Korea survey posed more detailed questions about initial arrest and detention, the types of facilities in which respondents were held, and the conditions they witnessed while incarcerated. The experiences of this second sample largely confirm those of our China survey sample. Just over one-third had been detained in the penal system and similar numbers reported witnessing extreme forms of abuse.

This pattern of detention, abuse, and release not only serves to intimidate but also may benefit corrupt officials extracting bribes from those seeking to avoid detention. The more painful the incarceration, the greater the bribe officials can demand for avoiding it. The repressive apparatus also appears to work. Despite the dissatisfaction with the North Korean regime documented in chapter 3, the surveys also reveal a highly atomized society in which barriers to collective action are profound and overt political opposition minimal; these issues are taken up in more detail in chapter 5.

Following brief overviews of the criminalization of economic activity, particularly in the 2004 and 2007 revisions of the criminal code, and the

2. Both the Criminal Law and the Criminal Procedure Law were revised in 2004.

North Korean penal system, this chapter provides a descriptive overview of respondents' experiences with the legal and penal systems. A striking finding is that conditions seen as characteristic of the country's infamous gulag of political penal-labor colonies—such as extreme deprivation and exposure to violence—exist across the entire penal system, including the work camps established to handle lower-level economic crimes. The incidence of such abuses is especially notable when taking into account the generally shorter periods of incarceration in the lower-level facilities.

An analysis of the determinants of arrest and incarceration reveals that the repressive apparatus disproportionately targets those involved in market-oriented activities. Such individuals were more than half again as likely to be arrested than the general sample.

This legal and penal system appears to play a dual role. On the one hand, it is an instrument of political repression and intimidation, including with respect to illicit economic activity. On the other hand, the criminalization of economic activity may be facilitating economic predation. As we saw in the previous chapter, the surveys provide evidence of an increase in bribery and corruption in North Korea. High levels of discretion with respect to arrest and incarceration abet shakedowns and extortion, facilitating corruption. From the standpoint of the central authorities, while these practices may constitute a kind of safety valve for low-level officials, unchecked, such malfeasance could ultimately threaten the political reliability of the internal security apparatus itself.

## Criminalization of Economic Activity

Political authorities in fraying and marketizing state socialist systems face a number of challenges to the integrity of the state sector and the ability to control economic resources. The criminalization of some activities, such as outright theft or destruction of government property, is arguably just the socialist counterpart of laws defending private property in capitalist economies. However, the effort of households and work units to engage in income-earning activities also poses economic as well as political challenges, even if these activities ultimately reflect the inability of the state sector to provide employment and basic necessities.

Individuals engaged in unauthorized private enterprise and trading do not show up at their work units. They, and their activities, are also difficult to tax. The postfamine reforms sought to regularize trade through markets, in part as a way of tapping new sources of revenue (particularly through market stand rental fees and sales taxes). But informal markets can evade such levies. In addition to these losses of labor and taxes is the political problem of individuals slipping through the elaborate net of political surveillance and monitoring, of which control of employment and the work unit are integral components.

**Figure 4.1   Response to "Government restrictions are increasing "** (percent)

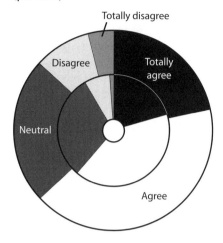

Note: The outer circle is the South Korea survey and the inner circle is the China survey. The question was worded slightly differently in the two surveys. The China survey's question was focused on restrictions regarding border crossing and defectors, whereas the South Korea survey's was a generalized question.

As a result, authorities have incentives to punish both failure to appear at work and the associated private activity. Not surprisingly, respondents in both surveys indicated that they believed that the level of repression had increased (figure 4.1). In the South Korea survey, the share agreeing or strongly agreeing that the government was increasing restrictions on the citizenry was 55 to 65 percent of the respondents across all four period subsamples; in each period, over half of respondents saw repression increasing.

Similar issues surround the complex principal-agent relationships between political authorities and enterprise and cooperative managers, even when the planning system is working as designed (Gregory 2004, Yang and Shepard 2009). Political authorities in communist systems appear to wield tremendous power, but they cannot single-handedly oversee the entire planning system. Decision making is necessarily delegated from the national planning commission, through the district planning commissions and economic ministries down to corporate groups and individual enterprise and cooperative managers. As the planning process collapsed, both acquisition of inputs and sale of final output increasingly took place through informal exchanges, making it more and more difficult for lower-level planning bodies to exercise effective oversight. "On-the-spot guidance" and special investigative units can be used to keep managers in line, but the leader and the inspectors cannot be everywhere at once and problems of asymmetric information abound. Party cadre are an additional instrument of control, but they too are vulnerable to the same principal-agent slack and opportunism that occurs with respect to managers. Paul Gregory (2004, 141) outlines the dilemma: "A benign interpretation of managerial opportunism was their desire for a quiet life. A more sinister interpretation was rent-seeking to enhance political and financial clout."

The emergence of market opportunities compounds these control problems immensely. Given the inefficiency of the planning process, managers can earn enormous rents by allocating resources more efficiently, engaging in trade—including foreign trade—and underreporting earnings. Political authorities have strong incentives to limit the diversion of state output to private use, including food grown on cooperatives, and the illegal use, profiteering from, or even sale of state assets. But the lack of coherent accounting mechanisms makes it difficult to observe these activities.

The evolution of economic crimes in North Korea exhibits a complex dialectic related to the government's tacking between reform and retrenchment (Yoon 2009). In the 1998 revision of the constitution, the government recognized income earned through legal economic activities as private property (Article 24); for a socialist system, this was potentially a major breakthrough (Frank 2005). Articles 20, 22, and 36 also expanded the scope for social organizations (such as professional organizations) and cooperatives to engage in commercial activity and even to own property and engage in foreign trade.

Yet the combination of system fraying and the partial economic reforms themselves gave rise to a variety of activities that went beyond what the state allowed or was comfortable with. Some economic crimes were subsequently managed through administrative punishments at the level of the work unit; the government introduced a new Administrative Penalty Law in 2004. But an increasing number of economic activities posed a substantial threat to socialist control. Even before the move away from reform, the government took a critical step of delineating these crimes with much greater precision, in part for legal reasons, in part because of the growing challenge these activities posed.[3] In the 1999 criminal code, the Chapter on Offenses against the Management of the Socialist Economy included

---

3. An important legal reason for the specification of economic crimes has to do with the formal commitment to the principle of *nullum crimen sine lege* in the 2004 revision of the criminal code: the principle that one cannot be prosecuted for a criminal activity unless there was a law specifically criminalizing the activity at the time it was committed. Under the old legal order—common to most Soviet-style legal systems—prosecutors and judges could prosecute and rule by analogy, allowing them to define activities as crimes if they resembled prohibited activity under statute. By moving toward this system, partly to nominally conform with global norms, the government simultaneously had to outline these crimes more precisely. Arguably, the legal changes are therefore less significant than they appear because individuals might well have been charged with similar activities even in the absence of corresponding statute.

eight articles. In 2004, it was retitled the Chapter on Offenses against the Management of the Economy and included 74 articles.

If taken literally, these laws prohibit a wide array of standard commercial activities and thus probably leave prosecutors the same level of discretion they enjoyed before the legal reforms. For example, Articles 110 and 111 of the 2004 criminal code provide for up to two years of labor training for individuals and firms engaging in "illegal commercial activities, therefore gaining large profits." Article 118 extends similar punishment to "gaining large profits through usury." Article 119 prohibits "illegally giving money or goods in exchange for labor." Violations of trade and foreign exchange controls receive particularly detailed attention (Article 104; Articles 1065–107; 116–117; 125–126). In sum, virtually all aspects of economic activity—commerce, financing, hiring of labor, foreign trade, and acquisition of foreign exchange—are potentially criminal activities.

Unauthorized movement is a critical feature of all of the activities listed above, and thus it, too, is criminalized. Leaving one's home without appropriate travel permits, overstaying travel permits, or leaving the country without authorization are all criminal offenses in North Korea. This last offense is of obvious significance to our consideration of refugees, as many seeking to leave are either caught in transit or apprehended by Chinese authorities and forcibly repatriated. Yet internal movement without a permit, for example, with the objective of trading, is also illegal.

It is noteworthy that this revision of the criminal code came only two years after the initiation of the country's most significant economic reform initiative in 2002. In 2007, a series of "additional clauses" (*bu-chik*) singled out a number of economic crimes for more severe punishment, including fixed prison terms and even death. Capital punishment was to be meted out for "extreme cases" of theft of state property and drug dealing, but increased punishments were also given for "illegally operating a business, such as a restaurant, motel or store," up to and including the death penalty (for running prostitution rings). We assume that these activities were criminalized because they were in fact taking place.

## The North Korean Penal System

The organization of the penal system provides a useful guide to the nature of crime and punishment in North Korea. The most notorious component of the prison system is the massive *kwan-li-so*, variously translated as political prison camps, labor colonies, or concentration camps; we will refer to them as political penal-labor camps. Built to incarcerate those guilty or suspected of political crimes, the number of these massive camps has recently been consolidated from 14 to about 5 sites. One camp (camp 22 near the Chinese border) is estimated to be 31 miles long and 25 miles wide and to hold 50,000 inmates (Harden 2009). With one exception, these camps are administered by the National Security Agency (NSA) (*bo-wi-bu*), an agency with wide-ranging external and internal security functions that include border and immigration control.[4]

The political suspects initially included counterrevolutionary social forces such as landlords, the religiously active, and members of purged political factions. Over time, this group came to encompass anyone guilty of political or ideological crimes or even suspected of disloyalty. Those with extensive knowledge of life outside North Korea have been particularly vulnerable to incarceration in these facilities, including repatriated Japanese-Koreans, those who have studied abroad, and those accused of trafficking people out of North Korea.

A distinctive feature of the management of political crimes is that there is little pretense of due process. Political crimes appear to fall outside of criminal statute altogether and are managed with a high level of discretion by the NSA. The NSA either apprehends those accused of political crimes directly or they are remanded to NSA custody; the NSA operates its own interim detention centers, including several dedicated to those caught attempting to cross the border or repatriated by Chinese authorities (Muico 2007). Prisoners accused of political crimes are detained in these interim facilities and tortured to extract confessions.

Once a case is deemed political, the NSA also assumes control of the detention process. A prosecutor from the NSA will hand down judgments in a closed-door local court session in the name of the central court in Pyongyang, including the decision of whether the criminal's family will also be sent with him. Group punishment in the form of incarceration of extended family and confiscation of property is a distinctive feature of the management of political crimes and incarceration in the political penal-labor camps. But the prosecutorial process is completely opaque from the perspective of the victim; inmates report being unaware of the precise nature of their crimes, incarceration is not the result of any meaningful judicial process, and sentences are effectively equivalent to time ultimately served.[5]

---

4. A useful summary of the history and functions of the NSA can be found in Namgung (2007).

5. The extrajudicial nature of political detention in North Korea is in clear violation of the Civil and Political Rights Covenant, to which North Korea is a state party. Inter alia, the covenant states that "anyone who is arrested shall be informed, at the time of arrest, of the reasons for his arrest…" and that "anyone who is deprived of his liberty by arrest or detention shall be entitled to take proceedings before a court, in order that that court may decide without delay on the lawfulness of his detention and order his release if the detention is not lawful" (Article 9). Some reported political detentions in North Korea resemble practices forbidden under the International Convention for the Protection of all Persons from Enforced Disappearance, or the so-called Desaparecido Convention (which has yet to enter into force and which North Korea has neither signed nor ratified). That convention defines "enforced disappearance"

Inmates of the political penal-labor camps (*kwan-li-so*) are typically assigned to hard labor in mining, logging, and farming enterprises in the highly inhospitable north and north-central part of the country; only in two political penal-labor camps is there reported evidence of efforts at political reeducation. Prisoners are also kept on starvation rations and many die of malnutrition and disease. Not surprisingly, the number of escapees from these camps is small; of the 300 refugees interviewed in the 2008 South Korea–based survey, only three report internments in a political penal-labor camp.[6]

Nonetheless, when asked if they were aware of the political penal-labor camps, 77 percent of the respondents in the South Korea survey responded affirmatively. When asked if they thought that those sent there were incarcerated justly, 93 percent responded "no."

Incarceration for standard criminal offenses, as well as the new economic crimes, is distributed through the remainder of the penal system. In addition to the political penal-labor camps, the government also maintains the *kyo-hwa-so*—literally, a "place to make someone better through education"—and sometimes translated as correctional or reeducation centers. In fact, there is little evidence that these facilities perform correctional or reeducation functions. Superficially, they resemble prisons for housing felons, and we will refer to them as penitentiaries. Prisoners in the *kyo-hwa-so* are presumably arrested for violations of the North Korean criminal code, subjected to a judicial process and given fixed-term sentences, which are described as "limited" if they are under 15 years and "unlimited" if longer than 15 years. The penitentiaries are administered by the People's Security Agency (PSA) (*an-jeon-bu*),[7] the national police force.

However, there are predictable differences with penitentiaries in

---

as "the arrest, detention, abduction or any other form of deprivation of liberty by agents of the State or by persons or groups of persons acting with the authorization, support or acquiescence of the State, followed by a refusal to acknowledge the deprivation of liberty or by concealment of the fate or whereabouts of the disappeared person, which place such a person outside the protection of the law" (Article 2).

6. Unfortunately, we have no information on the conditions under which these three either were released or escaped, but curiously the length of their incarceration does not differ significantly from that of the other respondents: one reported incarceration between one and five years, one of less than a year, but one reported being in a political penal-labor camp for less than a week. It is clearly difficult to draw inferences from three respondents, although the survivor testimony from these camps on these issues is now fairly extensive. See particularly Hawk (2003) and the memoirs of C. H. Kang (2002) and Y. Kim (2009).

7. The PSA replaced the Social Safety Agency in 1998, and the name of the police was changed from *an-jeon-bu* to *in-min-bo-an-sung*. The PSA was upgraded to the People's Security Ministry in April of 2010 (*in-min-bo-an-sung* to *in-min-bo-an-bu*). However, we use the term People's Security Agency because the change occurred after our second, South Korea survey and because the local police continue to be known colloquially as *an-jeon-bu*.

other penal systems. First, the definition of felony crimes in North Korea includes a range of activities that appear political rather than criminal. Table 4.1 outlines major categories of crimes, as defined by North Korean statute, the number of discrete crimes that fall under each type, the place of incarceration for the crimes in question and typical sentences. The list includes "anti-state, anti-people crimes," "crimes injurious to socialist economy," "crimes injurious to socialist culture," and "crimes injurious to socialist collective life." Hawk (2003) describes the case of a woman imprisoned in a penitentiary who had been convicted of disturbing the "socialist order" by singing a South Korean pop song in a private home. As table 4.1 also shows, however, correctional institutions house inmates convicted of a number of economic crimes.

As in the political penal-labor camps, prisoners in the penitentiaries are compelled to perform hard labor. Satellite imagery and refugee testimonies reveal that they are typically maximum-security compounds that combine buildings housing prisoners and administration with work units; some are located near mine faces. Refugees with experience in them report that they were subjected to brutal treatment and torture and deprived of adequate food and medical care. Many inmates do not live to serve out their sentences and escape may even be more difficult than from the sprawling political penal-labor camps (Hawk 2003, Muico 2007, KINU 2009). In the 2008 survey, 9 percent of those incarcerated reported spending time in a penitentiary.

The third and fourth components of the North Korean penal system manage lower-level crimes and misdemeanors. The *jip-kyul-so* ("collection centers") house low- or misdemeanor-level criminals for periods of up to six months of hard labor. As a study by the Korean Institute for National Unification (KINU 2009) describes this level of the penal system, "the cases handled by 'collection centers' include those whose crimes are not serious enough for [the penitentiaries] but too serious to send off to 'labor training camps.'" Examples would include violating a designated or restricted area or overstaying travel permits, but the KINU report also lists absence from work or group training sessions. Some North Koreans forcibly repatriated from China are also transferred to the "collection centers."

Finally, in addition to the collection centers for lower-level offenses there has been an explosive growth of *ro-dong-dan-ryeon-dae* (labor training centers), a network of facilities that dates to the 1990s. The labor training centers were not initially a statutory feature of the penal system. Rather, they emerged as an ad hoc response on the part of authorities to the fraying of socialist control during the famine and in its immediate aftermath, including unauthorized movement, black market activity, border-crossing, and the other economic crimes listed above (Noland 2000).

The labor training centers are operated at the municipal level. They constitute mobile labor brigades of relatively small numbers of prisoners—30 to 60—typically held for less than six months in small, mini-

**Table 4.1  Major categories of crime, number of discrete crimes falling under each category, place of incarceration, and typical sentences**

| Category | At correctional centers | | At designated locations (usually labor training centers) |
| --- | --- | --- | --- |
| | Unlimited term sentence | Limited term sentence (1 to 15 years) | Labor training sentence |
| Anti-state, anti-people crimes (14 types) | Conspiracy to overturn the state (5 types) | Conspiracy to overturn the state (14 types) | — |
| Crimes disruptive to national defense systems (16 types) | — | Neglecting preparedness for wartime production (15 types) | Neglecting preparedness for wartime production (10 types) |
| Crimes injurious to socialist economy (104 types) | Stealing state properties (6 types) | Stealing or robbing state properties (83 types) | Stealing or robbing state properties (76 types) |
| Crimes injurious to socialist culture (26 types) | Smuggling historical relics and smuggling and selling narcotics (3 types) | Importing and spreading depraved culture (25 types) | Importing and spreading depraved culture (16 types) |
| Crimes injurious to administrative systems (39 types) | — | Collective disturbance; interfering with official business (30 types) | Interfering with official business; creation or dissemination of false information (29 types) |
| Crimes harmful to socialist collective life (20 types) | — | Acts of hoodlumism or racketeering (15 types) | Acts of hoodlumism or racketeering (18 types) |
| Crimes injuring life or damaging property of citizens (26 types) | Willful murder or kidnapping (3 types) | Willful murder (25 types) | Excessive self-defense (13 types) |

*Source:* KINU (2009, table 2-4).

mally guarded and fenceless compounds. If not apprehended locally, these prisoners have already been through interrogations and shipped back to their hometowns for final release. Sometimes the detainees in the labor training centers are even allowed to go home for food or to recover from illness. Detainees do road repair, construction, and substitute for the lack of other forms of energy and transportation in the face of shortages, for example, by pushing train cars.

From 2001, this sort of labor training emerged as the preferred sentence not only for petty crimes but also for the growing range of economic crimes (table 4.1). In the 2004 revision of the penal code described above, "labor training sentence" was explicitly introduced as a new form of punishment, and the existence of the labor training centers therefore institutionalized (Han 2006, Yoon 2009, KINU 2009, B. Y. Kim 2010).

Labor training centers have played a particularly important role in the management of those caught crossing the border or repatriated from China (Muico 2007). Leaving the country without permission was initially considered equivalent to treason. The 1999 criminal law revision first distinguished defectors leaving for a subversive purpose from migrants who illegally leave the country for economic reasons; those in the first category were subject to much harsher punishments. Traveling abroad without permission remains a crime in the 2004 penal code, which provides for penalties up to and including death if such activity has a national security or antiregime dimension (Article 62). However, Article 233 of the revised penal code of 2004 permits sentences of up to two years in a labor training center.

Initial screening of repatriated North Koreans typically includes extensive questioning at special NSA detention facilities about contact with South Koreans while in China or exposure to South Korean propaganda, broadcasts, movies, or music; those involved in these more serious political offenses are liable to incarceration in the *kyo-hwa-so* (penitentiaries) or even the *kwan-li-so* (political penal-labor camps). The NSA retains discretion to either release those involved in border crossing after initial detention, which can last up to several months, or release them to the PSA for incarceration in locally managed *jip-kyul-so* ("collection centers") or *ro-dong-dan-ryeon-dae* (labor training centers).

Incarceration in these two types of lower-level facilities was by far the most common form of contact with the penal system among our respondents. Of the 102 South Korea–based survey respondents who reported some incarceration, 49 reported spending time in a labor training center and 68, or 23 percent of the 300 person sample, reported being detained in collection centers.

Table 4.2 summarizes the nature of the four main penal institutions including their administration, the nature of the offenses, the prosecutorial process and sentencing, and the number of respondents in our 2008 survey of South Korea–based refugees who ended up in each institution.

**Table 4.2   The North Korean prison system: An overview**

| Facility | Supervising institution | Offenses | Prosecutorial process and sentencing | Number in 2008 South Korea survey sample (n=300; number incarcerated = 102) |
|---|---|---|---|---|
| *Kwan-li-so* (political penal-labor camps) | National Security Agency (Bureau 7) | Serious political and ideological crimes but also "suspect" categories | Largely extrajudicial; high level of National Security Agency discretion, with effective life sentences, including for extended family, and confiscation of property | 3 (2.9 percent of those incarcerated) |
| *Kyo-hwa-so* (penitentiaries or long-term reeducation camps) | People's Security Agency | In addition to criminal felonies, serious crimes disruptive of national defense, injurious to the socialist economy, injurious to socialist culture, injurious to administration, and harmful to socialist collective life | Trial and court sentencing; "limited" terms of 1–15 years and "unlimited" terms of more than 15 years of correctional labor | 9 (8.8 percent) |
| *Jip-kyul-so* ("collection centers" or detention facilities) | People's Security Agency | More serious misdemeanors and economic crimes, including theft of state property, spreading "depraved culture," and some border crossing | Trial and court sentencing; sentences of six months to one year | 68 (66.7 percent) |
| *Ro-dong-dan-ryeon-dae* (labor training centers) | People's Security Agency, operated at county level | In addition to lower-level crimes, an expansive number of economic crimes, violations of labor administration, and rules governing socialist culture | Initially ad hoc rehabilitation facilities; institutionalized with 2004 revision of the penal code and expanded use of "labor training" as punishment; sentences of six months to two years | 49 (48 percent) |

Note: Numbers in last column do not sum to 100 percent because of multiple incarcerations.

Particularly noteworthy is the porous line between political and criminal activities and the wide range of activities that are subject to a labor training sentence under the revised criminal code (table 4.1).

## Who Gets Arrested and Imprisoned?

The first point of contact with the legal and penal system in North Korea is typically either the National Security Agency or the People's Security Agency, although ad hoc "antisocialist inspection units" have also been deployed to deal with border crossing and trafficking as well as economic crimes.[8] The NSA deals with political offenses and since about 2000 typically has conducted the first screening process of those apprehended for border crossing or repatriated by Chinese authorities. Just under 30 percent of the 2008 survey respondents reported being detained and questioned by the NSA. The exact same share reported being detained and questioned by the criminal police or PSA, with the remaining 40 percent reporting that they were detained and questioned by both.

It is probable that the high share detained by the NSA or both the NSA and the PSA reflects the greater propensity for refugees to have been detained for illicit border crossing efforts at some point. This suspicion gets support from results of our China survey reported in chapter 1. Roughly one-quarter of the respondents in our China survey had been repatriated, and of those repatriated, 26 percent had been repatriated twice and another 15 percent three or more times. However, some of those repatriated may also have been engaged in cross-border trafficking, business, or most likely survival efforts, which thus further increased their risk of capture and repatriation. About one-fifth of the respondents in the China survey had returned to North Korea voluntarily; taking money or food back were the overwhelming reasons cited (79 and 11 percent of those returning, respectively).

Multivariate analysis indicates that the probability of being arrested is highly correlated with involvement in private market activities; involvement in such activities generates a more than 50 percent increase in the likelihood of arrest. Detention is associated to a lesser extent with participation in the August 3 units described in chapter 3, a form of entrepreneurial activity operated through existing state-owned enterprises and other officially sanctioned entities. These findings are consistent with the regime's expansive definition of economic crime.

Among this sample of refugees, the likelihood of being arrested is also positively associated with having an advanced, postcollege education, even when controlling for occupation; being a professional is negatively

---

8. The multivariate analysis reported in the remainder of this chapter draws on Haggard and Noland (2011).

correlated with probability of arrest but with a smaller estimated impact. One possibility is that those with higher levels of education are better positioned than others to pursue illicit activities and thus run higher risks of incarceration. Another possibility is that the regime is more sensitive to the activities of the intelligentsia than other social groups.[9] Despite the ubiquity of "basic" illicit activities such as market trading, it is striking that laborers and housewives are less likely to be arrested, even though the involvement of housewives in the market is widespread. This fact may reflect at least some forbearance where market activities are seen as serving primarily survival purposes, although those arrested cut widely across all strata of the refugee population.

There is no robust statistical evidence of changes in propensity to get arrested over time. This could be because the government's overall propensity to incarcerate may also be unchanged, even if certain forms of punishment such as labor training have become more institutionalized over time, or it may reflect the fact that the respondent's date of exit is simply too imprecise a measure to get at changes in penal practices over time.

However, the strategy of intimidation includes not only detention and incarceration but also what happens to inmates once imprisoned.

## Nature of Punishment

Perhaps due to a desire to conform—at least superficially—to international norms, revisions of the legal code have gradually included a number of standard legal protections. *Habeas corpus* was introduced in the 1998 revision to the constitution. As noted above, the 2004 Criminal Procedure Law adopted the principle of *nullum crimen sine lege* (no crime without law) by stipulating that "no one shall be arrested or detained in a manner not provided for in the law or without following the procedures prescribed in the law" (Article 177). The law also now stipulates that no arrest shall be made without a warrant, that only investigators and "pretrial agents" can make an arrest (Article 180), and that a pretrial agent making an arrest must apply for, and receive, preapproval from a prosecutor (Article 181). A number of provisions in the 2004 criminal code revision even outline harsh penalties for those violating rules governing arrest, detention, search, and seizure.

A similar set of provisions appears to pertain to the criminal trial process. The NSA retains significant discretion with respect to all political crimes, which are handled through means that are largely extrajudicial.

---

9. Intriguingly, being assigned to a military unit is associated with a higher probability of being arrested in this sample, although the number of military respondents was too small (16) to make much of the result.

But revisions of the Criminal Procedure Law in 2004 and 2005 stipulate that "all criminal cases shall follow the principles, procedures and methods stipulated in the Criminal Procedure Law" and that "trials be conducted at appropriate levels of court, and the punishment levels shall be determined by court decisions."

Not surprisingly, these legal and procedural reforms do not seem to matter. Of the 102 respondents in the 2008 survey who had been incarcerated, only 13 reported even receiving a trial at all. Although the numbers are small, this share does not change significantly among those who left after 2005, following the revision of the code; of 25 leaving after that date, 3 (12 percent) reported receiving a trial but 22 (88 percent) did not. Moreover, the absence of a trial and conviction was by no means limited to those cases that ended up with detention in the *kwan-li-so* and *kyo-hwa-so*. On the contrary, the share of those reporting that they did not receive trials and convictions was even higher in the lower-level penal institutions: 86 percent of those incarcerated in the *ro-dong-dan-ryeon-dae* and 91 percent of those who served time in the *jip-kyul-so*. The North Korean legal and penal system clearly retains an extraordinary level of discretion with respect to political crimes and lower-level infractions such as economic crimes.

Discretion appears to be exercised with respect to both detention and release. Given the duration of statutory sentences we expected that those incarcerated would have spent a long time in prison. This did not prove to be the case (table 4.3). Average time in prison is certainly longer for the political penal-labor camps and the penitentiaries; although the numbers in our sample are very small, the lengthy sentences for political crimes are well-known. But the information on "collection centers" and labor training centers is significant. Virtually all of those incarcerated in the labor training centers were held for less than a year, even though sentencing guidelines typically allow holding prisoners for up to two years.[10] Sixty-three percent of those incarcerated in the "collection centers" were released within a month.

There is much about this system that we do not understand. It is possible that inmates are escaping or bribing their way out of detention. However, the information we have is consistent with a model of a police state in which authorities have a high level of discretion not only in detaining, arresting, and prosecuting people but also in their ability to release them.

One reason that such a model might be effective is because the conditions in the facilities are designed to be a powerful deterrent and even have a psychological impact, in effect terrorizing those who are detained.

---

10. Each day served at a correctional facility counts for two days against subsequent labor training sentences, which might partly account for the shorter duration of time served (KINU 2009, 91).

**Table 4.3    Length of imprisonment, by detention facility: South Korea
survey**

| Length | Number of respondents | Percent | Number of respondents | Percent |
|---|---|---|---|---|
| | Kwan-li-so (political penal-labor camps) | | Kyo-hwa-so (penitentiaries) | |
| Less than 1 week | 1 | 33.3 | 2 | 22.2 |
| Less than 1 month | 0 | 0.0 | 1 | 11.1 |
| Less than 1 year | 1 | 33.3 | 2 | 22.2 |
| Between 1 and 5 years | 1 | 33.3 | 3 | 33.3 |
| More than 5 years | 0 | 0 | 1 | 11.1 |
| Total | 3 | 100 | 9 | 100 |
| | Jip-kyul-so ("collection centers") | | Ro-dong-dan-ryeon-dae (labor training centers) | |
| Less than 1 week | 11 | 16.4 | 10 | 20.4 |
| Less than 1 month | 31 | 46.3 | 17 | 34.7 |
| Less than 1 year | 22 | 32.8 | 20 | 40.8 |
| Between 1 and 5 years | 3 | 4.5 | 2 | 4.1 |
| More than 5 years | 0 | 0 | 0 | 0 |
| Total | 67 | 100 | 49 | 100 |

Nearly one-quarter of the sample in the initial, China-based survey
reported having been arrested in China and repatriated to North Korea.
Nearly 10 percent of the respondents reported having been incarcerated in a political detention facility or penitentiary.[11] As we noted above,
90 percent of this group reported witnessing forced starvation, 60 percent
reported witnessing deaths due to beating or torture, and 27 percent
reported witnessing executions.

It has been alleged that pregnant women thought to be carrying children of suspected Chinese paternity have been subject to forced abortions or infanticide; 5 percent of the respondents indicated that they
had witnessed these practices. This pattern of a high rate of affirmative
response to general phenomena such as hunger in the prison system and a
much lower response to the highly specific practice of infanticide suggests
respondents were not simply providing answers that they had intuited
the interviewers wanted to hear. This reassurance makes the response to

---

11. Specifically, we asked whether they had been detained in either a penitentiary (*kyo-hwa-
so*) or other detention facility for political prisoners (*jung-chi-bum soo-yong-so*); the objective
was to also capture the NSA's detention facilities. This wording would leave out the so-called
collection centers and labor training centers, but the wording of the earlier questionnaire was
vulnerable to the respondent's interpretation.

**Table 4.4    Experiences of violence in the North Korean prison system: South Korea survey** (percent share of those imprisoned in each type of facility)

| While you were detained or imprisoned, did you see with your own eyes: | Kwan-li-so (political penal-labor camps) | Kyo-hwa-so (penitentiaries) |
|---|---|---|
| Executions | 66.7 | 77.8 |
| Forced starvation | 33.3 | 66.7 |
| Death from being tortured or beaten | 33.3 | 55.6 |
| Killing of newborns | 0 | 11.1 |

| | Jip-kyul-so ("collection centers") | Ro-dong-dan-ryeon-dae (labor training centers) |
|---|---|---|
| Executions | 50.8 | 47.9 |
| Forced starvation | 73.1 | 83.7 |
| Death from being tortured or beaten | 33.3 | 30.6 |
| Killing of newborns | 7.7 | 8.3 |

a final question all the more chilling: When asked if they believed that prisoners were used in medical experimentation, a practice alleged by Demick (2004) and Cooper (2005) among others, 55 percent of the respondents believed (but did not necessarily witness) that this had occurred at the facilities in which they were incarcerated.

The China survey did not differentiate these experiences by the precise type of penal institution, but this was a focus of the 2008 South Korea–based survey. Table 4.4 shows the share of respondents by level of penal institution that witnessed executions, forced starvation, deaths from beatings or torture, or the killing of newborns. The pattern of responses is quite similar to that of the earlier survey: a high response rate with respect to generalized forms of abuse and a much lower response rate on the highly specific question on infanticide, again lending credence to the responses on the other questions.

In the South Korea survey, the question concerning medical experimentation was posed as a direct interrogative about what respondents had witnessed, not merely heard. Had they seen with their own eyes medical experimentation on prisoners who had received capital punishment? In contrast to the China-based survey, none said that they had. One interpretation is that such experimentation does not occur. The second is that it occurs, but no one with direct knowledge lives to bear witness to it. Respondents in the China survey may have heard about such experimentation but not seen it or may have been traumatized enough to believe it was possible. By contrast, respondents in the South Korea survey answered negatively simply because the bar was set higher by the question: whether they had actually witnessed such experimentation, something that they were unlikely to have done.

What is striking about these findings is the ubiquity of violence and deprivation across the different initial points of contact with authorities and various levels of the prison system. The horrors of the *kwan-li-so* (political penal-labor camps) have now been thoroughly documented in memoirs and refugee testimony (C. H. Kang 2002, Hawk 2003, Y. Kim 2009). But the findings with respect to lower levels of the prison system are even more striking. In both the lower-level criminal facilities (*jip-kyul-so* or "collection centers") and the labor training centers (*ro-dong-dan-ryeon-dae*), nearly half of respondents reported seeing executions, roughly three-quarters reported forced starvation, and nearly a third reported witnessing deaths from beatings and torture.

Moreover, these levels of violence are witnessed despite the generally shorter periods of incarceration in these lower-level facilities. The mean period of incarceration in both types of facility was in the range of one month to one year. Prisoners experiencing this typical length of incarceration in a "collection center" witnessed abuses at the following rates: executions (75 percent), forced starvation (100 percent), and death by torture and beatings (50 percent). For the labor training centers incarceration for the typical period of time was associated with observing abuses at slightly lower rates: execution (60 percent), forced starvation (90 percent), and death by torture or beating (20 percent). The conclusion is clear. Even at the lower-level facilities, inmates are exposed to extreme levels of abuse. The findings in chapter 2 linking the incarceration of North Korean refugees to psychological distress are sadly comprehensible.

## Institutionalization of Repression

The refugee literature provides a much more eloquent testimony to the abusive nature of the North Korean system than anything we can add here. However, our brief review of the development of the criminal and penal system and evidence from the surveys do shed some additional light on the nature of repression in North Korea.

First, the development of the legal system exhibits some apparently contradictory trends. As with the broader pattern of economic reform and retrenchment, there is a parallel process of periodically relaxing the treatment of some crimes related to economic survival. The best-documented example of this forbearance is the legal treatment of border crossing, which at least until the renewed crackdown of 2008–09 was demoted from the equivalent of treason to a misdemeanor offense for those showing no political motives. More generally, we see the regime moving to adjust features of its legal system to international norms, at least on paper.

Yet at the same time, the range of economic activities deemed criminal has expanded dramatically. Also apparent is the institutionalization of "labor training" as a means of dealing with these and other low-level crimes. These two trends can be reconciled by noting that the government maintains a very high level of discretion; whatever the law says, the security apparatus is capable of making adjustments in detention and incarceration with few checks on its authority. One might expect an uptick in detention and incarceration whenever the government is intent on checking market activity, as it has been since 2005 in particular. Despite the relaxation of statute, for example, the 2008–09 period saw a clear increase in reports of sweeps, campaigns, detentions, and harsher punishments for border crossing.

The statistical analysis of detention experiences suggests that those involved in market activities are more than half again as likely to be incarcerated. Of course, incarceration in political penal-labor camps and penitentiaries carries much longer sentences than incarceration in labor training camps, and many prisoners end up dying in them. Yet, it is nonetheless surprising that there is very little difference in the propensity to witness extreme forms of violence and deprivation in the notorious political penal-labor camps and the lowest-level labor training facility.

Such a system obviously has the effect of sowing fear. "Labor training" has the additional benefit of constituting a form of corvée labor or tax. But this pattern of detention may also have an additional economic motivation. High levels of discretion with respect to arrest and sentencing and very high costs of detention, arrest, and incarceration have the effect of increasing bribe costs. The more arbitrary and painful the experience with the penal system, the easier it is for officials to extort money for avoiding it. Indeed, in another, smaller survey, "avoiding punishment" is the second most frequently cited motive for bribery after "being permitted to trade," and officials of police and security agencies are by far the primary recipients of these payments (B. Y. Kim 2010, table 2, figure 2).

These features of the penal system could provide incentives and opportunities for corruption of the internal security apparatus. Corruption may act as a safety valve in a fraying socialist system, a means of maintaining support among cadre by providing them access to economic rents. But predation on the part of officials in the security apparatus can also generate a divergence between the policy interest—and even survival interests—of the government and the private interests of security officials by generating more harsh repression and popular resentment than is optimal. This divergence could create substantial risks for the regime over the longer run, particularly as repression is harnessed not to ideological objectives—however cynically those are already viewed—but to private gain by government, party, and internal security functionaries. It is to the wider political implications of these developments that we now turn.

# 5

# Political Attitudes and Nascent Dissent

North Korea is probably the most repressive regime extant, scoring at the absolute bottom on all standard measures with respect to regime type, political and civil liberties, and human rights. Yet we also know that public sentiment can turn against apparently unshakable dictatorships with amazing velocity, as small oppositions swell into overwhelming majorities. Individuals may harbor very adverse views of the regime but lack information on the attitudes of others. As a result, they are effectively constrained by threats of coercion to silence or even to disguise their true beliefs, a phenomenon social scientists have dubbed "preference falsification."

However, once groups start to reveal their disaffection, or to defy the regime openly, others can be emboldened to do the same. If individuals reveal their real political preferences and willingness to resist, it can pose overwhelming challenges to security forces as large masses defect. Such "information cascades" help explain sharp political turning points, such as the collapse of the communist regimes of Eastern Europe (Kuran 1989, 1995a, 1995b; Lohmann 1994; Bikhchandani, Hirshleifer, and Welch 1998).

There are reasons to doubt that a dramatic political unraveling will occur in North Korea any time soon; outside analysts have underestimated the regime's capacity to survive before. The regime has cultivated a core base of supporters in the army, party, and state apparatus. The strength of the coercive apparatus is extraordinary, and the party provides the leadership a highly developed institution for social surveillance and monitoring. The North Korean regime not only has a highly developed propaganda apparatus (Lankov 2009, Myers 2010) but also jealously guards competitive sources of outside information, including those gleaned from unauthorized exit from the country, in order to limit comparisons that might call its portrayal of material circumstances into question. Above all, the regime has aggressively forestalled independent forms of social organization, permitting only state-sanctioned bodies such as youth leagues, which provide additional instruments of both elite recruitment and control. There are no independent unions, autonomous religious organizations, or forums of intellectuals, all of which have served as platforms for organizing dissent in countries that have democratized in recent decades.

However, the marketization process we have described in previous chapters signals a fraying of state control; indeed, the recourse to repression described in the previous chapter indicates that other instruments have lost effectiveness. Until the famine, the state's grip on the economy and the allocation of all employment by administrative fiat provided a powerful tool for controlling the lives of citizens, particularly given the link between employment and a variety of social benefits. With the collapse of the socialist social contract, individuals fended for themselves and in doing so created a second economy. The nonsanctioned market economy has the potential to develop into an autonomous social space—a civil society—through which not only income and consumption but also alternative sources of information can flow (Hassig and Oh 2009, chapter 5; Lankov 2009).

Moreover, we cannot rule out the possibility that retreat into private activity may have political motivations. In his classic work on "everyday forms of peasant resistance," James C. Scott (1985) catalogued a variety of strategies, such as shirking work or destroying elite property, that provided subordinated classes a means of challenging elite dominance and showing disaffection. The retreat from the state sector into the market and various forms of private activity may well constitute a parallel set of quasi-political activities in a state socialist system, a form of "everyday resistance" against what would otherwise appear an impregnable dictatorship.

This chapter examines underlying political attitudes and the prospects for more overt political behavior. As acknowledged in chapter 1, refugees may not be a good barometer of political attitudes in their home countries for two interrelated reasons: They may be unrepresentative in a demographic sense, and having voted with their feet they are likely to hold distinctively negative views of the regime that are unrepresentative of the remaining resident population. As we have seen in previous chapters, the first problem can be addressed in part through standard multivariate statistical techniques. The second problem of unrepresentative attitudes rooted in idiosyncratic and unobservable individual-level characteristics—in effect, in biography—is much more difficult to address. Nonetheless, important experiential factors that might influence attitudes, such as incarceration or ill treatment at the hands of authorities, can also be controlled for ex post. The use of refugee interviews to get at political attitudes must be approached with particular caution, but we believe some important insights can nonetheless be gained from both their attitudes and their insights into changing attitudes and behavior in North Korean society more generally.

We first examine respondents' evaluations of the regime's performance along a number of dimensions. Not surprisingly, the refugees' evaluations are negative. Although negative views of the regime are widely shared, there is some evidence that members of the core political class and government and party workers are particularly disaffected.

Although we do not have true panel data, we can exploit the timing of refugees' exit to gain some insight into changes in political views over time. Evaluations of the regime appear to be getting more negative. Although those who departed earlier were more willing to entertain the view that the country's problems were due to foreigners, respondents who left later were more likely to hold the regime accountable. Questions about both personal aspirations and the future of North Korea also suggest a declining hold of ideology and the regime's particularly virulent nationalism. Despite the regime's constant vilification of the United States, younger and more educated respondents showed a marginal preference for resettlement in the United States over South Korea. Virtually none of the respondents favored a "third way" in which North Korea would retain its independence, even if under alternative leadership. Refugees overwhelmingly favored unification on southern terms.

Following an analysis of attitudes, we turn to the prospects that these adverse views of the regime might be communicated. The barriers to communication are high; even among this highly disaffected share of the population, ability to communicate disaffection appears low. The scope for overt political activity remains even more limited.

However, there is evidence of an increasing willingness to defy the government through everyday forms of resistance, such as listening to foreign media. We show that not only is there a relatively constant willingness to engage in clandestine economic activities, as we showed in chapter 3, but also these activities may be associated with a greater propensity to communicate adverse information. Moreover, there is some evidence that the repressive response to these changes outlined in the previous chapter may contribute to politicizing the populace.

## Political Attitudes: Perceptions of Regime Performance and Their Determinants

As discussed in chapter 2, the share of North Korean refugees citing "political" motives for departure has been steadily rising over time. In order to gauge the sources of disaffection with the regime, respondents in both surveys were presented with a series of statements about the performance of the North Korean government and asked to indicate their

**Figure 5.1    Response to "Kim Jong-il's regime is improving"**
(percent)

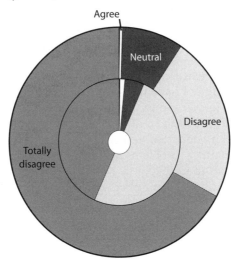

Note: The outer circle is the South Korea survey (n = 201) and the inner circle is the China survey (n = 1,306). In the China survey, 0.1 percent of the respondents "totally agreed."

agreement at the time they departed the country on a scale of 1 to 5.[1] Questions included assessments of whether the economy, education, and social conditions were improving, but the distribution of responses did not differ much across these discrete issue areas. We focus here on responses to the most general statement: "Kim Jong-il's regime is improving" (figure 5.1). Roughly 85 percent of the respondents in both surveys indicated that they "disagreed" or "strongly disagreed" with this statement.

By dividing the South Korea–based sample into four eras of departure, we were able to trace how attitudes have changed over time, if at all.[2] The respondents who left during the immediate postfamine period (1999–2002), about one-quarter of the sample, held the most negative views, although some of them saw some improvement in economic circumstances from the depths of the famine years. Those who left during

---

1. Where 1 = strongly disagree, 2 = disagree, 3 = neutral, 4 = agree, 5 = strongly agree.

2. It is possible that the respondents' perceptions were shaped by information that was contemporaneous with the administration of the survey. However, it is a plausible assumption that their impressions were shaped predominantly by conditions at the time they left; these were their last first-hand experiences with the country, and as we show in Haggard and Noland (2010c), their responses do not appear to correlate with time spent either outside of North Korea or in South Korea.

**Figure 5.2    South Korea survey response to "What makes the North
Korean economy  better or worse?"**

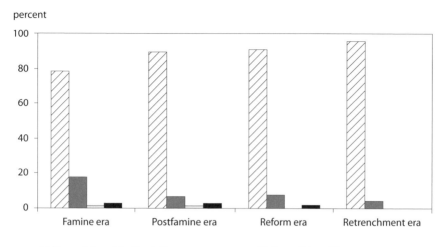

percent

☑ The policies of the North Korean government   ■ The policies of foreign governments
☐ The situation in the world economy in general   ■ Other/no opinion

the most recent, retrenchment period (2006–08), about 15 percent of the
sample, held the least unfavorable views, though even among this group,
81 percent of the respondents disagreed or strongly disagreed with the
statement that the regime was improving.

Given the negative evaluations on this indicator (and the economic
indicators discussed in chapter 3) it is important to gauge the extent to
which respondents believed that the poor performance was the result of
government actions. The respondents increasingly held the North Korean
government accountable for these adverse developments, with the share
placing primary responsibility on the North Korean government at more
than 95 percent in the retrenchment subsample (figure 5.2). The share citing
the policies of foreign governments as responsible for their predicament
fell steadily from 18 percent among the famine era leavers to 4 percent in
the retrenchment group.

Although views of the regime are widely shared, it is possible to use
multivariate statistical analysis of the pattern of responses in figure 5.1 to
tease out some of the demographic and experiential determinants of political attitudes.[3] Not surprisingly, political attitudes are correlated with political classification, with those in the core and wavering classes sometimes

---

3. The following draws on Chang, Haggard, and Noland (2009b) and Haggard and Noland
(2010d).

giving the regime higher marks than those in the hostile class.[4] Adverse personal experiences with the regime such as incarceration in the prison system, loss of family members during the famine, and the belief that they had not received assistance were also correlated with political opinions in predictable ways, lowering evaluations of the regime's performance.

It is notable that time spent in South Korea or other third countries is *not* robustly correlated with political attitudes. This suggests that the refugees' responses do not reflect socialization or learned behavior outside North Korea but rather their experiences in the country.

As in the results presented in chapter 3, it is possible to control ex post for some possible sample selection problems that could bias any inferences drawn from the refugee surveys to the wider population. We do that in this case by combining the estimated statistical models with national-level demographic data to derive estimated "approval ratings" for the population as a whole.[5] The sample and projected national means, along with their 95 percent confidence intervals, are displayed in figure 5.3.

With respect to the South Korea sample, the projected national approval ratings are about four to five percentage points higher than the raw scores generated by the survey itself, a result we would expect. In the China survey, however, the projected approval ratings are nearly the same. But in neither case are these differences statistically significant; in both surveys the results fall easily within the 95 percent confidence limits. Moreover, the point estimates for the national "approval rating" derived from both surveys are approximately 15 percent—and even the upper bound 95 percent confidence interval is well under 25 percent. At least controlling for the demographic and experiential factors that we can, we cannot rule out that mass support for the regime may be much weaker than is frequently believed.

---

4. Respondents from the far northeast provinces of North and South Hamgyong tended to regard the regime less malignly than those from other parts of the country. This result may be due to a sample selection effect. The northeast is regarded as the region of the country most severely affected by the famine. However, proximity to China also makes it easier to exit. Relative to other provinces, the profile of respondents from the northeast may include those who had less traumatic experiences than those from elsewhere but because of the relatively lower cost of exit were able to migrate anyway.

5. Specifically, the mean sample responses, originally scored on a 1 to 5 metric, are converted to a 0 to 100 scale to generate "sample approval ratings," which are simply the scaled mean score of each response variable. To project the nationwide approval ratings, the probability of observing each response conditional on estimated national values of each explanatory variable is predicted. The predicted probabilities sum to one. To estimate the mean response the products of each score and its predicted probability are summed, yielding a probability weighted mean response. This value is then converted to a 0 to 100 scale to generate the estimated nationwide approval ratings. The same procedure is applied to calculating minimum and maximum predicted probabilities of each outcome, which are estimated at the 95 percent confidence level and used to establish confidence intervals for each response estimate.

**Figure 5.3  Response to "Kim Jong-il's regime is improving": Samples versus national projections**

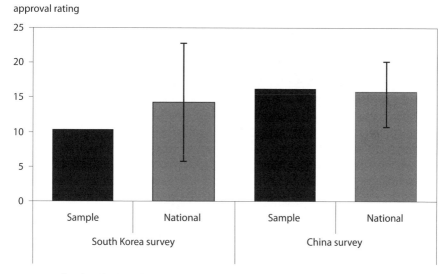

approval rating

Note: Vertical brackets display confidence intervals at the 95 percent confidence level.

## Aspirations for the Future

In addition to the "approval ratings," the respondents were asked two sets of future-oriented questions that provide insight into the hold of ideology and North Korean nationalism and also suggest increasing flows of information. The first involved personal aspirations. In the China survey, the respondents were asked where they wanted to permanently resettle. In the South Korea survey, the permanently resettled former residents of North Korea were asked the broader political question of what future they wanted to see for the peninsula itself.

### Preferences for Future Resettlement

Relatively few refugees in the China survey wanted to remain in China; the two most frequently identified preferred destinations for permanent resettlement were South Korea (65 percent) and the United States (19 percent) (figure 5.4).[6] In contrast to the indicators of psychological status reported in chapter 2, multivariate analysis suggests that demographic variables generally appear to be more correlated than experien-

---

6. Results reported in this section are from Chang, Haggard, and Noland (2009a).

**Figure 5.4  Preferred destinations for permanent resettlement: China survey** (percent)

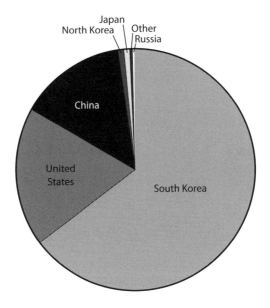

tial variables with preferences about location of permanent resettlement. The most striking findings have to do with education and age. Secondary and postsecondary education are statistically significant predictors of the preference to live in the United States; in contrast, they are negatively associated with a preference for South Korea as the final destination. Similarly, age is strongly negatively correlated with a preference to emigrate to the United States, and in some of the statistical models, the occupational category of "student" is negatively associated with a preference for South Korea.[7]

In short, older and less-educated respondents prefer South Korea. The United States is the favored destination for younger, better-educated respondents, possibly reflecting better English language ability, less affinity for or family ties to South Korea, and a greater willingness to take risks. This result

---

7. Unlike many of the issues under consideration, provincial origin mattered when it came to dreams of permanent resettlement. The refugees who originated in the northeastern provinces had a distinct disinterest in the United States as a destination for permanent resettlement. One possible explanation, consistent with the economic analysis presented in chapter 3, is that refugees originating in provinces further from the border represent a more enterprising self-selected group, which might be consistent with the notion that younger, better-educated, and possibly more risk-tolerant refugees are interested in migrating to the United States.

is striking given this group's lifelong exposure to virulently anti-American propaganda and suggests a breakdown in the North Korean government's monopoly over information, which is more directly confirmed below.

### Aspirations for North Korea

Further insight into political attitudes can be gained by considering the refugees' aspirations not only for themselves but also for the Korean peninsula as a whole. In the South Korea survey respondents were asked three questions concerning their preferences for the political organization of the Korean peninsula. They were first asked which alternative most accurately represented their views while in North Korea: maintenance of the current North Korean government; installation of a new non-Kim Il-sungist government in North Korea; unification with South Korea; or don't know/none of the above. They were then posed the same alternatives asking what they believed now and what they believed were the preferences of people they knew in North Korea.

Unification was supported overwhelmingly; given their predominantly negative perceptions of the current North Korean regime, respondents clearly preferred unification under South Korean leadership. There was little support for the maintenance of the status quo (only a single respondent out of 300) nor for "third way" solutions in which North Korea would remain independent under an alternative political regime (figure 5.5). Although exposure to South Korea appears to intensify these preferences at the margin, the responses so strongly supported unification that it is effectively impossible to do multivariate analysis; there simply is not enough sample variation. The respondents also indicated that their own views mirrored those of their peers remaining in North Korea, though obviously there is no way of judging the accuracy of this projection.

## From Attitudes to Behavior: Political Communication

It may not be surprising that North Korean refugees, and even citizens remaining in the country, harbor adverse attitudes about the regime or believe that these have gotten worse over time.[8] Yet a crucial question for the future of the regime is the extent to which such views are communicated and become the basis for collective action. In the model of information cascades, the political stability of the authoritarian regime is dependent on silence: on the inability of citizens to know what others are thinking and therefore to make common cause with them. Is such communication taking place?

---

8. The statistical analysis in this section draws on Haggard and Noland (2010d).

**Figure 5.5    South Korea survey respondents' views on Korean unification**

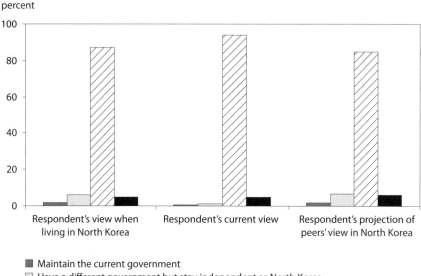

percent

Maintain the current government
Have a different government but stay independent as North Korea
Unify with South Korea
None of the above/don't know

In the South Korea–based survey the refugees were presented with a series of statements about their experiences in North Korea and asked that they grade their responses on a 1 to 5 scale.[9] These questions, however, were not about the respondent's attitudes and behavior but about "people" in North Korea. From the standpoint of political anthropology, these questions can be interpreted as a kind escalating ladder of dissent, beginning with the extent to which people joke, followed by complaining and organizing:

- "People make jokes about the government" (JOKES).
- "People speak freely about the government" (SPEAK).
- "People complain about the government" (COMPLAIN).
- "People feel they can speak freely about their opinions of Kim Jong-il" (LEADER).
- "Some people are organizing against the government" (ORGANIZING).

The shares affirming the statement that people make jokes about the government, while rising, never exceeded 45 percent in any of the four

---

9. Where 1 = strongly disagree, 2 = disagree, 3 = neutral, 4 = agree, 5 = strongly agree.

period subsamples, and the share supporting the statement that people complain about the government never reached 40 percent. Even among an unusually disaffected subgroup of the population—refugees—and despite their overwhelmingly negative assessment of the regime, less than half of the sample reported that their peers joked or complained about the government.

Kim Jong-il appears sacrosanct. Although perceptions that people are freely discussing the Dear Leader rise steadily among those who left the country after 1998, even among those who fled most recently (the retrenchment cohort) only 8 percent reported that people spoke freely about Kim Jong-il. Indeed, the shares who reported their peers speaking freely about Kim Jong-il almost precisely mirrored the shares reporting that people were organizing against the government.

What determines differences in views with respect to the restrictiveness of the regime (reported in figure 4.1 in the previous chapter) and the extent of political communication and dissent? The share of household income derived from market sources is positively associated with both perceptions of tightening restrictions and joking with peers about the government, providing at least some support for the idea that the market provides greater space for at least limited forms of political communication.

Of course, these findings may reflect the fact that the refugees are more likely to move in what amounts to a criminal subculture in North Korea, at least from the perspective of the regime. But it is equally plausible that repression and low-level dissent are mutually reinforcing. Detention by the political, as distinct from regular, police was associated with a greater likelihood of reporting joking or complaining about the government among one's peers. The direction of causality is debatable; it could be that the system is correctly identifying those engaged in politically deviant behavior. Yet it is notable that the minority (less than 13 percent) who reported that they had formal legal proceedings prior to incarceration had significantly more positive assessments of the regime than the majority who did not, at least suggesting that the government's treatment may be shaping attitudes rather than the other way around.

The results again provide mild support for the existence of greater cynicism if not outright dissent among some elite groups. Older respondents, members of the core class, residents of the capital city Pyongyang, and those working in party or government offices were somewhat *more* likely to report a perception that restrictions were increasing but also that citizens were joking and speaking freely about the government among peers. There is also some evidence that party membership is significantly correlated with joking about the government, although in all of these cases the results could reflect the fact that privileged groups are less constrained than nonelites rather than reflecting any trends in society.

Again, counterfactual projections are made in an attempt to check whether overweighting particular groups in the sample has distorted the picture provided by the survey respondents. The "national sample" provides an estimate of what the underlying population's answer might be to these questions (figure 5.6). It does not appear that the survey sample systematically overweights or underweights groups perceiving higher levels of social communication. In some cases the projected national averages are above the sample means and in some cases below. In all cases the null hypothesis of equality in the two distributions cannot be rejected at the 95 percent level.

## From Attitudes to Behavior: Everyday Forms of Resistance

Answers to the question about whether peers are organizing against the government comport with a wide array of evidence on the limits of collective action in North Korea. Organizations that maintain clandestine networks within the country—which have an interest in spotlighting antiregime actions—have very little to report in this regard; overt antiregime action remains sporadic at best (Haggard and Noland 2010b).

This does not mean, however, that citizens are quiescent; disaffection may be channeled into private actions that while not overtly political may nonetheless have longer-run implications for the stability of state socialism. One example of such action is the willingness of citizens to access alternative sources of information that are likely to conflict with official mythology. Figure 5.7 reports responses to a question on access to foreign media. It is evident that the informational barrier is increasingly permeable: A rising share, a majority in the retrenchment period, reported watching or listening to foreign media, and critically, a falling share (nil in the retrenchment period) reported having access to foreign media but declining to watch or listen. Not only is foreign media becoming more widely available but also inhibitions on its consumption are disappearing. And it is foreign news media that are being consumed: When the respondents were asked to differentiate between access to and consumption of entertainment and news, the share consuming foreign news reports was almost 30 percentage points higher than the share consuming foreign entertainment products.

Moreover, we find evidence that access to information is correlated with political attitudes. Consumption of foreign media was associated with more negative assessments of the regime and its intentions. This finding is of particular policy as well as analytic significance, as it suggests the crucial role that control over information plays with respect to the effectiveness of government propaganda and mythmaking (Lankov 2009, Myers 2010). The availability of alternative sources of information undermines the heroic image of a workers' paradise and may help explain the phenomenon of younger and better-educated refugees preferring resettle-

**Figure 5.6    Level of repression in North Korea: Sample (South Korea survey) versus national projection**

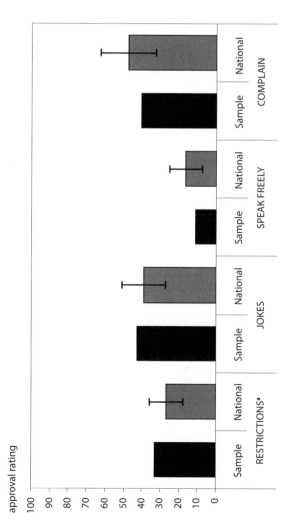

approval rating

a. RESTRICTIONS is inverted such that a lower number equates to a more adverse assessment of the intensity of repression. In the raw data a higher number equates to a more adverse response.

Note: Vertical brackets display confidence intervals at the 95 percent confidence level.

**Figure 5.7    Access to foreign media: South Korea survey**

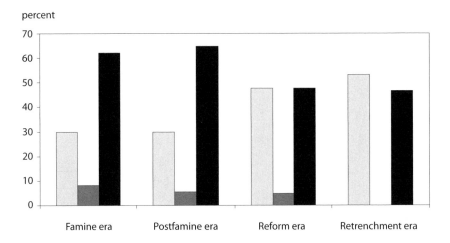

percent

Famine era    Postfamine era    Reform era    Retrenchment era

☐ You watched or listened to foreign news or entertainment programs including videos
   or DVDs
◼ You had access to foreign news or entertainment programs but did not watch
■ You did not have access to foreign news or entertainment programs

ment in the United States.[10] The existence of an "alternative narrative" also threatens to unleash the information cascades that can be extremely destabilizing to authoritarian rule.

The consumption of foreign media is but one aspect of a much larger phenomenon of engagement in private economic activities documented in chapter 3. To what extent might the market become the locus of political communication or even more overt political organization? Although reports of such activity are few, they are not altogether absent. As the government has acted to control markets, most recently in connection with a confiscatory currency reform announced on November 30, 2009, scattered news reports have emerged of incidents in which market traders, mostly women, have protested restraints on trade (Haggard and Noland 2010b).

In the South Korea survey, we asked respondents whether traders cooperated with each other. The share of respondents agreeing or strongly agreeing ranged from 32 to 42 percent across the four periods, although with no perceptible trend. Likewise, when asked whether traders in the

10. To be clear, our results do not suggest that consumption of foreign news or entertainment media is purely a youth or urban phenomenon as some have claimed. The highest reported rates of consumption are among the middle-aged, and there is little difference in the pattern of consumption across urban and rural populations, at least in recent years. Rather, the main identifiable trend is a significant secular increase in consumption of these products over time.

market were beginning to organize to protect their interests, the affirmative response rate was 28 to 29 percent in all time periods. Although this is a minority of the full sample, it is nonetheless surprising; the market may hold at least some opportunity for cooperation and collective action.

## Conclusion

The constraints on independent collective action and the corresponding atomization of civil society are a recurrent theme in the analysis of authoritarian regimes. In North Korea, as in other highly repressive political systems, pervasive surveillance, a highly developed internal security and monitoring apparatus, and the liberal use of the penal system all serve to reduce trust in the society as a whole. Even making jokes about the government is risky, let alone complaining, disparaging the leader, or organizing against the regime.

If approached with appropriate caution, however, refugee surveys can provide insights into public opinion and behavior in authoritarian systems that substantially nuance the simple assessment that "repression works." First, repressive regimes are able to control behavior but not private perceptions and political attitudes (Hassig and Oh 2009, chapter 6). Objective measures of the horrendous economic performance of the North Korean regime are mirrored in the extremely adverse opinions refugees have about the regime's performance. If anything, the state's attempts to reassert control over the economy, which become visible from 2005, exacerbated adverse perceptions of the regime.

It should be stressed that all of these results are derived from surveys of refugees. One would expect this group to have negative assessments of the regime, and multivariate analysis confirms that their views are often more negative than the projected attitudes of the resident population. But at least controlling for identifiable demographic and experiential markers, these differences are not as stark as we expected; all counterfactual projections of the views of the resident population fall within the 95 percent confidence bound around the sample averages. At least on the basis of observable characteristics, the highly negative evaluations may well represent the unarticulated views of large swaths of the North Korean public.

There is some evidence that growing politicization is correlated with membership in the core class and employment in the government, party, or military. These findings are interesting, given that these respondents occupy relatively—even substantially—favored positions. Intraelite schisms are the Achilles' heel of authoritarian regimes. To the extent that even relatively privileged groups are expressing discontent, it suggests either that the regime may not be as stable as is often thought or—more plausibly—that at least lower-level elites might be more open to reform.

A second finding concerns the limits on the ability of such regimes to deflect accountability. A common tactic of authoritarian leaders is to rally support for the government by displacing blame for poor performance onto external and internal enemies. Respondents in our surveys, however, were decreasingly inclined to believe state propaganda, which has consistently stressed North Korea's "hostile environment." Respondents also showed an increasing propensity over time to hold the North Korean government accountable for the country's problems, with the share placing primary responsibility on the North Korean government at more than 95 percent among those who left in the retrenchment period (i.e., after 2005). The reaction to the November 2009 currency reform—an obviously self-inflicted disaster, incompatible with the regime's narrative ascribing all ills to foreign "hostile forces"—adds a contemporaneous exclamation point to these trends.

These attitudes were reflected in questions posed about aspirations for the peninsula. Partial reforms of the political system were rejected in favor of the much more radical step of outright absorption by the South.

A third set of findings has to do with political behavior. Although there is little evidence of overt political activity in North Korea, there is ample evidence not only of growing cynicism but also of communication of disaffection and a growing willingness to engage in a kind of quiet exit from the system. This has occurred first and foremost by engaging in market activity and to a lesser extent by consuming alternative media that effectively challenges the regime's narrative. With respect to the latter, there is evidence that inhibitions against consumption of foreign media are declining and that consumption of foreign media has contributed to disaffection.

A crucial issue for the future of North Korea—as for other authoritarian regimes—is the extent to which these activities might provide the basis for a more robust and independent civil society. Small restaurants and the provision of other services are not merely businesses; they provide the space for communication outside of heavily monitored official work units (W. Y. Lee 2009).

Taken together, our findings underline a classic dilemma facing highly repressive regimes. Despite the adverse views of the regime and a growing tendency to hold the government accountable, there is little evidence that adverse views of the regime were communicated widely or that markets were becoming the locus of collective action, at least until the wildly disruptive currency reform of 2009. When authoritarian governments pursue policies that diverge so widely from the public interest and have such disastrous consequences the only way to maintain power is through coercion and surveillance. In this sense, the extraordinary repressiveness of the regime is probably a rational strategy. Yet such a strategy only has the effect of making the public more alienated, thus requiring still higher levels of coercion and surveillance. The post-2005 backsliding with respect to reform appears to reveal just such a dynamic.

The second conclusion that can be drawn, however, is that loyalty to the regime may be in shorter supply than is thought. If challenged, the leadership is not likely to find champions among the public. Campaigns to defend the regime through continued and increased sacrifice, 100-day campaigns, and other Stakhanovite appeals may not generate outright dissent, but they are less and less likely to work as individuals engage in more and more extensive "everyday forms of resistance." The unprecedented February 2010 apology to low-level cadre in the wake of the currency reform disaster may signal that the stumble may have exceeded even this regime's coercive capacity and that at least some accountability is required to sustain elite if not mass support.

Taken together, these results point to a kind of "market syndrome" in which participation in market activities is associated with higher arrest rates, more consumption of foreign news, more negative assessments of the regime, a greater willingness to communicate those views to one's peers, and a greater propensity to cite political motives for emigration. On its own terms, the regime is right to fear the market.

# 6

# Conclusion

Our interests in North Korean refugees are twofold: The first is a humanitarian, and ultimately human rights, impulse. This book has documented the precarious existence of this community: the personal trauma of displacement, vulnerability, and the difficulties of integration in new settings. These problems are compounded in the North Korean case by the draconian controls exercised over exit, the severe punishments meted out for those involved in border crossing, and the particularly inhospitable environment in China, through which virtually all refugees have transited. How should the international community respond to the ongoing problems faced by North Korean refugees?

The refugees, however, represent only the tip of the much larger North Korean iceberg. As we and many others have documented, North Korean refugees have good reason to fear persecution because of the abysmal human rights record in the country. The refugee issue is ultimately inseparable from the broader question of how to formulate an effective human rights agenda for North Korea.

Our second set of interests arises from the fact that the refugees are witnesses to North Korea's ongoing political, economic, and social transformation. North Korea's changing internal political dynamics include a reversal of reform and a highly uncertain succession process, both of which carry risks of wider instability. Since at least 2005, we have seen a distinct trend toward tighter state control; the disastrous November 2009 currency reform is only the most recent manifestation of "reform in reverse." During the same period, North Korea's external behavior has been marked by continuing belligerence as well, including missile and nuclear tests (followed by sanctions), the sinking of the South Korean naval vessel, the *Cheonan*, and most recently the shelling of Yeonpyeong Island.

In this concluding chapter, we first consider the insights that can be gleaned from the refugee experience to inform our expectations about the future direction of the North Korean political economy. We then turn to the specific needs of the refugees and human rights concerns more broadly. In each case, we outline the implications of our analysis for current developments and suggest policies that would facilitate positive changes in North Korea.

## Whither North Korea?

For the first four decades of its existence, the North Korean economy was organized as a classic, Soviet-style planned economy notable only for the rigor with which markets were suppressed. The economy was nearly autarkic; the North Koreans even timed their central plans to frustrate linkage with their allied socialist brethren. Yet claims of self-reliance notwithstanding, the economy depended crucially on the Soviet Union for aid in the form of food, fuel, and weaponry. In the late 1980s this model had already begun to experience significant problems. The subsequent collapse of the Soviet Union and dissolution of the Eastern Bloc was a blow from which the economy has still not fully recovered. Unlike Vietnam, which responded to similar external shocks by accelerating reforms, North Korea stood pat as first its industrial and then agricultural sectors imploded, resulting in a famine in the mid-1990s that killed as many as 3 to 5 percent of the precrisis population.

At the level of the individual, our surveys document the traumas of the famine that continue to reverberate through the refugee diaspora. At a societal level, the surveys detail the rapid collapse of the centrally planned economy during the first half of the 1990s and the emergence in its wake of nonsanctioned market activities. Small-scale social units—households, workplaces, local government and party offices, even military units— were forced to act entrepreneurially in order to access food and survive. This bottom-up marketization began with the food economy but spread to other products in the domestic market and even extended to barter and later monetized cross-border transactions with China.

Since the famine ended in 1998, government policy has grappled with these changes—with great ambivalence. Much market-oriented behavior was technically illegal. But with the state unable to uphold the traditional socialist social compact, it was uneasily tolerated. Continually struggling to make socialist theory and existing practices consistent, the government has sometimes acquiesced, even ratified, facts on the ground, only to retreat by attempting to limit and contain the scope of private and market activity. Yet we find a consistent tendency in the postreform period for the government to reassert the state's lost control, demonstrated most obviously in the extraordinary criminalization of economic activity that our surveys reveal. For understandable reasons, the regime is highly insecure with respect to the potential domestic political implications of economic change.

Although there is evidence of a brief reformist opening (roughly 1998–2002), the growth of markets has been primarily a function of state failure rather than a proactive reform process. Even at its peak in 2002, policy evinced ambivalence: Measures were introduced, albeit clumsily, to increase both the flexibility and responsibility of enterprise managers in the context of the plan and to enhance limited material incentives in agriculture. But at the same time, monetary and financial policies were undertaken to undercut the class of traders—effectively black marketeers—that had sprung up as the state-run system failed. In this and several other important respects, even the much-touted reforms of 2002 foreshadowed the failed currency reform that would occur seven years later in the "great confiscation" of 2009. The implicit goals of policy were not to fundamentally change the state socialist system in favor of a more decentralized, market-oriented economy but rather to reconstitute and improve the centrally planned economy.

A closely related motivation was to address a profound fiscal crisis and loss of macroeconomic control. With the near collapse of the state-owned enterprise sector, the government's ability to raise revenues through traditional channels had been severely compromised. Yet the country's bloated military, and the tensions it generated, posed enormous resource requirements as did the ongoing commitment to inefficient state-owned enterprises.

For a variety of reasons, including external ones, the modest reform attempts of 2002 did not deliver as expected and in fact generated some altogether new problems such as high inflation. Since roughly 2005, the trend in economic policy has been unambiguously illiberal. There appear to have been a number of personnel changes around this time that brought conservatives to the fore, and the onset of the second nuclear crisis no doubt contributed to the ascendance of hardliners. Since 2008, the succession process further dampened the appetite for undertaking reforms that carry political risk.

Yet the state lacks the capacity to fully displace the market; its latest attempt, the November 2009 currency reform, was a political as well as economic fiasco, ending in an unprecedented apology, the scapegoating of senior officials, and tactical retreats, for example, in allowing markets to reopen and citizens to hold foreign exchange. Yet even these partial reforms are ambiguous and thus send only mixed signals; similar episodes have been followed by retrenchment in the recent past. Because the state's capacity for raising revenue has been so severely impaired, and because the state is able to at least partly tax participation in formal markets, the government's acquiescence in the return of the markets could reflect fiscal exigencies rather than a more fundamental change in course.

The government's erratic and mixed policy course over the last decade and the ensuing poor economic performance have clearly increased cynicism. As the socialist social compact has broken down, households have been forced to supplement state-sector wages with income from market activities. Our surveys document the market's emergence as an alternative avenue to wealth and prestige and a semiautonomous zone of social communication that could, at least in theory, provide the locus of independent political power and even organization.

Corruption appears to be a pervasive feature of the new hybrid economy. Even accepting that the refugees may hold disproportionately negative views about the regime, the surveys paint a picture that is highly consistent with basic economic theory. Extensive, and in significant part arbitrary and even capricious, state intervention generates both opportunities and incentives for corruption at all levels. A survey we conducted of Chinese businesses operating in North Korea confirms the capacity of firms to make money but also the uncertainty of the policy environment and the corresponding requirement to pay off public officials in order to do business. We can certainly imagine growing disaffection among those victimized by this policy environment—most recently in the massive savings destruction associated with the currency reform.

The implications of these dynamics for political stability are ambiguous, however. The institutional capacity of the regime has been underestimated in the past. Although personalist in nature, the party, military, and security apparatus are extraordinarily large and to date have remained loyal, in part because of intricate structures for monitoring and in part because they enjoy at least some fruits from their elite status. Although reports of internal splits within the elite are to be expected during successions, there are also powerful incentives for the regime's elite supporters to rally around the existing system and the designated successor. Recent institutional changes, such as the strengthening and expansion of the National Defense Commission (NDC) and special sessions of the Supreme People's Assembly—the highest government body—and the party congress appear designed precisely to rally critical bases of support. Yet as the NDC has a privileged position, we can expect that the political forces that it represents—most notably the military, security apparatus, and military-industrial complex—will have privileged access to resources when compared with the traditional functions of the state, such as maintaining infrastructure and improving the health care and educational systems. These public goods are pivotal for any future reform process to succeed.

At lower levels, corruption may act as a kind of safety valve, providing additional payoffs for officials otherwise squeezed by the country's ongoing economic misfortune. But the growth of the informal economy and its associated corruption signals that the personal interests of state officials may increasingly diverge from policy established by central decision makers. Survey respondents who worked in government offices attested to growing abuse of office among their former colleagues coupled with increasing amounts of time devoted to political indoctrination in an effort to harness work effort and maintain control. Yet exhortation is unlikely to override powerful incentives generated by the massive distortions that riddle the economy. The most significant political splits in the regime may exist not at the top of the system but in the fissiparous pressures generated by the continued weakness of the state sector and the lure of the market and other illicit sources of income.

What is the likelihood that these developments would generate a reaction from below? Although our surveys show considerable discontent, they also depict an atomized society characterized by very low levels of trust. While one can document widespread antiregime sentiments, considerable inhibitions against even the private expression of dissenting views continue. Civil society institutions capable of channeling mass discontent into any constructive action appear to be completely absent. The November 2009 currency reform, implemented after the conclusion of our surveys, provides a test of the surprising resilience of the political system. Households adjust to incremental deterioration in their well-being with coping strategies. But the impact of the currency reform was widespread across the population, sudden, and nakedly inconsistent with the regime's meta-narrative that foreign forces are largely to blame for the country's misfortunes. The surveys document the declining hold that this narrative had on the population even prior to the currency reform; the shock of the conversion no doubt further damaged the regime's credibility, perhaps irreparably so.

Yet this massive shock generated only sporadic civil disobedience with no evidence that it might cascade into a wider movement. Given the strength and ferocity of the repressive apparatus evident in our surveys, the reasons are not surprising.

Nonetheless, elites do not operate in a vacuum; no matter how repressive the political system, the regime must figure out ways to elicit adequate compliance and work effort to permit the system to function. The government's backtracking on the currency reform shows clearly that even highly repressive governments may be forced to accommodate disaffection from below, even if only on tactical grounds. Indeed, as observed at the conclusion of the preceding chapter, participation in the market is associated with a number of characteristics—greater likelihood of arrest, more consumption of foreign news, more negative assessments of the regime, a greater willingness to communicate those views to one's peers, and a greater propensity to cite political motives for emigration—that might be thought of as a "syndrome" to adopt a medical metaphor. What we have called "everyday forms of resistance" may not generate regime change as traditionally conceived, but marketization could increasingly constrain the economic and political policy choices of the regime. From this perspective, the regime's antipathy toward the market is comprehensible.

How might this occur? In this regard, our characterization of North Korean cynicism and corruption as "increasing" is potentially important in a crucial respect. Kim Byung-yeon (2010), working with a similar, if slightly smaller, survey of refugees concludes that while the level of corruption is quite high, it has been relatively constant over time, suggesting a kind of political equilibrium.

Corruption in some forms can be good, "greasing the wheels," introducing a degree of flexibility in systems that would otherwise be self-debilitating.[1] However, other forms of corruption—particularly "cascading" corruption, which drives up transaction costs all along the value chain—can impose large deadweight losses, impede the initiation of productivity-enhancing activities, and distort the allocation of resources. When such corruption takes the form of street-level extortion and sheer predation of almost unimaginable brutality documented in our surveys, it not only impairs the informal sector's contribution to growth but surely undermines the credibility of and allegiance to the political regime as well.

Moreover, the inability of the state sector to provide adequate income and even the most basic elements of the social contract, such as food, continues to create incentives for managers and households to exit the planned economy and enter the market. As this process continues and the state sector shrinks, it could at some point generate adequate constraints that some process of economic—if not political—reform of the state would be necessary for its very fiscal survival. Indeed, it could be that the revival of markets is tolerated because they have become necessary sources of revenue as some of the less privileged parts of the state grasp for "dedicated" revenue streams that they can control.

If our findings of tepid support for the regime together with perceptions of rising corruption correctly characterize attitudes held by large swaths of the North Korean public, the long-term implications for political stability are potentially explosive.

The North Korean regime confronts two major, ongoing, and related challenges. The first is ideological. The very raison d'être of the North Korean regime is the alternative it poses to democratic, capitalist South Korea. Yet it appears unable to both deliver on the promise of the socialist model and eradicate the market despite its apparent desire to do so. Second, the regime continues to grapple with a basic fiscal challenge

---

1. For example, maintenance of slush funds by enterprise managers in centrally planned economies allows them to cope with input disruptions by sourcing outside the plan, in effect responding to underlying scarcities permitting them to fulfill their targets and generating adequate resources back to the state sector to keep it afloat. This might be considered a "good" form of corruption as opposed to the alternative, the consistent underestimation of productivity and the stockpiling of inputs, which would be even less efficient.

posed by its large expenditures, questionable ability to extract resources from the economy, and a scramble for resources that pits the rising power and prerogatives of the military-industrial complex against the traditional economic functions necessary for good governance and the social well-being of the population.

The international community has a strong interest in fostering the continued growth of internal markets, both as a badly needed tool to provide for an impoverished population and as a mechanism to encourage long-term internal political change in a more humane direction. External economic engagement additionally holds the prospect, though no guarantee, of moderation of the regime's belligerent foreign policy and nuclear ambitions.

If engagement with North Korea is appropriate, the policy community needs to think in a nuanced way about the modalities of engagement that will be appropriate for an economy as poor and distorted as that of North Korea. What kinds of reforms might work—and be politically palatable—were the regime or its successor to consider a new course? Can a strategy of selective political and economic engagement contribute to this process and, if so, how?

## Engaging North Korea

The rehabilitation of North Korea's failing economy poses two interrelated challenges. The first is to raise per capita incomes to address the country's widespread poverty and food insecurity. The second is to encourage a fundamental reorientation away from the state and toward effectively functioning market-oriented institutions. The latter has a political dimension as well: Apart from improving the functioning of the economy and better addressing the population's material needs, the development of more market-oriented institutions, even if not fully independent of state control, would lessen the pervasive control over people's lives, which is a constant theme in refugee testimony.

Arguments for economic engagement by external actors are also motivated by the premise that they might induce North Korea to engage politically, to pursue talks that would check its nuclear ambitions and moderate tensions on the peninsula. A closely related argument for engagement, however, is that increased economic integration will contribute to a deeper transformation of North Korea, which will, as a result, come to have a much greater stake in international cooperation and the development of robust foreign economic relations (see, for example, Asia Society 2009).

However, we cannot assume that any and all forms of economic engagement will have similarly transformative effects. In a country such as North Korea, even nominally private economic exchanges can be monopolized by the state and military sectors. And external actors also may not be comfortable rocking the boat. Some strategic thinkers in South Korea have acknowledged openly that a central objective of an engagement strategy is precisely to avoid a messy collapse of the regime (e.g., Moon 2004). As a consequence, the transformative effects of economic integration will depend crucially on the nature of the economic ties that develop between North Korea and its partners and the extent to which such ties can be appropriated by politically connected groups such as the Kim family clique, the party, and/or the military.

In order to assess the prospects for different strategies of engagement, it is important to provide some sense of what a reformed North Korea might look like. Although there is more than one path out of the difficulties the North Korean economy now faces, the basic contours of the reform process are surprisingly clear. Given the economy's small size and location in the dynamic, high-growth Northeast Asian region, the country would benefit from a dramatic expansion in international trade and investment ties, particularly with its neighbors South Korea, China, and Japan. The share of international trade in national income could quintuple from where it is today (Noland 2000).

There would be corresponding changes in the composition of output. Given that the country does not have a comparative advantage in the production of food crops, the agricultural sector would shrink and production would shift away from bulk grains, which can be imported much more cheaply, toward higher value-added products aimed at urban consumers, both locally and abroad. Both mining and manufacturing would expand, generating foreign exchange through exports. Within manufacturing, production would shift from capital goods, where North Korea has no comparative advantage, toward the production of labor-intensive, mid-technology manufactures for the world market.

The services sector is normally underdeveloped in centrally planned economies, and North Korea appears to be no exception. A reformed economy would have an expanded services sector, fed by the entry of entrepreneurial North Koreans into a variety of services that require minimal investment but that would have tremendous welfare-improving effects: restaurants, barbers and beauty parlors, retail shops, and construction. There is even a role for services exports. North Korea already has a small animation industry, and strong education in certain technical niches could generate opportunities in other select sectors. Export of labor and increased earnings from remittances might also be a component of a more open North Korean economy.

In light of the weak institutional linkages between North Korea and the global economy, foreign firms are likely to play a key role in this process of transformation, providing the product specifications and global procurement and marketing networks North Korea currently lacks. This injunction by no means suggests a single model based on the Washington Consensus; if nothing else, the experience of Asia over the last half century has demonstrated that there is more than one way to skin a cat. Some economies in Northeast Asia, notably South Korea, have implemented policy packages characterized by a heavy reliance on domestic entrepreneurship, indigenous technical skills, and government intervention, with foreign firms playing a role as buyers as well as producers. China developed by initially relying on export-oriented enclaves, which gradually expanded. Others, such as Singapore, implemented much more neutral policy regimes and relied much more on multinational corporations to drive manufacturing growth. But in all three cases, an orientation toward global markets and some role for foreign entities were key.

There are multiple paths from here to there, and detailed blueprints are less important than the general direction of policy and a willingness to experiment and learn. The sequencing of key reforms has varied considerably. It is probably sufficient to get a few important things right initially; not all reforms have to be implemented at once. What is certain, however, is that a dynamic North Korean economy will involve increased foreign trade and investment and quite fundamental shifts in output as a result. Institutional reforms will be required not only to support the market but also to marry the latent potential of the domestic economy to the demands of the world market. In thinking about engagement with North Korea it is critical to keep in mind that this is more than a technocratic exercise or one aimed at the alleviation of poverty in the short run. The goal is more fundamental: to encourage and assist North Korean authorities and officials to effect a fundamental institutional change (see figure 6.1). What types of engagement might be most effective in this regard?

## Humanitarian Assistance

Before examining commercial involvement with North Korea, it is worth considering international humanitarian assistance to the country. Since the devastating famine in the 1990s, large segments of the North Korean populace have remained chronically food insecure (Haggard and Noland 2009a). In response to these pressing humanitarian needs, the UN's World Food Program has been in operation in the country since 1995, as have a number of nongovernmental organizations (NGOs). The humanitarian presence represents the most sustained engagement between the government of North Korea and the world community.

In his final report as UN special rapporteur for North Korean human rights, Vitit Muntarbhorn emphasized that ensuring access to food is a basic human right (United Nations Human Rights Council 2010), and we strongly concur. Given the recurrence of famine or near-famine conditions in North Korea during the "reform in reverse" period, it is particularly important to restate the principle that humanitarian assistance be divorced from high politics. The international community, as well as North Korea's neighbors, should stand ready to provide assistance on the basis of need.

**Figure 6.1  Engaging North Korea**

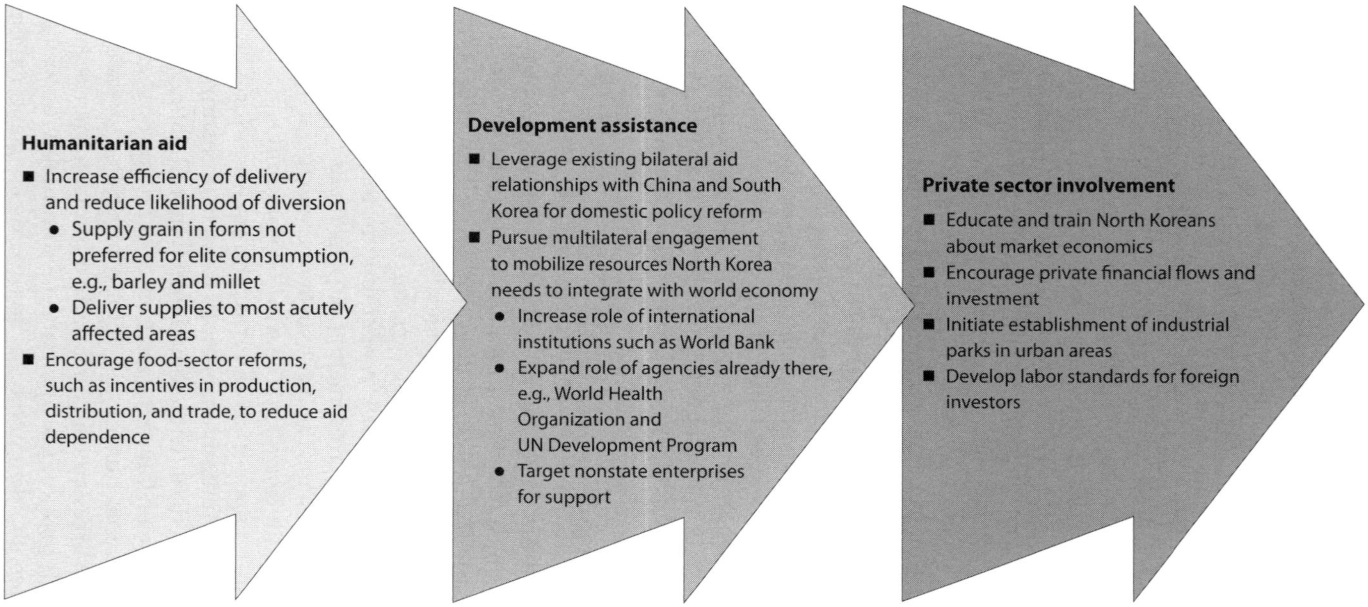

**Humanitarian aid**
- Increase efficiency of delivery and reduce likelihood of diversion
  - Supply grain in forms not preferred for elite consumption, e.g., barley and millet
  - Deliver supplies to most acutely affected areas
- Encourage food-sector reforms, such as incentives in production, distribution, and trade, to reduce aid dependence

**Development assistance**
- Leverage existing bilateral aid relationships with China and South Korea for domestic policy reform
- Pursue multilateral engagement to mobilize resources North Korea needs to integrate with world economy
  - Increase role of international institutions such as World Bank
  - Expand role of agencies already there, e.g. World Health Organization and UN Development Program
  - Target nonstate enterprises for support

**Private sector involvement**
- Educate and train North Koreans about market economics
- Encourage private financial flows and investment
- Initiate establishment of industrial parks in urban areas
- Develop labor standards for foreign investors

Nonetheless, even the provision of humanitarian aid requires thought. Donors should insist to the extent possible on a transparent and accountable aid program, a standard our surveys make clear has not always been met in the past. For both humanitarian reasons and the crucial political purpose of maintaining support for such aid, outside donors must remain committed to core humanitarian principles and programmatic reforms that increase the efficiency of aid delivery and reduce the likelihood of its diversion away from the intended recipients.

Such reforms would include supplying grain in forms not preferred for elite consumption, such as barley and millet, and delivering aid supplies to the most acutely affected areas, so that even if it was diverted from its intended use and sold in markets, it would likely remain in the areas where it will do the most good. While the United States, the main donor to the UN's World Food Program, has addressed the second issue, American policies still require US food aid to be sourced in the United States and transported on US vessels; as a natural consequence, US food aid largely takes the form of staples like corn, which the United States produces in abundance. Reforms in *US* practices could improve the effectiveness of the aid programs it supports in North Korea.

To the extent possible such assistance should also be guided by the longer-run objective of weaning the country from the need for humanitarian aid. The humanitarian program needs to be coupled with a dialogue over reforms of the food sector that will make it less dependent on food aid over time. These include reforming incentives in the production and distribution of food, as well as broader reforms, such as adequate incentives for exports, that will allow North Korea to import food on commercial terms.

Yet no matter how well designed, such assistance will inevitably have ambiguous effects on economic reform and regime transformation. Ironically, the existence of food aid and the incentive to monetize it through diversion into markets acted as an important stimulus for the development of markets in the 1990s. But given that most food aid is channeled through the public distribution system, it almost of necessity has the consequence of strengthening the power of the state; humanitarian engagement must always be alert to ways to mitigate this effect.

## Development Assistance

Long-term development assistance, as distinct from humanitarian aid, is typically extended with some policy conditionality and thus could play a key role in encouraging reform. A growing body of scholarly research on the political economy of aid suggests that it is most likely to be effective when coupled with domestic reform. In the absence of reform, aid may have little impact or may even encourage temporizing behavior by governments, large public sectors, clientelism, and corruption. Problems of moral hazard abound in the North Korean case in particular. Proffering aid—which may help address real needs in North Korea and make the regime feel more secure—may also discourage precisely the long-run evolution in the North Korean system that the policy seeks.

We return to the question of how to design a multilateral aid strategy in more detail below. To be clear, the signals emanating from Pyongyang, at least at the moment, are not auspicious in terms of economic reform and the political prerequisites that would make interaction with multilateral development banks and other aid agencies productive. But a consideration of bilateral assistance from China and South Korea provides some important clues to the structuring of foreign aid and its reform-leveraging effect.

### China

At present, China is North Korea's main patron. Although it has tried to persuade North Korea of the benefits of economic reform it does not appear to have introduced any policy conditionality into its aid program, or if it has, it has been less than successful in enforcing it. Nor has it shown any interest in enforcing UN Security Council sanctions against North Korea in response to its missile and nuclear tests (Noland 2009b).

China's influence on the North is not entirely negative, however. To the extent that its engagement contributes to economic rehabilitation, Chinese trade and aid raise income and alleviate poverty. China also provides a proximate model of a ruling communist party that has managed to introduce reforms while maintaining political power, an important fact to emphasize in appealing to the self-interest of the North Korean leadership. Much of China's economic engagement with the North also appears to be occurring on market-conforming terms; indeed, China has been increasingly explicit that it would like the state to guide the economic relationship but markets to do the work. Through the process of marketizing the North Korean economy, Chinese engagement has the long-term indirect effect of constraining North Korean economic policy away from some of its more self-destructive impulses.

The initiation of a state development bank in early 2010 is rumored to have been initiated by the Chinese, frustrated by the degree of corruption in North Korea and fearful of the expropriation risk facing Chinese investors. The centralization of investment relations between China and North Korea through the formation of the state development bank could be interpreted as an attempt by China to focus accountability with the North Korean state and protect Chinese investors from cascading corruption and could thus provide an example of how to leverage aid for policy reform.

To the extent that economic integration proceeds between China and North Korea, it is unlikely to promote the sort of transparency and governance agenda promoted by the World Bank or Transparency International;

China is hardly an exemplar of the Washington Consensus. Nonetheless, if Chinese engagement continues to downplay the role of aid, or at least emphasizes its complementarity to private activity, China's deep engagement will probably have strong, if indirect, marketizing effects.

### South Korea

The country's second most important donor is South Korea, although under the Lee Myung-bak administration, and particularly since the sinking of the *Cheonan*, South Korean aid has dried to a trickle. Inter-Korean engagement was originally conceived by Kim Dae-jung as an instrument: The point of engagement was to encourage sufficient systemic evolution in North Korea to establish a meaningful basis for reconciliation and, ultimately, national unification. However, critics of this strategy noted that engagement gradually became an end in itself, with financial inducements offered simply to keep talks moving forward or as a hedge against collapse. Although most South Korean assistance has been in the form of humanitarian assistance, some has taken the form of "cooperation projects," such as the Kaesong Industrial Complex, that were designed to leverage a broader reform process.

We do not rule out the long-run effect of such experiments, and their positive social consequences for the workers involved are important, even though a substantial share of those benefits are captured as a result of wage payments passing through the state. But these semipublic, semiprivate ventures do not appear to have been successful to date in leveraging reform. This limited effect arises in part because of their confinement to enclaves, although this was true of export-processing zones earlier in Asia's history. But the effect of reform is also mitigated because various South Korean subsidies make them less than fully commercial undertakings. Looking forward, South Korea will want to consider the types of support that will encourage system transformation when North Korean authorities decide to move, while avoiding the temptation to provide assistance that simply transfers resources or is effectively captured by the state.

While China will pursue its own agenda, South Korea should commit to the principle that investment in such projects should be done on efficient, transparent terms. As long as the South Korean government maintains direct and indirect influence over specific capital allocation decisions by financial intermediaries, it will be tempted to use this influence to promote its policy toward the North.[2] Cooperation projects should minimize discretionary state involvement either directly or indirectly through public-sector financial institutions or other state-owned enterprises.

---

2. The Hyundai Asan corruption trials in which five South Korean government officials were convicted of illegally channeling funds through the Korean Development Bank to Hyundai Asan for use in the North is exhibit A in this regard (Noland 2004).

To be clear, there is an economic case for intervention. Economic integration between the North and South may have positive externalities, and the social rate of return on South Korean investment in the North may exceed the private rate of return. Moreover, subsidization of engagement may promote evolutionary economic and political change in the North. As a consequence, there is a public policy justification for encouraging investment in the North.

Public-sector initiatives by the South, and even subsidies, could support private investment in a variety of ways. Examples include multilateral assistance for the development of export processing zones and engaging South Korean institutions, such as the Korea Trade Investment Promotion Agency and the Korea Ex-Im Bank, in North Korea. But many discussions of the rehabilitation of the North Korean economy have overemphasized public investment and have failed to consider the crucial complementarities between public-sector investment, economic reform, and the engagement of the South Korean private sector. At least some of the massive costs of modernizing the North Korean economy can be borne by the private sector through foreign direct investment. This is even true with respect to infrastructure, where a number of developing countries have benefited from private investment in projects ranging from telecommunications to highways and even the provision of power and water. South Korea has a long history undertaking exactly this sort of investment in the developing world. Egyptian conglomerate Orascom is currently undertaking an expansion of North Korea's cellular phone network.

But the existence of a justification for support does not mean that all support works equally well; interventions should be clear, limited, and transparent and implemented as neutrally as possible with respect to specific projects and firms. The most efficient way of accomplishing these objectives would be for the South to introduce broad tax incentives for investment in the North, which would encourage firms to invest there rather than other offshore destinations such as China or Southeast Asia. A tax-based policy would separate the overarching societal goal of investment in the North from state influence on particular investment decisions and would thus preserve the microeconomic efficiency of private firms selecting among potential investment projects on the basis of expected rates of return. Market-compatible engagement would have the added benefit of encouraging learning on the part of the North Koreans, whose interaction with the outside world has been on largely nonmarket terms.

## Mobilizing International Finance

Bilateral assistance, while essential, is likely to prove inadequate to successfully revitalize the North Korean economy. Multilateral cooperation not only will reduce the chances that North Korea will play the interests of outside parties against one another but also will provide additional resources for the tremendous scale of investment ultimately required for North Korea to successfully integrate into the global economy. International financial institutions such as the World Bank and Asian Development Bank have a role to play in this process as providers of nonpoliticized technical assistance and policy advice as well as capital. The International Finance Corporation—the World Bank's private-sector arm—could have a particularly important role to play insofar as a core goal is to encourage the development of non-state-controlled entities, and the multilateral development banks work largely through existing state institutions. The Six Party Talks or some successor scheme could spawn regional economic initiatives and embed the process of inter-Korean reconciliation in a broader regional fabric (Haggard and Noland 2009b).

North Korea is in need of depoliticized technical assistance on a panoply of issues running from the mundane but critical, such as developing meaningful national statistical capabilities, through basic agricultural and health technologies to the social infrastructure of a modern economy. This infrastructure should incorporate policy mechanisms to manage macroeconomic policy, including through a reform of the central bank; specify property rights and resolve commercial disputes; regulate markets, including financial markets as they emerge; establish and implement international trade and investment policies; and so on.

The possibility of a Northeast Asian Development Bank has been floated as a vehicle for undertaking these tasks. However, it would be a mistake to construct a new institution that would duplicate the activities of existing global and regional institutions in which the five other countries are already well represented. Rather, both advice and multilateral lending will be facilitated by North Korea's entry into the World Bank, International Monetary Fund, Asian Development Bank, and the World Trade Organization and an expansion of the activities of agencies that are currently engaged there, such as the United Nations Development Program, World Health Organization, and United Nations Children's Fund (UNICEF). In our view, the sooner this happens, the better. There could well be a role for subregional initiatives, possibly growing out of the existing Six Party Talks or some future equivalent as we have discussed in detail elsewhere (Haggard and Noland 2009b).

One model of multilateral engagement of North Korea would be to allow the World Bank to play a coordinating role as the administrative arm of a consultative group. The Bank would engage in more detailed analysis of the North Korean economy and become the repository for a dedicated North Korea fund that would initially support technical assistance and the building of local institutional capacity. These early actions would eventually support direct lending and investment guarantee activity. Japanese postcolonial claims payments could be one source of financing for such a facility as the two countries normalize relations. Calibration on the basis of Vietnam's experience in joining the World Bank suggests that the North

Koreans might expect an eventual lending program on the order of $150 million to $250 million annually; given South Korea's interest in revitalizing North Korea and the prospects of Japanese postcolonial payments, the actual lending from such a facility might be substantially larger.

But the Tumen River project provides a case study of how well-intentioned multilateral schemes can go nowhere in the absence of complementary domestic policies (Tsuji 2004). Similarly, the efforts by the Korean Peninsula Energy Development Organization to provide North Korea with lightwater reactors—whatever their political merits—proved a complete white elephant from an economic perspective. Infrastructure projects, such as pipelines and the energy grid, might provide the opening wedge for multilateral cooperation. But as we have argued above, undertaking such initiatives in the absence of a shift in North Korean policy is unlikely to garner either public or private support and could send misleading signals to North Korea given the vast resources such projects would demand.

## Commercial Engagement

In the end, however, the role of both humanitarian and developmental aid must be put in proper perspective. To the extent that North Koreans have any interactions with foreigners, it is often with government agencies or NGOs. Given the North Korean milieu, it is quite natural for North Koreans to think of such engagement as a form of political bargaining. But an important long-run task of engagement is a sort of political-economic socialization: to educate North Koreans about the functioning of market economics and to reorient their conception of engagement away from politically driven resource transfers or political tribute and toward mutually beneficial exchange. As the previous section suggested, the private sector will ultimately play the key role not only in the process of integration but also in this socializing function: through trade, foreign direct investment, private capital flows, and technology transfer through expertise. Participation of foreign firms means that projects would be subject to the market test of profitability and would encourage North Korean authorities to think of economic engagement in terms of joint gain rather than as political tribute.

In such a context, not all forms of public and private engagement are equally transformative. One can imagine a hierarchy of modalities of engagement that combine public involvement with private investment and trade, each with differential effects on the long-run objective of reform. From the standpoint of encouraging systemic transformation in North Korea, energy pipelines or even transportation links would have the least impact. Although North Korean infrastructure is in desperate need of repair, rehabilitation of the transportation sector will only promise enduring gains once there are clear signs of reform that would allow infrastructure investment to support wider marketization; at that point, such investments would jump the queue and become more central. But we should not believe in a "field of dreams" approach in which the public sector builds and the private sector comes; we have ample experience, including in the North-South rail links, of infrastructure projects that have gone nowhere.

Next in this hierarchy would be projects such as Mt. Kumgang, which can literally and figuratively be fenced off from the rest of the North Korean economy and society and as a result have limited effects on institutional transformation. Given the historical enmity and distrust between the North and the South, the Mt. Kumgang tourism project may have been a necessary first step to build confidence and trust. But future projects should be evaluated with a more critical eye. Marginally preferable to the Mt. Kumgang project would be mining concessions or special economic zones in remote areas such as Rason (formerly Rajin-Sonbong). However, it is important to note that these are classic enclave projects, with limited spillover into the broader society, and should be seen only as tactical steps on the road to a broader opening.

Industrial parks, bonded warehouses, and other preferential investment zones in urban areas would be preferable, and investment by South Korean and third-country firms throughout North Korea would be the best of all. To be sure, industrial parks, bonded warehouses, and preferential investment zones have a mixed record around the world but in the North Korean milieu represent a substantial second-best improvement over the status quo. Industrial parks are justifiable insofar as the most natural South Korean investors in the North are small- and medium-sized industrial enterprises that are increasingly uncompetitive in South Korea but could remain viable given access to lower-wage North Korean labor. Extending the public provision of physical infrastructure and effective political guarantees to these small enterprises makes a certain sense, particularly if the alternative is for these firms to move their operations to China or Vietnam. Yet the North Korean decision in 2009 to close the border and interfere with the operation of the Kaesong Industrial Complex suggests that these risks pertain even—and perhaps particularly—to such high-visibility projects.

More decentralized investment throughout the country would not only permit location decisions to be driven by profit opportunities but also maximize the contact between North and South Koreans and third-country nationals (and thus provide the demonstration or educational effects with respect to the operation of a market economy). Such an approach would also create competition between local authorities to attract investment.

Whatever the specifics, these limited or more expansive openings would be the key modality through which emerging industrial and service activities would expand (through the creation of new capacity made possible by foreign investors) and be linked to the world economy through global supply, procurement, and marketing networks. Sadly, it is apparent that Pyongyang understands the implications of these different modalities of engagement and prefers precisely the ones that generate hard currency earnings without requiring significant alteration of existing practices. It appears sufficiently comfortable with the existing enclaves to replicate them elsewhere, for example, in the form of a Mt. Paekdu tourism venture (on the Chinese border) and Kaesong-like industrial enclaves in Haeju and elsewhere, per the October 2007 North-South summit agreement.

To the extent possible, this approach should be eschewed in favor of more decentralized and free-ranging establishment of foreign-invested enterprises in the country. Yet even under the most propitious conditions, it is evident that the government will attempt to steer economic engagement through state-controlled entities rather than the emerging nonsanctioned market-based actors our surveys documented. One implication is the necessity of developing Sullivan-type principles of labor standards, similar to those implemented by US investors during the apartheid period in South Africa, to ensure that foreign investors do more than simply exploit virtual slave-labor conditions. For investors from South Korea, Japan, the United States, and other Organization for Economic Cooperation and Development (OECD) members, adherence to the OECD's Guidelines for Multinational Enterprises, including those ensuring that North Korean workers are aware of their rights and how to exercise them, would be another way of trying to ameliorate the impact that engagement with state-owned entities in North Korea could have in terms of reinforcing state control.

## Private Lending

The North Korean government will eventually seek to resolve the overhang from its past international defaults (probably with South Korean government assistance) and reenter international capital markets as a borrower; at the time of this writing, there is intriguing evidence of North Korean efforts to settle outstanding debts with a number of East European creditors (at pennies to the dollar and even barter terms). Such borrowing has been important in financing infrastructural development in Vietnam once reform makes such investments viable.

The tendency for commercial lenders to lend to the state will be intensified in the North Korean case: by the tenuous legal status of nonstate entities, their lack of credit histories, and absence of freely held collateral. Under such conditions, there may be a public policy justification to tilt the playing field away from state-connected borrowers.

For tactical reasons and because of the state-socialist nature of its economy, the North Korean government has historically blurred distinctions between private and public capital flows, particularly in its interactions with South Korea. Nominally private flows have been embedded in larger political bargains between the two countries and carried public subsidies and guarantees. For example, much of South Korea's food aid to the country was technically in the form of loans, although this was well-known fiction. As a result, such flows have not been fully subject to market tests of viability and profitability. This blurring of public and private flows has created a host of moral hazard problems. Private actors are encouraged to undertake projects that are not sustainable, and the North Korean government is not held accountable for enabling a positive rate of return on foreign investment.

Moreover, North Korea has repeatedly undercut private investors, reneging on financial commitments, interfering with the management of foreign-invested facilities, and elevating political over economic concerns to the detriment of foreign investors. The country remains in default on several billion dollars of commercial bank debt and has continually changed the rules governing foreign investment in ways that make it difficult if not impossible to realize a competitive risk-adjusted rate of return.

Private capital flows are an absolute necessity if the North Korean economy is to be revitalized. This principle is not ideological; rather, it stems from several quite pragmatic considerations. First, international aid flows are unlikely to have their desired effect in the context of government policy that remains hostile to private financial flows; aid will simply be wasted. Second, the international donor community is unlikely to support large aid flows in the context of a hostile policy toward foreign investors. Even if political relations were to improve, it would be extremely difficult for South Korea to mobilize large-scale multilateral support for its North Korea policy without some sign of a change of course from Pyongyang in this regard. The demand for foreign assistance has always exceeded its supply, and donors have become increasingly selective about where funds go. Third, international aid flows are unlikely, on their own, to provide the scale of financing needed to turn the North Korean economy around. Finally, foreign direct investment constitutes the institutional mechanism for both technology transfer and the links to marketing and distribution networks that North Korea currently lacks. Aid should seek to complement and encourage such private flows, not provide a substitute for them.

## Constructive Engagement: A Reprise

In short, the broad contours of what a reformed North Korean economy would likely look like are surprisingly well understood, even if those contours permit substantial variation in the precise sequencing and pace of policy change. Opening and reform will look at least something like the export-oriented strategies pursued by North Korea's neighbors, integrating the country into the dynamic region in which, ironically, it has the good fortune to dwell. Aid, both humanitarian and developmental, bilateral and multilateral, will play an important role given the magnitude of the challenges the North Korean economy faces.

But two simple rules of thumb should be observed to ensure that engagement is constructive. First, it needs to occur in the context of a strategic decision on the part of North Korea to adopt complementary reforms, even if partial. The problem is not so much uncertainty about the contours of advisable economic policy reform, but rather the apparent absence of the political leadership that would make the implementation of such a program feasible. Second, and closely related, aid must operate in the context of incentives for the private sector, both domestic and foreign, to play a larger role in North Korea's future. Without an adequate private-sector presence, aid will simply strengthen the state sector, encourage politicization of projects, and intensify rent seeking.

## The Humanitarian and Human Rights Imperative

The problems North Korea faces are not just material in nature, and it is misguided to think that economic solutions alone are adequate to move the country forward. What can be done to improve the plight of the North Korean people if the aim of the regime is to preserve the essential outlines of the existing political economy? How do we address the problems of existing refugees and the possibility that future economic or political crises might generate a new flood of them? How do we deal with the humanitarian and human rights issues in North Korea itself?

One can conceptualize a humanitarian and human rights policy for North Korea along two distinct dimensions. First it is important to distinguish policies to address the human rights and humanitarian problems in North Korea from the distinct issues surrounding the refugee population. Second, the international community can pursue policies that engage the government of North Korea and require its cooperation; we begin with a discussion of an agenda to engage North Korea on these issues, which we label "direct policies." But given that the current regime is likely to resist fundamental alterations in the status quo, the international community must entertain policies that operate "indirectly," regardless of the stance of the North Korean government. Policy options along these two dimensions are summarized in table 6.1. We first discuss "direct," then "indirect" policies toward the resident population of North Korea and move on to refugee-specific issues.

### "Direct" Engagement Policies Regarding the Resident Population of North Korea

North Korea engages in the systematic denial of human, civic, and political rights through brutal repression. Despite the fact that it routinely ignores its obligations under international covenants, North Korea is nonetheless party to four key human rights treaties including those on civil and political rights; economic, social, and cultural rights; women's rights; and child rights.[3] In response to concerns about the implementation of North Korea's commitments, the United Nations appointed a special rapporteur for North Korean human rights. During his six years in this position, North Korean authorities did not once permit Thai law professor Vitit Muntarbhorn to visit the country. In his final report to the Human Rights Council of the UN General Assembly, he described the human rights situation in North Korean as "*sui generis* given the... many instances of human rights violations which are both harrowing and horrific," surprisingly direct language given the often anodyne and diluted style of UN treatment of human rights abuses (United Nations Human Rights Council 2010, 1).

Vitit's successor, Indonesian human rights lawyer Marzuki Darusman, submitted his first report to the UN General Assembly in September 2010, and North Korea's deputy UN ambassador, Pak Tok-hun, responded later in October that Darusman's report was "a political plot fabricated by hostile forces in an attempt to isolate and stifle our system." He went on to say that "the purpose is clear, the promotion of human rights is only words but in reality what they try to do is change the ideology and system of our country."[4]

It is not difficult to identify numerous actions that the North Korean government could take to begin to address the human rights situation in the country. The examples we cite here are illustrative and do not exhaust the possibilities; many track the recommendations of the Committee for Human Rights in North Korea (2010). But they should not be seen as reflecting a distinct national agenda; indeed, to the extent that they are identified with particular countries, the force of the argument weakens. It falls to the democracies and NGOs to continually raise these issues as matters of principle and policy. In this regard, Europe and the new developing-country democracies have a particularly important role to play in reminding North Korea that human rights are not simply an American preoccupation but a more widely shared concern. Indeed, these actions should be taken up by all countries seeking to engage North Korea.

First, it is important to simply open a dialogue. North Korea should allow access to the Office of the UN High Commissioner for Human Rights, the Special Rapporteur on Human Rights, the Special Rapporteur on Torture, and the UN Commission on Human Rights Working Group on Arbitrary Detention.

---

3. North Korea is a party to the United Nations International Covenant on Civil and Political Rights, International Covenant on Economic, Social and Cultural Rights, Convention on the Elimination of Discrimination against Women, and Convention on the Rights of the Child (United Nations Human Rights, Office of the High Commissioner for Human Rights 2010).

4. Louis Charbonneau, "North Korea Says UN Rights Talk Is a Plot," Reuters AlertNet, October 22, 2010, www.alertnet.org (accessed on November 10, 2010).

**Table 6.1　Human rights policy matrix**

| Policies toward | "Direct" policies involving engagement with the North Korean government | "Indirect" policies not requiring engagement with the North Korean government |
|---|---|---|
| Resident population of North Korea | ■ Initiate official dialogue<br>　• Seek access to UN Special Rapporteur<br>　• Monitor compliance with existing obligations<br>■ Seek penal system reform<br>　• Close political penal-labor colonies<br>　• Release political prisoners and family members<br>　• Improve treatment of prisoners and World Food Program access<br>　• Open dialogue with International Labor Organization on prison labor<br>■ Improve humanitarian relief<br>　• Conduct aid operations according to international standards<br>　• Seek access to UN Special Rapporteur on Food and Hunger<br>　• Condition development assistance on improvements in human rights, refugee, and humanitarian relief practices<br>　• Design development assistance to encourage citizen participation<br>■ Seek full accounting of prisoners of war and abductees<br>■ Encourage nonofficial exchange and contact<br>■ Encourage family reunifications | ■ Promote news and information dissemination<br>■ Develop labor standards for foreign investors |

(continued on next page)

Refugees

■ Seek decriminalization of exit

■ Seek release of citizens incarcerated due to forced repatriation from China

■ Assist and protect trafficked North Koreans in China who may wish to return to North Korea

■ China
  - Cease forced repatriation
  - Permit UNHCR access to border area

■ South Korea
  - Enhance assimilation of defectors
  - Continue funding for refugee egress

■ United States
  - Improve implementation of the North Korea Human Rights Act
  - Publicize the availability of support for North Koreans who seek asylum in the United States
  - Establish a hotline with UNHCR and South Korea
  - Provide scholarships to refugees

■ Create a "hole in the fence"
  - Actively promote refugee flows through temporary refugee resettlement facilities

UNHCR = United Nations High Commissioner for Refugees

Second, as we have seen in chapter 5, a host of issues surround the regime's use of the legal and penal system to punish behaviors that are crucial not only for a more open polity but also for the functioning of a market economy. The change in the underlying laws may ultimately depend on a process of political liberalization, but the international community can begin by focusing on the prison system itself. North Korea should be called on to

- close the notorious *kwan-li-so* network of political penal-labor camps and allow the UN Working Group on Arbitrary Detention, the International Committee of the Red Cross (ICRC), Amnesty International, Human Rights Watch, or a similar group to certify that these prison camps have been closed;

- release family members, including children, of those convicted of political crimes;

- release political prisoners held in violation of their rights under the International Covenant on Civil and Political Rights to which North Korea is a state party or allow review of the cases of prisoners of conscience with the ICRC or a similar group with a view to their release;

- end brutal treatment of prisoners in the *kyo-hwa-so* (penitentiaries) including forced starvation; permit the World Food Program access to these facilities;

- initiate a dialogue between North Korea and the International Labor Organization (North Korea is not a member of this organization) on how practices in the *kyo-hwa-so*, *jip-kyul-so* ("collection centers"), and *ro-dong-dan-ryeon-dae* (labor training centers) can be brought up to international norms against forced and slave labor; and

- ratify the United Nations Convention against Torture and Other Cruel, Inhuman or Degrading Treatment or Punishment and its Optional Protocol (United Nations General Assembly 2010).

As we noted in the previous section, the provision of aid has an important role to play in North Korea, but its provision should always be attentive to the possibility of expanding human rights and political participation. A third set of prescriptions would be to

- permit public and private humanitarian relief organizations to conduct their operations according to well-established international norms and protocols. The basic principles governing delivery of humanitarian aid are straightforward. Aid should go to those in greatest need based on objective and systematic assessment and access to aid should not discriminate on the basis of age, gender, social status, ethnicity, or political beliefs (Ziegler 2002). Aid delivery should be transparent, enabling agencies to confirm that it is distributed to the target group and to assess its impact. These processes require that aid agencies have direct and ongoing contact with the affected populations and are able to collect (or monitor the collection of) data on the status of the populations.[5] In the process, the North Korean government will hopefully develop the capability to more accurately assess human needs in the country, a crucial first step to understanding the very scope of the humanitarian challenges it faces;

- permit the UN Special Rapporteur on Food and Hunger access to the country; condition development assistance on meaningful improvements in human rights, refugee, and humanitarian relief practices; and

- design development assistance to permit citizen participation—in line with well-established best practice—and encourage the presence of NGOs both foreign and, over time, domestic.

A fourth area is for the North Korean government to provide a full accounting of prisoners of war from the Korean War and abductees missing from South Korea, Japan, and other nations. Although the Japanese abductees have received the most attention, those missing or abducted are estimated to exceed 1,000 people and many are South Korean.

A fifth area that is of particular importance is to develop multiple channels of exchange and contact (Lankov 2009). Although it may appear odd to include this injunction in the context of humanitarian and human rights concerns, it is in fact a crucial step given the closed nature of North Korean society and the dearth of information about the outside world. Access to information plays an essential political role. All societies, even democracies, are vulnerable to government propaganda and misinformation. But in closed societies, authoritarian governments have particular leeway to develop elaborate propaganda machines that fundamentally distort information about the outside world. Connecting individuals to the outside world serves the crucial function of undermining these distortions by providing information, forcing the government to respond to a

---

5. These basic norms are embodied in the World Food Program's handbook, which lays out a standard operating procedure embodying reciprocal obligations on the part of donors and recipients. The NGO community is much more diverse than the public humanitarian aid machinery. Confrontation with difficult ethical dilemmas in Bosnia and Central Africa in the 1990s pushed the NGO community to codify voluntary norms that overlapped at a number of points with those governing the multilateral aid effort. The most prominent of these exercises is the Inter-Agency Code of Conduct arising out of the Sphere Project (2004) and later, in recognition of the absence of a formal accountability mechanism, the establishment of the Humanitarian Accountability Project International (Young et al. 2004). Among the norms embodied in the Sphere codes are understanding of basic conditions; evaluation of effectiveness; participation in the design, management, and monitoring of programs; distribution of aid through a transparent system that can be monitored and adequately audited; and impartiality, or the distribution of aid in a fair and equitable manner.

more informed public. Our surveys suggest that the North Korean public is receptive to alternative, non-state-controlled sources of information. In addition to these political functions, outside exchanges also constitute a crucial channel for technology transfer, broadly conceived: the flow of information not only expands freedom of thought but increases capabilities as well.

A strategy for such engagement might begin with less political exchanges, such as visits of orchestras and sports teams and academic exchanges; the last are particularly important in fields such as agronomy, medicine, and management that might contribute to wider reforms. Yet the most powerful way to influence future political developments is by encouraging educational opportunities abroad, bringing the youth of North Korea into contact with the world.

A final cluster of policies is to accelerate and expand family reunifications. South and North Korea have held 18 rounds of family reunions for those divided as a result of the war. Approximately 127,600 South Koreans have applied to take part in the meetings; 86,400 are still living, yet only about 17,000 have met their families. Given the advanced age of those surviving the Korean War, and their shorter life span in North Korea, this is an issue of great urgency.

The problem, of course, is that all of these actions require at least the North Korean government's acquiescence, if not its active cooperation. And while there is much to be said for holding the North Korean government to international obligations into which it has voluntarily entered, one should not be overly optimistic about cooperation from the present regime. The Committee for Human Rights in North Korea (2010) suggests that if the proposals of the UN Human Rights Council remain unimplemented despite the Universal Periodic Review and access to North Korea continues to be denied to the special rapporteurs and other UN human rights bodies, a more robust strategy should be pursued. These could include adoption of a resolution on North Korean human rights by the UN Security Council (UNSC) referring the matter of crimes against humanity in North Korea to the International Criminal Court for investigation and prosecution. A similar tack could be adopted via the "responsibility to protect" doctrine, since the prison system and other practices could be shown to constitute crimes against humanity.

But this approach has a practical problem: China sits on the UNSC and is unlikely to accede to any such UNSC resolutions, particularly ones that could set a precedent in terms of its own internal practices. This approach is also unlikely to have concrete effect. Rather, the measures noted here should be approached in a dispassionate way, as a wide-ranging and long-run reform agenda on which the democracies seek to engage North Korea if and when it seeks to reenter the international community. As with the economic reform process, the human rights agenda should be seen as a component of a broader process of political change, which, even if falling well short of regime change or democratization, would nonetheless limit the most egregious abuses.

## "Indirect" Policies Toward North Korean Residents

Although it would be preferable to have sustained cooperation with North Korea on humanitarian and human rights issues, the current regime's unwillingness to engage on these issues leaves the international community little choice but to consider policies that do not require its assent. These measures naturally place the international community in a more confrontational stance vis-à-vis the regime, but given the lack of success in engaging North Korea and the seriousness of the issues in question, the risks are warranted.

As documented in the preceding chapter, the information North Korean people receive about their own country and the world outside is highly restricted, but they are also increasingly willing to listen to outside information sources. At present, more than a dozen public and private groups in South Korea, Japan, and the United States broadcast radio into North Korea (Beck 2010). These efforts should be expanded along with other efforts to provide information directly to the North Korean people. In the United States, the administration should seek additional funding under the North Korean Human Rights Act (NKHRA) to bolster the existing activities of Radio Free Asia and Voice of America. In addition to the current short-wave broadcasting, the United States should redouble its efforts to persuade North Korea's neighbors to host transmission facilities for more easily accessed medium-wave (AM) broadcasting. We have no illusions that such information will lead to fundamental political change, but it has the marginal effect of undercutting the North Korean propaganda machine and thus increasing pressure on the North Korean government for greater accountability.

Likewise, as economic engagement proceeds, it is important to ensure to the extent possible that it is a mechanism of transformation, not simply an instrument to reinforce the status quo. One possibility noted above would be to encourage the development of codes of conduct similar to the Sullivan Principles, which were used in South Africa during that country's apartheid period, for foreign companies investing in North Korea. For OECD members such as South Korea, Japan, the United States, the European Union, and Russia, this could also involve ensuring that their multinational corporations implement the OECD's Guidelines for Multinational Enterprises when investing in North Korea, including in the Kaesong Industrial Complex. The labor laws in the complex could be amended to incorporate the core labor standards of the International Labor Organization, including the right to freedom of association and collective bargaining, the right to strike, prohibition against sexual discrimination and harassment, and a ban on child labor. Admittedly, the firms' scope for implementing such norms would be constrained by the North Korean government, but as the case of apartheid-era South Africa demonstrates, it is possible for businesses to make marginal improvements in working conditions, even in the context of a highly repressive legal environment if sufficient pressure is brought to bear.

## Policies Regarding Refugees

Most of the refugees we interviewed left North Korea because they believed conditions in China were better than those in North Korea. Even with modest improvements in the North Korean economy through the mid-2000s, North Korean refugees continued to leave. The turn away from reform after 2005, and particularly the disastrous 2009 currency conversion, provides additional motives for leaving even in the face of escalating efforts by both China and North Korea to raise the costs of doing so. With the gap between living standards in North Korea and China continuing to widen and with little prospect for significant improvement in political conditions in North Korea, the incentives to migrate will remain high over the foreseeable future.

Despite the importance of economic motivations, and the government of China's desire to portray the North Koreans as "economic migrants," it is important to underline that North Koreans crossing the border in search of permanent resettlement elsewhere are in fact refugees. Under the 1951 Convention Relating to the Status of Refugees (Article 1), the basis of refugee status is a legitimate fear of persecution on return to one's country of origin. Whatever their stated motives for exit, the fear of persecution can hardly be in doubt given the fact that exit is criminalized (also in contravention of international law) and the accumulating evidence on the internment of those seeking to leave or returning to the country when caught doing so.[6]

Nor as we saw in chapter 4 can there be any doubt about the abuses committed against prisoners, from forced starvation to torture and arbitrary execution. As a consequence, many North Koreans have a prima facie case for being considered *refugees sur place*; whether or not they

---

6. Article 12(2) of the International Covenant on Civil and Political Rights, to which North Korea is a state party, states unambiguously that "everyone shall be free to leave any country, including his own." The Refugee Convention holds that refugees must fear persecution based on race, religion, nationality, membership of a particular social group, or political opinion. To claim that the refugees are not protected under the Convention, one would have to hold the view that they did not fall under one of the five protected categories. But clearly, any North Korean leaving the country in search of resettlement or asylum would hold the "political opinion" that the criminalization of exit was unwarranted, quite apart from those who face persecution for their political views or simply fall into suspect categories (the "hostile classes"). For more on the legal grounds for protecting North Korean refugees, see Cohen (2010).

would have qualified for refugee status when they left North Korea, the North Korean government's policies upon their repatriation confer on them refugee status. The United Nations concurs and explicitly asks for "neighboring countries and the international community…to provide protection to those fleeing the Democratic People's Republic of Korea in order to seek asylum" (United Nations General Assembly 2010). Under the Refugee Convention, those seeking refugee status—and those appropriately entitled to it—should be given access to accepted processes through which their refugee status can be determined.[7]

The UN High Commissioner for Refugees (UNHCR) has been subjected to substantial criticism for not pushing the case of North Korean refugees more aggressively, in part because of several technicalities.[8] It is clear, however, that the agency faces a difficult balancing act. The proposal to take the Chinese government to arbitration over this issue is unlikely to succeed and could well be counterproductive. The UNHCR needs to continue its constructive activities in Beijing on behalf of the North Korean refugees, while at the same time urging the Chinese government to grant it access to the border region for establishing refugee determination procedures and providing protection for refugees as appropriate. North Korea should be encouraged to decriminalize movement within North Korea and across the border and to end the persecution of those who return voluntarily or are forced back into North Korea. A "direct" agenda concerning refugees would include demands that North Korea:

- adhere to its obligations under the Refugee Convention and end the criminalization of exit;

- release citizens currently incarcerated due to forced repatriation from China; and

- assist trafficked North Koreans in China who may wish to return to North Korea, ensuring that they are not persecuted and are protected in the process of repatriation.

---

7. It is important to acknowledge, however, that some North Koreans crossing the border may not seek or even want refugee status but rather a normalization of their status, for example, as traders or in the case of marriage to Chinese nationals.

8. The first issue was whether North Koreans were economic migrants lacking in legitimate fear of persecution. By 2003 the UNHCR had clearly stated that any assessment of protection needs must take into account the human rights situation in North Korea; the existence of groups that are particularly prone to persecution, in particular on account of their family or political background; the practice of penalizing unauthorized departures; and the abusive conditions in "reeducation" facilities (United Nations General Assembly 2007, 10). A second issue concerns citizenship. Article 1A (2) of the 1951 Convention also excludes from refugee status those with dual nationality, who have the ability to seek protection from the other nationality. According to South Korea's Constitution, North Koreans are also citizens of the Republic of Korea, but they clearly do not enjoy access to this benefit.

But in the end, the actions of China, South Korea, and the United States are likely to be more consequential than direct engagement with North Korea on these questions, and we therefore focus on these "indirect" policies next.[9]

## China's Obligations Regarding Refugees

Because China is the first port of entry for the overwhelming share of all North Korean refugees, China's position with respect to them is critical. In policy discussions in the United States, the phenomenon of North Korean refugees in China is sometimes likened to that of Mexican immigrants in the United States as a way of acknowledging Chinese concerns. There is some validity in this comparison. In both cases, the gap in income creates strong incentives for migration offset only by the stringency of controls. In both cases, immigrants provide labor but also confront a variety of social problems and difficulties in being integrated. But the government of Mexico celebrates its emigrants and the remittances they send home; it does not criminalize exit, imprison returnees, or stage public executions of those who help migrants cross the border. Although some sympathy with Chinese concerns is warranted, we cannot allow these concerns to trump the basic rights of the refugees.

China has fallen far short of its international obligations in this regard (Kurlantzik and Mason 2006, Freeman and Thompson 2009). China acceded in 1982 to both the 1951 Convention Relating to the Status of Refugees and the 1967 Protocol Relating to the Status of Refugees. Moreover, Chinese policy contravenes a 1995 UN-Chinese agreement stating explicitly that "UNHCR personnel may at all times have unimpeded access to refugees and to the sites of UNHCR projects in order to monitor all phases of their implementation."[10]

---

9. The North Korean regime has vehemently rejected the actions of the UN Council on Human Rights, a political body subsidiary to the UN General Assembly, which since 2003 has passed annual resolutions on North Korea's human rights record. North Korea has also refused to meet with special rapporteurs or the High Commissioner for Human Rights. North Korea takes a different stance toward the UN Human Rights Committee, however, a "treaty body" or technical committee that reviews implementation reports on the International Covenant on Civil and Political Rights through its Working Group on the Universal Periodic Review. North Korea submits such implementation reports and sends representatives to the review sessions of this body, most recently in 2009. In 2009, North Korea secured at least some diplomatic support from other developing and authoritarian regimes during this review. The government also simply rejected 50 of the recommendations forwarded to it under the review process, a number having to do with the treatment of refugees. In 2010, its response was even more unequivocal, in effect rejecting every single proposal advanced by the committee.

10. Article III(5), United Nations (United Nations High Commissioner for Refugees) and China, Agreement on the Upgrading of the UNHCR Mission in the People's Republic of China to UNHCR Office in the People's Republic of China, UNTS Volume 1898/1899, I–3237, December 11, 1995, 61–71.

The very presence of large numbers of North Korean refugees in China reflects in part the difficulty of patrolling a long land border but also some combination of corruption and acquiescence on the part of local Chinese border authorities. A distinct issue is the status of a growing number of children born to North Korean women in China, who are without documentation and effectively stateless, regardless of specific provisions of either the Chinese or North Korean legal codes.

But as a matter of policy, China does not treat fleeing North Koreans as refugees, and over the last five years it has steadily tightened controls and undertaken more detailed contingency planning (Freeman and Thompson 2009). Any North Korean escapee in China is subject to punishment as an "illegal transgressor." China has also signed several agreements with North Korea on the border. China cooperates with North Korean persecution of its refugees: through forcible repatriations, permitting North Korean security forces into China to track down refugees, fining Chinese citizens who assist refugees, and detaining and deporting foreigners who assist this population and publicize their plight. Refugees detained by Chinese authorities are also subject to abuse and even torture prior to repatriation (Amnesty International 2000, 2001, 2004; K. Lee 2006).

Repatriation is particularly troubling as it is explicitly prohibited under the Refugee Convention; the treaty does not permit the return (*refoulement*) of refugees to their country of origin.[11] China's obstinacy has blocked an appropriate international response through the UNHCR despite the country's membership in the Executive Committee of the High Commissioner's Program and its nominal commitment to refugee rights as a signatory to core protocols.

However morally justified, it is unlikely that appeals to China on the basis of shared values are likely to succeed. Rather, China must be reminded that current North Korean practices are a threat to basic security interests. North Korea's failed economic policies and human rights abuses are not just humanitarian problems. They have the potential to create a variety of negative transborder externalities, including drug smuggling, human trafficking, and even public health problems, as the outbreak of swine flu in the North Korean border region in late 2009 demonstrated clearly. Since refugees are unable to work and difficult to integrate, they are vulnerable not only to abuse but also to the lure of crime and other antisocial behaviors.

Regrettable as China's behavior is, it does reflect legitimate concerns about the presence of undocumented North Koreans within the country's borders, and these apprehensions should be taken seriously and

---

11. Article 33 of the Convention states, "No contracting party shall expel or return (*refouler*) a refugee in any manner whatsoever to the frontiers of territories where his life or freedom would be threatened on account of his race, religion, nationality, membership of a particular social group, or political opinion."

addressed. Moreover, there is no reason for China to bear the burden of resettling all North Korean refugees.

Ideally, these concerns could be addressed through the establishment of temporary refugee resettlement camps in China itself together with third-country commitments to accept the refugees for permanent resettlement. However, given Beijing's resistance to allow direct UNHCR access, a more likely modality would be for the United States to work with South Korea and other interested parties in the Asia Pacific and Europe to establish multilateral first asylum arrangements, as was done for the Vietnamese boat people in the late 1970s. These arrangements would be negotiated with countries in the region willing to provide temporary asylum, such as Mongolia or Southeast Asian countries, with the assurance that the refugees will be permanently resettled elsewhere. Interested countries including South Korea, the United States, and Japan would commit to both financing such an effort and accepting refugees for resettlement, discussed further below. The goal of third-party action should be to make it as costless as possible for China to accept the North Koreans as refugees and, failing that, to provide a multilateral safety net and convince China to let them transit and exit. In the meantime, the United States and other third parties should seek to persuade China to establish some process of regularization that would permit the refugees to remain in China on a temporary protected basis as an interim solution.

## A Hole in the Fence?

The foregoing recommendations attempt to address North Korean human rights and the refugee question frontally, through direct engagement or negotiation with the North Korean government and through appeal to Chinese obligations and interests. In the absence of any real improvement in the North Korean human rights situation, an alternative would be to actively promote refugee flows: If we cannot influence the rights of the population under the existing regime, we should get them out of the country. One possibility would be for the United States, South Korea, the United Nations, and other concerned parties to urge China to establish temporary refugee resettlement camps, either under UN administration or through some coalition of the willing, with the intention that the refugees would be allowed to on-migrate to third countries. This solution would compound the refugee problem in the short run but have two more salutary effects: It would institutionalize a concerted effort to increase those able to escape and also induce the North Korean regime to think hard about its domestic policy and political choices.

China claims that its most basic concern is the potential for instability that a flood of refugees might generate both in China and in North Korea itself if such solutions were pursued (Freeman and Thompson 2009). It is not obvious that these expressed concerns are genuine. The three Chinese provinces that constitute the border region have a combined population roughly four times that of North Korea. Average per capita income in them is in excess of $4,000, multiples of North Korea's. An existing ethnic Korean population accounts for well under 2 percent of the populace; even in the Yanbian autonomous region ethnic Koreans now account for less than one-third of the populace. North Korea's northern provinces are generally sparsely populated (the population belt is in the south, along the demilitarized zone), so the idea that a flood of refugees from this relatively sparsely populated zone could upend the political order of these much larger and richer Chinese provinces is far-fetched. Rather, the "refugee flood" argument distracts attention from China's strategic uses of North Korea in its rivalries with the United States and India and its propensity to protect North Korea, including in the context of the Six Party Talks.[12]

Given China's strategic commitment to the Kim regime, however, its concerns are not unwarranted in light of the catalytic role that Hungary's opening of its border with Austria played in the collapse of the East German regime. Some observers have explicitly argued that opening the door to North Korean refugees could be a route to regime change in North Korea (Eberstadt and Griffin 2007, Kirkpatrick 2006), a proposal that quite naturally arouses Chinese suspicions. However, Chinese cooperation with respect to refugees does not commit it to a weakening of its border security or to any particular strategy toward North Korea. There is no reason why China could not uphold its international obligations with respect to North Korean refugees, maintain whatever level of border security it deems appropriate, and continue its preferred strategy of political and economic engagement with North Korea.

At a minimum, however, China should meet its obligations under the Refugee Convention, permit the UNHCR to assess the asylum claims of North Koreans in China, and make clear that North Korea's and China's commitments under the Refugee Convention trump any bilateral agreement that they may have struck. Our China-based survey indicated that under current policy, relatively few North Korean refugees wanted to settle in China permanently. But if China provided some pathway to legalization, the numbers willing to live peacefully in China might increase substantially. This might be the most practical and humane outcome for this community, at least until developments in North Korea provide a more welcoming environment for refugees to return.

---

12. There is increasing evidence of debates in Chinese policy circles on the merits of continuing to support North Korea. See in particular International Crisis Group (2010) and Snyder (2009).

## South Korea's Role with Respect to Refugees

If China's stance has been unconstructive, under the Sunshine Policy pursued by the Kim Dae-jung and Roh Moo-hyun governments, South Korea's could be described as ambivalent. Despite its constitutional claim over the whole of the Korean peninsula and its designation of North Korean refugees as citizens of the Republic of Korea, Seoul became increasingly unwelcoming toward them over the first half of the 2000s. The government maintains a debriefing and educational program for arriving refugees as well as cash support for them, and NGOs have stepped into the breach as well. But open support for refugees complicated a delicate North-South diplomacy, which was in any case continually veering off track. South Korea has also been concerned about problems of assimilation. As Andrei Lankov (2006) notes, the total number of North Koreans currently living in South Korea is less than the number West Germany managed to absorb in a typical year during the Cold War. Nonetheless, the problems of assimilating even this small number have proven large, particularly as the demographic profile of the refugees has shifted away from elite defectors to those who are older and lacking in skills and education.

One manifestation of the new caution with respect to refugees was a reduction in direct support payments under the Roh Moo-hyun government (though admittedly other educational or training incentives were introduced or expanded). This decision has probably had complex ramifications. Many North Korean refugees entering South Korea now do so via distant countries in Southeast Asia or Mongolia. These long journeys are expensive and must be financed in some way. In the past, the cash award given to North Korean refugees upon arrival in South Korea constituted an important bond, establishing the refugee's capacity to repay debts incurred in passage. The reduction of the cash grant has, in effect, made the commitment to repay less credible. This change in policy will have two probable effects. First, it will make it harder for refugees to finance their journey. Second, criminal gangs will become more prominent in the migration process. Unable to avail themselves of the cash bond, refugees are increasingly likely to enter into arrangements resembling indentured servitude to finance their passage. This regrettable situation could be particularly pertinent with respect to women, who have already experienced the depredations of trafficking in their efforts to reach China.

The election of Lee Myung-bak marked a substantial turn in South Korean policy toward the North, including a greater willingness to raise human rights concerns. In 2010, a revised Bill for the Protection of North Korean Defectors and Settlement was passed. The bill

- accelerated the screening process;
- widened the definition of "defector" or "refugee" to include North Koreans who had spent up to 10 years in third countries;

- expanded the incentives for companies to hire refugees and expanded the eligibility of North Korean refugees to work in the South Korean public sector;
- strengthened housing guarantees for refugees leaving government processing centers;
- provided special schooling for refugees in light of the educational disruptions that they may have experienced; and
- increased adjustment support including job search and mental health counseling.

A North Korean Human Rights Act, which had stalled in the National Assembly due to objections by the opposition party, was revived following the sinking of the *Cheonan* as well. The legislation would either establish a North Korea Fund to deal with refugees or allow funds appropriated to the Inter-Korean Exchange Fund to be used for refugee-related purposes. Other ideas under consideration include establishing microfinance projects (some of the refugees are nothing if not entrepreneurial) and addressing the problem of how to pay brokers who may have assisted the refugees in transit. Solutions could involve using state funds to compensate the brokers or providing legal representation in potential extortion cases or instances in which brokers attempt to alter contractual terms ex post.

## US Policy on North Korean Refugees

The United States also has policy obligations with respect to North Korean refugees, but it is fair to say that neither Democratic nor Republican administrations took a particularly strong interest in the issue until the mid-2000s. Until 2004, the State Department had generally taken the position that US obligations to North Korean refugees were attenuated because they were in fact South Korean citizens. North Korean human rights abuses were occasionally the subject of analysis by nongovernmental human rights organizations, but it was not until 2001, with the establishment of the US Committee for Human Rights in North Korea (subsequently renamed the Committee for Human Rights in North Korea) that there was an American organization dedicated to addressing North Korean human rights.[13] In its wake, other NGOs such as LiNK and the North Korean Freedom Coalition sprang up, each with somewhat differing emphases, approaches, and constituencies. The National Endowment for Democracy, unable to pursue its usual approach of working with local human, civil, and political rights groups in the case of North Korea, instead works with North

---

13. In the interest of full disclosure, one of the authors of this book was a founding member of this organization and remains on its board, and both have coauthored research reports under its imprint (Haggard and Noland 2005, 2006).

Korean refugee and other groups attempting to promote North Korean human rights from outside the country.

In response to agitation by these and other human rights groups, the US Congress passed the North Korean Freedom Act of 2003 and the following year the NKHRA, which was reauthorized in 2008 through 2012 (North Korean Human Rights Reauthorization Act, 110th Congress, HR 5834; see M. Kim 2008 for a summary). The intent of the initial legislation and its reauthorization is to promote human rights by improving the efficiency of humanitarian aid; providing financial support to NGOs promoting human rights, democracy, rule of law, and the development of a market economy; increasing the amount of information available within North Korea through operations such as Radio Free Asia; and providing humanitarian and legal assistance to North Koreans who have fled the country. The law also established an envoy position within the State Department for the promotion of North Korean human rights, which was elevated to a full ambassadorship in the reauthorization.

As we have already noted in our discussion of China, international cooperation is important. Even if convincing China to act more forcefully is not likely to bear fruit, the United States should clearly state its position that it views the North Koreans in China as refugees deserving international support and work to provide the international safety net that would facilitate their resettlement. The NKHRA clarified the eligibility of North Koreans for refugee or asylum status in the United States, instructed the State Department to facilitate the submission of applications by North Koreans seeking protection as refugees, and authorized up to $24 million per year for humanitarian assistance for North Koreans outside North Korea.

Yet in the immediate aftermath of its passage, resettlement activities were limited by the difficulty of screening North Korean candidates for resettlement, and money that had been appropriated under the act was not in fact spent. The 2008 reauthorization adjusted the original 2004 provisions for the US resettlement of North Korean refugees while criticizing the slow implementation of the original bill. A report by the United States Government Accountability Office found that between October 2004 and March 2010, the United States resettled only 94 North Korean refugees—fewer than resettled in the United Kingdom or Germany (GAO 2010). One explanation offered for the slow rate of processing North Korean applications and the small number of successful asylum seekers was the policies of third-country governments, which did not permit easy access to asylum claimants. The "blame the foreigners" excuse begs the question of how the British and Germans managed to elicit better cooperation from the same group of countries, particularly given our findings that the United States is the favored country for resettlement after South Korea.

Implementation of the NKHRA could be strengthened in a variety of ways. The government could establish or designate an office with the specific responsibility for implementing the NKHRA refugee resettlement mandate (Committee for Human Rights in North Korea 2010). Steps to strengthen implementation would include but not be limited to

- improving the implementation of the policy by US embassies, particularly in Asia. There is a need to better educate embassy personnel in countries where North Koreans have fled to understand their rights under the NKHRA and to increase staffing of Korean speakers in the relevant diplomatic facilities where North Koreans have made asylum claims;

- publicizing the availability of support within the Korean-American community for North Korean family members or others who might seek asylum in the United States;

- establishing a hotline together with the UNHCR and South Korea, as recommended by the Committee for Human Rights in North Korea, so that North Korean refugees in danger have some way to contact those who can offer them immediate protection; and

- providing scholarships to refugees. Apart from a justifiable humanitarian gesture, such an action could contribute to the formation of a post-Kim regime elite. As governments begin extending scholarships to North Koreans selected by their government, refugees should not be left behind. In the case of the United States, such scholarships could be modeled after those provided to South Africans during the apartheid period. With respect to other countries, an informal division of labor could be worked out—for example, while Sweden provides scholarships to North Koreans selected by their government, Norway might provide them to refugees.

## Final Thoughts

The testimonies that emerge from the surveys reported in this book depict a society under stress, undergoing changes that we ignore at our own peril. It is impossible to sidestep the question of how one should address these economic reform and humanitarian issues in the context of the broader negotiations that will inevitably arise between the United States and North Korea. Yet the trends revealed in the experiences of the more than 1,600 refugees interviewed in these surveys may inform our expectations about how those diplomatic activities may play out.

The Six Party Talks remained in suspended animation as this book went to press. The United States has continued to resist the opening of a stand-alone bilateral track but has consistently stated that bilateral discussions can take place in the context of the revived multilateral talks. Indeed, if adequate progress on denuclearization is made through the Six Party Talks or some successor initiative, the normalization of diplomatic relations between the United States and North Korea would require quite extensive negotiations.

Discussions over both economic reform and human rights are likely to be a dialogue of the deaf at the outset, and on some issues North Korea will certainly invoke a sovereignty defense. Nonetheless, interest in human rights has been an enduring feature of US foreign policy, and the political process will no doubt continue to cast a light on human rights abuses in North Korea. Any concessions that the United States is called on to make to North Korea will come only as North Korea addresses issues of interest to the United States, and these are by no means limited to the nuclear question and security agenda. The linkage is most clear in the case of economic assistance and the need for reform. It will be extremely difficult to justify anything more than humanitarian assistance to North Korea if the regime remains committed to policies that undermine the effectiveness of aid.

Particularly as the United States moves to normalize diplomatic relations with North Korea, humanitarian issues, refugees, and human rights will necessarily enter the picture. Such items are a component of the very complicated bilateral agenda that the United States has with China and other authoritarian regimes, and even if the track record of success is limited, the effort to exercise influence at the margin will continue. It may not be appropriate to push humanitarian and human rights to the top of the Six Party Talks agenda—if only for the practical reason that support for such a change in the agenda would be lacking—but there is no reason why the United States should shy away from these issues in the bilateral negotiations that will inevitably ensue.

Much will ultimately depend on what happens within North Korea itself, and on this score the findings of this book are, unfortunately, not reassuring. In the end, the North Korean leadership can pursue only two broad paths. Under one, the regime will rally core bases of support in the military, security apparatus, and state sector to revive the state socialist system—politically, economically, and ideologically—or at least muddle through its ongoing economic difficulties. This path entails the continued imposition on the populace of the crushing burdens that our surveys have documented. This attempt would exploit external support from China, other developing countries, and problematic regimes such as Iran, Syria, and Venezuela. The regime would stonewall the Six Party Talks to hold on to its nuclear weapons and remain isolated from the advanced industrial states as a result. Unfortunately, much of the evidence that we report here suggests just such a strategy, albeit with the ongoing changes that are arising as a result of the marketization process and a high vulnerability to crisis, including recurrent food shortages.

Under a more hopeful scenario, the North Korean leadership would take the strategic decision to return to the reform process, through either an ambitious reform plan or a more gradual, learning-by-doing approach.

Progress in the Six Party Talks would unlock external benefits, more or less rapidly depending on core decisions with respect to nuclear weapons. This more hopeful path may come in an effort for Kim Jong-il to salvage his unfortunate legacy of secular economic and social decay. Alternatively, it might emerge as some successor leadership consolidates power and confronts its dubious inheritance.

Admittedly, the instruments available to the outside world to influence this choice, beyond promising to support the higher path, are limited. Nevertheless, we have sketched out a program to address the needs of both the North Korean refugees and those they have left behind, an agenda that goes beyond simply waiting for a change for the better.

# Appendix A
# The Surveys: Implementation, Method, and Inference

This study draws on two surveys of North Korean refugees. The first survey was conducted from August 2004 to September 2005 in China by a team of South Korean researchers in collaboration with Chinese nongovernmental organizations (NGOs) and church groups. A total of 1,346 refugees were interviewed in Jilin, Liaoning, and Heilongjiang provinces.

The second survey of 300 refugees was conducted in Seoul, South Korea between August and November 2008 with assistance from two refugee organizations. This survey was administered under much more hospitable circumstances. It is reassuring that this survey largely confirms the results obtained in the earlier one in China. Nonetheless, both surveys are ultimately samples of convenience, as we have little information on the underlying refugee populations in either location, particularly in China.

The two surveys used different questionnaires. This was partly a result of a learning process; no matter how well crafted a survey instrument, information is always revealed in the process, which forces a revision of priors and opens new issues for analysis. Yet there are a number of common questions on both surveys so that results could be compared, and as noted the results of the two surveys are broadly consistent. Where there was divergence between the two surveys, we have attempted to devise tests that might explain it.

We begin with an explanation of how the surveys were conducted. We then turn to some particular methodological issues that affect the inferences that can be drawn from the surveys and necessary caveats with respect to this kind of survey work.

# Implementation of the Surveys

## The China Survey

The China survey was conducted under the auspices of the US Committee for Human Rights in North Korea (subsequently renamed the Committee for Human Rights in North Korea) through a grant from the Smith Richardson Foundation. The survey instrument was designed by members of the committee (including one of the present authors) in collaboration with Professor Yoonok Chang of Hansei University.

The survey was implemented by a team led by Professor Chang from August 2004 to September 2005 in 11 Chinese cities or counties across the three provinces constituting Northeast China: Shenyang, Dandong, Harbin, Changchun, Tonghua, Jilin, Helong, Hunchun, Tumen, Yanji, and Wangqing. For reasons of security the location of the interviews was not included in the questionnaire. The sites were selected on the basis of the presence in the locale of institutions and individuals who had worked with North Korean refugees, mostly Korean-Chinese churches and pastors, NGOs, and other sympathetic Korean-Chinese.

Forty-eight individuals were recruited from this network and trained by the South Korean team in Yanji before conducting the interviews. The interviewers were responsible for identifying and consenting refugees into the study on the basis of their networks. The purpose of the study was explained to the interviewees—that this was an academic research project, but one that sought to publicize the plight of the refugees—and they were assured that all answers would be held confidential. Those not wishing to participate were excluded. To avoid interviewing the same individuals, the refugees were not paid for participating. Given the use of multiple interviewers over an extended period, however, the possibility of a single individual having been interviewed more than once cannot be categorically excluded.

In a small number of cases, after consenting to participate in the survey, respondents indicated some anxiety in having their responses recorded on paper in their presence; in these cases the responses were memorized by the interviewer and recorded on paper ex post.

Obviously, surveys conducted under these difficult conditions cannot be expected to meet the normal standard of contemporary social science research. Because of tightened security in the border region, doing another such survey has become much more difficult if not altogether impossible. In part due to these concerns, with the support of the Smith Richardson Foundation, a second survey was conducted in South Korea in a more supportive legal environment. Nonetheless, we believe that the China survey—used primarily in chapter 2—in fact conveys important information about the refugee experience. Moreover, we are heartened by the fact that the results of the China and South Korea surveys are generally consistent.

## The South Korea Survey

The South Korea survey was implemented with the cooperation of the Association of Supporters for Defecting North Korean Residents (ASDNKR), a quasi-governmental organization established to assist incoming North Korean defectors through services such as counseling and introducing the newly arrived North Koreans to academic or job opportunities.[1] A pilot survey was conducted in August and September 2008 of refugees who visited the ASDNKR for personal business. A central issue was to guarantee that the Korean-language survey instrument was fully intelligible to the refugees. Respondents in both the pilot and subsequent surveys were informed that their participation was voluntary, that the identity of respondents would be held confidential, and that the survey was part of an academic research project based in the United States. Participants in both the pilot and full surveys received modest gift certificates for their participation.

Following the pilot survey, the ASDNKR facilitated contact with the Sung-ui Association, a private civic organization of North Korean defectors with about 7,000 members and 16 offices in South Korea, to recruit staff to conduct the full survey. The Sung-ui Association introduced seven defectors who agreed to administer the survey in neighborhoods with concentrations of North Korean refugees; the staff were compensated for their work.[2] Two training sessions were held for the survey administrators to explain the purpose of the research, the nature of the survey instrument, and the requirements of the research project. The survey was stratified on one dimension with respect to which there was some confidence about the underlying population: gender. An effort was made to contact defectors who had recently arrived in the South in order to capture changing views over time, but many refugees had left during the famine period, while others reached South Korea only after having spent months or years in third countries.

The full survey was administered from October to November 2008. First, the survey administrators contacted individuals in their neighborhoods to conduct face-to-face interviews, yielding about 100 respondents. Second, small groups were recruited to meet for a free lunch or dinner in addition to the gift certificate. Third, a final group was contacted directly through ASDNKR in order to reach the desired sample of 300.[3]

---

1. Later, subsequent to the completion of the survey, ASDNKR was replaced by the Foundation for North Korean Defectors by the 2010 revision of the North Korean defectors law in order to improve and expand services for newly arrived North Koreans.

2. The seven administrators were residents of the Seoul area: two from Nowon-gu, a district in northwestern Seoul with a large defector population; two from Gangseo-gu; two from Yangcheon-gu; and one from Songpa-gu.

3. A total of 313 surveys were administered; 13 were invalid and had to be discarded.

# Drawing Inferences

As observed in chapter 1, the two surveys are samples of convenience and pose particular problems of inference. First, they do not constitute a random sample with respect to the refugee population. Neither we nor anyone else knows the underlying characteristics of that group, and each sample might be subject to idiosyncratic forms of bias. The characteristics of those who were able to get to South Korea might have been somewhat different from those who remained in China. More generally, those who did not respond to questions may have been different from those who did. Nor do we have any way to control for the veracity of responses.

A second and arguably more important problem of inference has to do with sample selection issues and our ability to project any conclusions from refugee surveys onto the resident population of North Korea. Three important examples make the point about possible sources of bias and how it can be addressed.

First, relative to the actual population of North Korea, residents of the northeast provinces were overrepresented in both surveys, as has been the case with previous surveys conducted in both China and South Korea. In the China survey, North Hamgyong province accounted for most of the respondents (57 percent), followed by South Hamgyong province (19 percent). Similar biases were evident in the South Korea survey, where half of the respondents were from North Hamgyong province, with another 15 percent from South Hamgyong. These distributions actually make these provinces somewhat *less* overrepresented than in most earlier surveys (cf. Robinson et al. 1999, 2001a, 2001b; Lee et al. 2001; Chon et al. 2007), but these provinces do nonetheless account for only about 23 percent of the North Korean population (United Nations Statistics Division 2009). As we argue in chapter 2 in more detail, this bias is a result partly of proximity and partly of the uneven effects of the famine, which hit the northeast particularly hard.

A second example of the difficulty in drawing inferences about the North Korean population has to do with possible demographic or other socioeconomic sources of bias. Early defectors from North Korea were typically elites: higher-ranking party or military personnel. Many of them took strongly ideological positions vis-à-vis the North and were in some cases handsomely rewarded for doing so. Over time, however, the demographics of the refugee population have shifted dramatically, looking more and more like the population of North Korea as a whole. As we show in chapter 2, refugees reaching South Korea are now dominated by workers and farmers, many with only a basic education. Indeed, it is possible that our sample now underweights high-ranking officials and military personnel (even though we have some of the latter in both samples).

This overweighting with respect to the northeast provinces and with respect to the demographic profile probably does not present a problem for drawing inferences about the North Korean refugee community, which is also almost certainly dominated by migrants from the northeast and has come to include more members of the working class and rural residents. Such biases do present a problem with respect to drawing inferences about the larger population. But as demonstrated in the text, we can use data on the North Korean population and multivariate regressions to control for these possible regional and demographic sources of bias and even to generate counterfactual projections of how a sample drawn from the entire population might have responded.

Third, and most importantly, it is likely that refugees differ from the remaining North Korean resident population in some unobservable ways. In particular, it is likely that the refugees are particularly disaffected with the regime; that is why they left. As a consequence, it is important to draw upon whatever experiential information we have (such as experiences during the famine period or at the hands of North Korean authorities) to control for observable life experiences in making inferences about the resident population.

# References

Alesina, Alberto, and Allan Drazen. 1991. Why Are Stabilizations Delayed? *American Economic Review* 81, no. 5: 1170–88.

Anderson, Penelope, and Paul Majarowitz. 2008. *Rapid Food Security Assessment: North Pyongan and Chagang Provinces, Democratic People's Republic of Korea* (June 30). Washington: Mercy Corps, World Vision, Global Resource Services, and Samaritan's Purse.

Amnesty International. 2000. *Persecuting the Starving: The Plight of North Koreans Fleeing to China*. London.

Amnesty International. 2001. *Human Rights in China in 2001—A New Step Backwards*. London.

Amnesty International. 2004. *Starved of Rights: Human Rights and the Food Crisis in the Democratic People's Republic of Korea*. London. Available at http://web.amnesty.org.

Armstrong, Charles. 2002. *The North Korean Revolution*. Ithaca, NY: Cornell University Press.

Asahi Shimbun. 2010. China and Japan Jointly Engaged in "Hunting Down Defectors" on Entire Chinese Land—Repatriate Them Back to North Korea [in Japanese], September 27. Available at www.asahi.com (accessed on October 12, 2010).

Asia Society. 2009. *North Korea Inside Out: The Case for Economic Engagement*. Report of an Independent Task Force convened by Asia Society Center on US-China Relations and the University of California Institute on Global Conflict and Cooperation. New York.

Bank of Korea. 2010. Economic Statistics System. Available at http://ecos.bok.or.kr (accessed on October 29, 2010).

Baubet, Thierry, Marine Buissonnière, Sophie Delaunay, and Pierre Salignon. 2003. Réfugiés nordcoréens en Corée du Sud: De l'importance d'un "tiers" humanitaire. *L'Autre* 3, no. 4: 455–69.

Bauer, Raymond, Alex Indeles, and Clyde Kluckhohn. 1956. *How the Soviet System Works: Cultural, Psychological and Social Themes*. Cambridge, MA: Harvard University Press.

Beck, Peter. 2010. North Korea's Radio Waves of Resistance. *Wall Street Journal*, April 16.

Bechtol, Bruce E. 2007. *Red Rogue: The Persistent Challenge of North Korea*. Potomac Books Inc.

Bikhchandani, Sushil, David Hirshleifer, and Ivo Welch. 1998. Learning from the Behavior of Others: Conformity, Fads, and Informational Cascades. *Journal of Economic Perspectives* 12, no. 3 (Summer): 151–70.

Bureau of Justice Statistics. 2003. *Prevalence of Imprisonment in the U.S. Population, 1974–2001.* Washington. Available at http://bjs.ojp.usdoj.gov (accessed on January 4, 2010).

Carlin, Robert L., and Joel Wit. 2006. *North Korean Reform: Politics, Economic, Security.* Adelphi Working Paper no. 382. London: International Institute for Strategic Studies.

Carothers, Christopher. 2010. China's New Source of Cheap Labor. *Wall Street Journal,* July 14.

Chang, Yoonok, Stephan Haggard, Marcus Noland. 2009a. Migration Experiences of North Korean Refugees: Survey Evidence from China. In *Korea Yearbook 2009,* ed. Rüdiger Frank, James E. Hoare, Patrick Köllner, and Susan Pares. Leiden, the Netherlands: Koninklijke Brill.

Chang, Yoonok, Stephan Haggard, and Marcus Noland. 2009b. Exit Polls: Refugee Assessment of North Korea's Transition. *Journal of Comparative Economics* 37, no. 2: 144–50.

Chon, Hyun-joon, Moon-young Huh, Philo Kim, and Chin-soo Bae. 2007. *An Assessment of the North Korean System's Durability.* Studies Series 07-03. Seoul: Korea Institute for National Unification.

Cohen, Jerome. 1968. *The Criminal Process in the People's Republic of China, 1949–63: An Introduction.* Cambridge, MA: Harvard University Press.

Cohen, Roberta. 2010. *Legal Grounds for Protection of North Korean Refugees.* Seoul: Citizens' Alliance for North Korean Human Rights (September 13, 2010). Available at www.brookings.edu (accessed on November 15, 2010).

Committee for Human Rights in North Korea. 2009. *Lives for Sale: Personal Accounts of Women Fleeing North Korea to China.* Washington.

Committee for Human Rights in North Korea. 2010. *Ten Specific Practical Measures for Advancing Human Rights in United States Policy toward North Korea.* Washington.

Cooper, Abraham. 2005. Toxic Indifference to North Korea. *Washington Post,* March 26.

Cumings, Bruce. 2003. *North Korea: Another Country.* New York: The New Press.

Database Center for North Korean Human Rights. 2008. *White Paper on North Korean Human Rights Statistics 2007.* Seoul.

Demick, Barbara. 2004. North Korea's Use of Chemical Torture Alleged. *Los Angeles Times,* March 3.

Demick, Barbara. 2009. *Nothing to Envy: Ordinary Lives in North Korea.* New York: Spiegel & Grau.

Demick, Barbara. 2010. Nothing Left; Letter from Yanji. *New Yorker,* July 12.

Dowty, Alan. 1987. *Closed Borders: The Contemporary Assault on Freedom of Movement.* New York: Twentieth Century Fund.

Drazen, Allan. 2000. *Political Economy in Macroeconomics.* Princeton: Princeton University Press.

Eberstadt, Nicholas. 2007. *The North Korean Economy.* New Brunswick, NJ: Transaction.

Eberstadt, Nicholas, and Christopher Griffin. 2007. Saving North Korea's Refugees. *New York Times,* February 19.

Faiola, Anthony. 2004. North Korean Women Find Abuse Waiting in China. *Washington Post,* March 3.

Fischer, Stanley, and Alan Gelb. 1991. The Process of Socialist Economic Transformation. *Journal of Economic Perspectives* 5, no. 4 (Autumn): 91–105.

Foster-Carter, Aidan. 1994. Korea: Sociopolitical Realities of Reuniting a Divided Nation. In *One Korea?* ed. Thomas H. Hendricksen and Kyong-soo Lho. Stanford: Stanford University Press.

Frank, Ruediger. 2005. Economic Reforms in North Korea (1998–2004): Systemic Restrictions, Quantitative Analysis, Ideological Background. *Journal of the Asia Pacific Economy* 10, no. 3 (August): 278–311.

Freeman, Carla P., and Drew Thompson. 2009. *Flood Across the Border: China's Disaster Relief Operations and Potential Response to a North Korean Refugee Crisis.* Washington: US-Korea Institute at SAIS, Paul H. Nitze School of Advanced International Studies, Johns Hopkins University.

GAO (US Government Accountability Office). 2010. *Humanitarian Assistance: Status of North Korean Refugee Resettlement and Asylum in the United States.* Washington (June).

Gey, Peter. 2004. *North Korea: Soviet-Style Reform and the Erosion of the State Economy.* Bonn, Germany: Friedrich-Ebert-Stiftung. Available at www.fes.or.kr (accessed on July 28, 2009).

Good Friends. 1999. *People Who Have Crossed the Tumen River* [in Korean]. Seoul.

Good Friends. 2010. After Two Years, Professional Counterfeiters in Pyongsung Finally Arrested. *North Korea Today* 348 (July).

Goodkind, Daniel, and Lorraine West. 2001. The North Korean Famine and Its Demographic Impact. *Population and Development Review* 27, no. 2: 219–38.

Gregory, Paul R. 2004. *The Political Economy of Stalinism: Evidence from the Soviet Secret Archives.* Cambridge: Cambridge University Press.

Grossman, Gregory. 1977. The Second Economy of the USSR. *Problems of Communism* 26, no. 5 (September–October).

Grossman, Gregory, ed. 1988. *Studies in the Second Economy of Communist Countries.* Berkeley: University of California Press.

Haggard, Stephan, and Marcus Noland. 2005. *Hunger and Human Rights: The Politics of Famine in North Korea.* Washington: US Committee for Human Rights in North Korea.

Haggard, Stephan, and Marcus Noland, eds. 2006. *The North Korean Refugee Crisis: Human Rights and International Response.* Washington: US Committee for Human Rights in North Korea.

Haggard, Stephan, and Marcus Noland. 2007. *Famine in North Korea: Markets, Aid, and Reform.* New York: Columbia University Press.

Haggard, Stephan, and Marcus Noland. 2008. North Korea's Foreign Economic Relations. *International Relations of the Asia-Pacific* 8, no. 2: 219–46.

Haggard, Stephan, and Marcus Noland. 2009a. Famine in North Korea Redux? *Journal of Asian Economics* 20, no. 4: 384–95.

Haggard, Stephan, and Marcus Noland. 2009b. A Security and Peace Mechanism for Northeast Asia: The Economic Dimension. *Pacific Review* 22, no. 2: 119–37.

Haggard, Stephan, and Marcus Noland. 2010a. Sanctioning North Korea: The Political Economy of Denuclearization and Proliferation. *Asia Survey* 50, no. 3: 539–68.

Haggard, Stephan, and Marcus Noland. 2010b. *The Winter of Their Discontent: Pyongyang Attacks the Market.* Policy Briefs in International Economics 10-1. Washington: Peterson Institute for International Economics.

Haggard, Stephan, and Marcus Noland. 2010c. Reform from Below: Institutional and Behavioral Change in North Korea. *Journal of Economic Behavior and Organization* 73, no. 2: 133–52.

Haggard, Stephan, and Marcus Noland. 2010d. *Political Attitudes under Repression: Evidence from North Korean Refugees*. East-West Center Working Papers, Politics, Governance, and Security Series 21. Honolulu, Hawaii: East-West Center. Available at www.eastwestcenter.org (accessed on March 30, 2010).

Haggard, Stephan, and Marcus Noland. 2011. Economic Crime and Punishment in North Korea. *Political Science Quarterly* (forthcoming).

Han, In Sup. 2006. The 2004 Revision of Criminal Law in North Korea: A Take-Off? *Santa Clara Journal of International Law* 5, no. 1: 122–33.

Harden, Blaine. 2007. As More Take a Chance on Fleeing North Korea, Routes for All Budgets. *Washington Post*, November 18.

Harden, Blaine. 2009. N. Korea's Hard-Labor Camps: On the Back Burner. *Washington Post*, July 20.

Hassig, Ralph, and Kongdan Oh. 2000. *North Korea Through the Looking Glass*. Washington: Brooking Institution.

Hassig, Ralph, and Kongdan Oh. 2009. *The Hidden People of North Korea: Everyday Life in the Hermit Kingdom*. Lanham, MD: Rowman & Littlefield Publishers, Inc.

Hawk, David. 2003. *The Hidden Gulag*. Washington: US Committee for Human Rights in North Korea.

Hawk, David. 2010. *Pursuing Peace while Advancing Rights: The Untried Approach to North Korea*. Washington: US-Korea Institute at SAIS, Paul H. Nitze School of Advanced International Studies, Johns Hopkins University.

Human Rights Watch. 2002. *The Invisible Exodus: North Koreans in the People's Republic of China*. New York.

Hunter, Helen-Louise. 1999. *Kim Il-song's North Korea*. Santa Barbara: Greenwood.

IFES (Institute of Far Eastern Studies). 2010. *DPRK Strengthens Control Mechanisms with Revised Law on the People's Economy*. NK Brief 10-11-26-1. Seoul.

International Crisis Group. 2010. *North Korea under Tightening Sanctions*. Update Briefing. Asia Briefing 101. Seoul and Brussels.

Jeon, Woo Taek. 2000. Issues and Problems in Adaptation of North Korean Defectors to South Korean Society: An In-Depth Interview Study with 32 Defectors. *Yonsei Medical Journal* 41, no. 3: 362–71.

Jeon, Woo Taek, Chang Hyun Hong, Chang Ho Lee, Dong Kee Kim, Mooyoung Han, and Sung Kil Min. 2005. Correlation between Traumatic Events and Posttraumatic Stress Disorder Among North Korean Defectors in South Korea. *Journal of Traumatic Stress* 18, no. 2: 147–54.

Kang, Chayeun. 2006. The Relationship Between Stress Coping Style and Mental Health among Female North Korean Refugees in China. *Korean Journal of Women's Psychology* 10, no. 1: 61–80 [in Korean].

Kang, Chol-hwan. 2002. *The Aquariums of Pyongyang*. New York: Basic Books.

Kato, Hiroshi. 2006. Remarks before meeting hosted by the United States Commission on International Religious Freedom, Washington, May 25.

Kim, Byung-jo. 2000. The Structure of North Korean Social Conflict and its Causes. *Yeon-gu Non-mun Jaryo* 2000–1 [in Korean]. Available at www.koreascope.com (accessed on July 28, 2009).

Kim, Byung-yeon. 2010. *Markets, Bribery, and Regime Stability in North Korea*. EAI Asia Security Initiative Working Paper no. 4 (April). Seoul: East Asia Institute.

Kim, Byung-yeon, and Dongho Song. 2008. The Participation of North Korean Households in the Informal Economy: Size, Determinants, and Effect. *Seoul Journal of Economics* 21, no. 2: 361–85.

Kim, Hyunah, Yesang Yoon, and Sunyoung Han. 2007. Development and Evaluation of PTSD Index in North Korean Refugees. *Korean Journal of Counseling and Psychotherapy* 19, no. 3: 693–718 [in Korean].

Kim, Mike. 2008. *Escaping North Korea: Defiance and Hope in the World's Most Repressive Country*. Lanham, MD: Rowman & Littlefield Publishers, Inc.

Kim, Soo-am. 2006. *The North Korean Penal Code, Criminal Procedures, and their Actual Applications*. Studies Series 06-01. Seoul: Korea Institute for National Unification.

Kim, Sung Chull. 2006. *North Korea under Kim Jong Il: From Consolidation to Systemic Dissonance*. Albany: State University of New York Press.

Kim, Yong. 2009. *Long Road Home: Testimony of a North Korean Camp Survivor*. New York: Columbia University Press.

Kim, Young Kwon. 2010. China Builds Patrol Offices for Tighter Surveillance on North Korean Defectors. Voice of America News, January 27. Available at www.voanews. com (accessed on February 25, 2010).

KINU (Korea Institute for National Unification). 2009. *White Paper on Human Rights in North Korea 2009*. Seoul.

Kirkpatrick, Melanie. 2006. Pastor Buck Is a Rescuer…Helping North Korea's Refugees Is the Key to Regime Change. *Wall Street Journal*, December 18.

Koh, Byung-chul. 2005. *Military-First Politics and Building a Powerful and Prosperous Nation in North Korea*. Nautilus Institute Policy Forum Online. Available at www.nautilus.org.

Korean Bar Association. 2009. *White Paper on Human Rights in North Korea*. Seoul.

Kuran, Timur. 1989. Sparks and Prairie Fires: A Theory of Unanticipated Political Revolutions. *Public Choice* 61, no. 1: 41–74.

Kuran, Timur. 1995a. The Inevitability of Future Revolutionary Surprises. *American Journal of Sociology*, no. 100: 1528–51.

Kuran, Timur. 1995b. *Private Truths, Public Lies: The Social Consequence of Preference Falsification*. Cambridge, MA: Harvard University Press.

Kurlantzick, Joshua, and Jana Mason. 2006. North Korean Refugees: The Chinese Dimension. In *The North Korean Refugee Crisis: Human Rights and International Response*. Washington: US Committee for Human Rights in North Korea.

Lankov, Andrei. 2004. North Korean Refugees in Northeast China. *Asian Survey* 44, no. 6: 856–73.

Lankov, Andrei. 2006. Bitter Taste of Paradise: North Korean Refugees in South Korea. In *The North Korean Refugee Crisis: Human Rights and International Response*, ed. Stephan Haggard and Marcus Noland. Washington: US Committee for Human Rights in North Korea.

Lankov, Andrei. 2009. Changing North Korea: An Information Campaign Can Beat the Regime. *Foreign Affairs* 88, no. 6 (November/December).

Lankov, Andrei, and Kim Seok-hyang. 2008. North Korean Market Vendors: The Rise of Grassroots Capitalists in a Post-Stalinist Society. *Pacific Affairs* 81, no. 1 (Spring): 53–72.

Lee, Keumsoon. 2006. *The Border-Crossing North Koreans: Current Situations and Future Prospects*. Studies Series 06-05. Seoul: Korea Institute for National Unification.

Lee, Kyo-duk, Soon-hee Lim, Jeong-ah Cho, Gee-dong Lee, and Young-hoon Lee. 2008. *Changes in North Korea as Revealed in the Testimonies of Saetomins*. Studies Series 08-05. Seoul: Korea Institute for National Unification.

Lee, Suk. 2003. Food Shortages and Economic Institutions in the Democratic People's Republic of Korea. Unpublished doctoral dissertation. Department of Economics, University of Warwick, Coventry.

Lee, Tae-hoon. 2010. Female North Korean Defectors Priced at $1,500. *Korea Times*, May 5.

Lee, Won-woong. 2010. North Korean Human Rights Policy Roadmap: Basic Concepts and Strategies. Paper presented at the International Symposium on North Korean Human Rights, Washington, September 8.

Lee, Woo-young. 2009. The Rise of Personal Discussion and Individualism in North Korea. *North Korea Newsletter* 83 (December 3). Seoul: Yonhap.

Lee, Young-hoon. 2007. *Survey of the State of Economic Transformation in North Korea as Told Through DPRK Defectors* [in Korean]. Seoul: Bank of Korea.

Lee, Yunhwan, Myung Ken Lee, Ki Hong Chun, Yeon Kyung Lee, and Soo Jin Yoon. 2001. Trauma Experience of North Korean Refugees in China. *American Journal of Preventive Medicine* 20, no. 3.

Leeson, Peter T. 2007. Better off Stateless: Somalia Before and After Government Collapse. *Journal of Comparative Economics* 35, no. 4: 689–710.

Lim, Wonhyuk. 2005. *North Korea's Economic Futures: Internal and External Dimensions.* Washington: Brookings Institution. Available at www.brookings.edu (accessed on May 24, 2009).

Lintner, Bertil. 2005. *Great Leader, Dear Leader: Demystifying North Korea Under the Kim Clan.* Silkworm Books.

Lohmann, Susanne. 1994. The Dynamics of Informational Cascades: The Monday Demonstrations in Leipzig East Germany, 1989–91. *World Politics* 47 (October): 42–101.

Michell, Anthony R. 1998. The Current North Korean Economy. In *Economic Integration of the Korean Peninsula*, ed. Marcus Noland. Washington: Institute for International Economics.

Moon, Chung-in. 2004. Managing Collateral Catastrophe: Rationale and Preconditions for International Economic Support for North Korea. In *A New International Engagement Framework for North Korea*, ed. Ahn Choong-yong, Nicholas Eberstadt and Lee Young-sun. Washington: Korea Economic Institute.

Moon, Chung-in. 2008. Managing the North Korean Nuclear Quagmire: Capability, Impacts and Prospects. In *The United States and Northeast Asia: Debates, Issues, and New Order*, ed. G. John Ikenberry and Chung-in Moon. Lanham, MD: Rowman & Littlefield Publishers, Inc.

Moon, Chung-in, and Jong-yun Bae. 2003. The Bush Doctrine and the North Korean Nuclear Crisis. *Asian Perspective* 27, no. 4: 9–45.

Muico, Norma Kang. 2005. *An Absence of Choice: Sexual Exploitation of North Korean Women in China.* London: Anti-Slavery International.

Muico, Norma Kang. 2007. *Forced Labor in North Korean Prison Camps.* London: Anti-Slavery International.

Myers, B. R. 2010. *The Cleanest Race: How North Koreans See Themselves and Why It Matters.* Melville House.

Nam, Sung-wook. 2007. Chronic Food Shortages and the Collective Farm System in North Korea. *Journal of East Asian Studies* 7: 93–123.

Namgung, Min. 2007. What Kind of Organization is North Korea's National Security Agency? *Daily NK*, September 9. Available at www.dailynk.com.

National Human Rights Commission of Korea. 2010. *Research into Human Rights Violence in the Process of Defection and Settlement of Defector Women* [in Korean]. Seoul.

Natsios, Andrew. 2002. *The Great North Korean Famine.* Washington: US Institute of Peace.

Noland, Marcus. 2000. *Avoiding the Apocalypse: The Future of the Two Koreas.* Washington: Institute for International Economics.

Noland, Marcus. 2004. *Korea After Kim Jong-il*. Washington: Institute for International Economics.

Noland, Marcus. 2009a. Telecoms in North Korea: Has Orascom Made the Connection? *North Korea Review* (Spring).

Noland, Marcus. 2009b. The (Non) Impact of UN Sanctions on North Korea. *Asia Policy* 7: 61-88.

Ofer, Gur, and Joyce Pickersgill. 1980. Soviet Household Saving: A Cross-Section Study of Soviet Emigrant Families. *Quarterly Journal of Economics* 95, no. 1: 121–44.

Powell, Benjamin, Ryan Ford, and Alex Nowrateh. 2008. Somalia after state collapse: Chaos or improvement? *Journal of Economic Behavior and Organization* 67, no. 3/4: 657–70.

Robinson, Courtland. 2010. Population Estimation of North Korean Refugees and Migrants and Children Born to North Korean Women in Northeast China. Unpublished paper, April 9.

Robinson, W. Courtland, Myung Ken Lee, Kenneth Hill, and Gilbert Burnham. 1999. Mortality in North Korean Migrant Households: A Retrospective Study. *The Lancet* 354, no. 9175: 291–95.

Robinson, W. Courtland, Myung Ken Lee, Kenneth Hill, and Gilbert Burnham. 2001a. Famine, Mortality, and Migration: A Study of North Korean Migrants in China. In *Forced Migration and Mortality*, ed. Holly E. Reed and Charles B. Keely. Washington: National Academy Press.

Robinson, W. Courtland, Myung Ken Lee, Kenneth Hill, Elbert Hsu, and Gilbert Burnham. 2001b. Demographic Methods to Assess Food Insecurity: A North Korean Case Study. *Prehospital and Disaster Medicine* 16, no. 4: 286–92.

Roland, Gérard. 2000. *Transition and Economics*. Cambridge, MA: MIT Press.

Scott, James C. 1985. *Weapons of the Weak: Everyday Forms of Peasant Resistance*. New Haven: Yale University Press.

Sheridan, Michael. 2006. Nation Under a Nuclear Cloud: "Racially Impure" Children Killed. *Sunday Times*, October 15.

Smith, Hazel. 2005. *Hungry for Peace: International Security, Humanitarian Assistance, and Social Change in North Korea*. Washington: US Institute of Peace Press.

Smith, Hazel. 2009. North Korea: Market Opportunity, Poverty, and the Provinces. *New Political Economy* 14, no. 2: 231–56.

Snyder, Scott. 2009. *China's Rise and the Two Koreas: Politics, Economics, Security*. Boulder, CO: Lynne Rienner Publishers.

Sphere Project. 2004. *Humanitarian Charter and Minimum Standards in Disaster Response*. Geneva.

Thaxton, Ralph A. 2008. *Catastrophe and Contention in Rural China: Mao's Great Leap Forward Famine and the Origins of Righteous Resistance in Da Fo Village*. New York: Cambridge University Press.

Tsuji, Hisako. 2004. *The Tumen River Area Development Programme: Its History and Current Status as of 2004*. ERINA Discussion Paper no. 0404e (April). Nigata: Economic Research Institute for Northeast Asia.

United Nations Economic and Social Council. *Implementation of the International Covenant on Economic, Social and Cultural Rights*. Second Periodic Report Submitted by States Parties under Articles 16 and 17 of the Covenant Addendum, Democratic People's Republic of Korea. E/1990/6/Add. 35 15 (May): 6 & 33.

United Nations General Assembly. 2007. *Situation of Human Rights in the Democratic People's Republic of Korea: Note by the Secretary General*. A/62/264 (August 15).

United Nations General Assembly. 2010. *Situation of Human Rights in the Democratic People's Republic of Korea: Report of the Secretary General.* A/65/391 (September 24). Available at http://ap.ohchr.org (accessed on November 1, 2010).

United Nations Human Rights, Office of the High Commissioner for Human Rights. 2010. *Democratic Republic of Korea.* Available at www.ohchr.org (accessed on October 13, 2010).

United Nations Human Rights Council, United Nations General Assembly. 2010. *Report of the Special Rapporteur on the Situation of Human Rights in the Democratic People's Republic of Korea, Vitit Muntarbhorn.* A/HRC/13/47 (February 17).

United Nations Statistics Division. 2009. *Democratic Republic of North Korea 2008 Population Census: National Report.* Available at http://unstats.un.org (accessed on February 23, 2010).

United Nations Statistics Division. 2010. *National Accounts Main Aggregates Database.* Available at http://unstats.un.org (accessed on October 29, 2010).

WFP (UN World Food Program). 2008. *WFP/FAO Rapid Food Security Assessment—Democratic People's Republic of Korea.* Final Report (June/July).

Wong, Paul. 1968. Storage and Retrieval of Data on Communist China. *Asian Survey* 8, no. 5 (May): 378–83.

Yang, Dali. 1996. *Calamity and Reform in China: State, Rural Society, and Institutional Change since the Great Leap Famine.* Stanford: Stanford University Press.

Yang, Moon Soo, and Kevin Shepard. 2009. Changes in North Korea's Corporate Governance. In *The Dynamics of Change in North Korea: An Institutionalist Perspective*, ed. Phillip Park. Seoul: Kyungnam University Press.

Yonhap News Agency. 2010. *North Korea Newsletter* no. 126, October 7. Seoul.

Yoo, Gwan Hee. 2010. Tax? What Tax? The North Korean Taxation Farce. *Daily NK*, April 5. Available at www.dailynk.com.

Yoon, Dae-Kyu. 2009. Economic Reform and Institutional Transformation: A Legal Perspective. In *The Dynamics of Change in North Korea: An Institutionalist Perspective*, ed. Phillip H. Park. Seoul: Kyungnam University Press.

Young, Helen, Anna Taylor, Sally-Anne Way, and Jennifer Leaning. 2004. Linking Rights and Standards: The Process of Developing 'Rights-Based' Minimum Standards on Food Security, Nutrition, and Food Aid. *Disasters* 28, no. 2: 142–59.

Ziegler, Jean. 2002. *Economic, Social, and Cultural Rights: The Right to Food.* Report by the Special Rapporteur on the Right to Food. Commission on Human Rights, 58th session. E/CN.4/2002/58. United Nations Economic and Social Council.

# About the Authors

Stephan Haggard, visiting fellow at the Peterson Institute, is the Lawrence and Sallye Krause Distinguished Professor at the Graduate School of International Relations and Pacific Studies, University of California, San Diego (UCSD). He is the author of *The Political Economy of the Asian Financial Crisis* (2000) and *Pathways from the Periphery: The Politics of Growth in the Newly Industrializing Countries* (1990) and coauthor of *The Political Economy of Democratic Transitions* (1995) and *Development, Democracy, and Welfare States* (2008) with Robert Kaufman and of *Famine in North Korea: Markets, Aid, and Reform* (2007) with Marcus Noland. He is a member of the Institute's Advisory Committee.

Marcus Noland, senior fellow, became deputy director of the Peterson Institute in September 2009. He has been associated with the Institute since 1985. He is concurrently a senior fellow at the East-West Center. He was a senior economist for international economics on the Council of Economic Advisers (1993–94); visiting professor at Yale University, Johns Hopkins University, the University of Southern California, Tokyo University, Saitama University (now the National Graduate Institute for Policy Studies), and the University of Ghana; and a visiting scholar at the Korea Development Institute. He is author, coauthor, or editor of *The Arab Economies in a Changing World*

(2007), which was selected as Choice Outstanding Academic Title for 2007, *Famine in North Korea: Markets, Aid, and Reform* (2007), *Korea after Kim Jong-il* (2004), *Industrial Policy in an Era of Globalization: Lessons from Asia* (2003), *No More Bashing: Building a New Japan–United States Economic Relationship* (2001), *Avoiding the Apocalypse: The Future of the Two Koreas* (2000), which won the 2000–01 Ohira Memorial Award, and *Economic Integration of the Korean Peninsula* (1998).

# Index

Kim Kyong-hui, 10
Kim Yong-il, 10*n*, 10–11
Korea Ex-Im Bank, 132
Korean Institute of National Unification, 89
Korean Peninsula Energy Development
    Organization, 134
Korean unification, attitudes toward, 109,
    110*f*, 116
Korean War, prisoners of war from, 143
Korean Workers' Party, 9, 13
Korea Trade Investment Promotion Agency,
    132
*kwan-li-so. See* political prison camps
*kyo-hwa-so. See* correctional centers;
    penitentiaries

labor colonies. *See* political prison camps
labor standards, 136, 145–46
labor training centers (*ro-dong-dan-ryeon-
    dae*), 82, 89–91, 92*t*
    abuse in, 97*t*, 97–98
    human rights issues, 142
    legal process and, 95
    length of imprisonment in, 95, 96*t*
labor training sentence, 91
Lee Myung-bak, 131, 152
legal risks of emigration, 3, 27–29, 149
LiNK, 153
living standards, as push factor, 146
loyalty to regime, 117

male refugees
    food access, 54*n*
    number of, 20–21
    psychological state, 36, 37*t*–39*t*, 39
market creep, 46
marketization from below, 5–8, 45–79. *See
    also* private business activities
    food economy, 47–58, 120
    household earnings, 58–62
    reforms (*See* economic reform)
    social changes and, 75–77, 76*f*, 79, 102
    state response to, 8–12, 81, 102, 120–21
market syndrome, 117, 123
market traders, age restrictions on, 10
marriage brokers, 35
medical experiments, 41*n*, 97–98
memoirs, 4, 17
Mexico, 148
microeconomic reforms, 63–64
militarization, 13–14
military-first politics (*Songun*), 14, 77*n*
military personnel
    food aid to, 57*t*, 57–58

likelihood of arrest, 94*n*
    social advancement of, 77*n*
missile program, 13–14, 130
missionaries, 34
Mt. Kumgang tourism project, 12, 135
Mt. Paekdu tourism venture, 136
multilateral cooperation, 132–34
Muntarbhorn, Vitit, 127, 139

National Defense Commission (NDC), 122
National Endowment for Democracy, 153
national ideology (*Juche*), 12
National Security Agency (NSA), 29, 87,
    91, 93
national values, economic reforms and,
    74–75, 75*f*
necessity entrepreneurship, 46
nongovernmental organizations (NGOs),
    127, 143*n*, 153
Northeast Asian Development Bank, 133
North Korea, lack of data on, 4, 4*n*
North Korean Freedom Act of 2003, 154
North Korean Freedom Coalition, 153
North Korean Human Rights Act
    (NKHRA), 145, 153–55
North Korean population
    "direct" engagement policies, 138–45
    economic reform and, 74–75, 75*f*
    educational attainment, 21*t*, 21–22
    food access, 54–55, 55*f*
    income from private business activities,
        61–62, 62*f*
    political attitudes, 106, 107*f*
    political attitudes of, 112, 113*f*
    survey inferences about, 162–63
North-South summit (2000), 5, 65
nuclear crisis
    first (1992-94), 13
    second (2002), 5, 8, 121
nuclear tests, 13–14, 130
*nullum crimen sine lege* (no crime without
    law), 85*n*, 94
number of refugees, 2*b*

occupational status
    assessment of well-being and, 73*n*
    generational mobility in, 22–24
    likelihood of arrest and, 94*n*
    political attitudes by, 111
    private business activities and, 58–59, 61,
        70, 72*t*
    psychological health and, 41–42
    in refugees, 22–24, 23*t*
official social status (*seong bun*), 15

opportunity entrepreneurship, 46
Orascom, 132
Organization for Economic Cooperation
    and Development (OECD), 136, 145
output, composition of, 126

Pak Tok-hun, 139
Park Nam-ki, 9, 10, 10*n*
party officials
    corruption (*See* corruption)
    political attitudes of, 111
    private business activities of, 58–59, 61,
        70, 72*t*
PDS. *See* public distribution system
penal code
    on border crossing, 11, 27, 29, 91, 98
    crime categories, 89, 90*t*
    economic versus political refugees, 29
    2004 reforms of, 82, 85*n*, 86, 94–95
penal system, 13, 86–93. *See also*
        incarceration; prisoners; *specific type
        of prison*
    corruption in, 82–83, 95, 99
    human rights issues, 142
    institutionalization of repression, 98–99,
        115
    nature of punishment, 94–98
    overview of, 91, 92*t*
    repatriation, 27–28
penitentiaries (*kyo-hwa-so*), 91, 92*t*
    abuse in, 97*t*, 97–98
    human rights issues, 142
    legal process and, 95
    length of imprisonment in, 95, 96*t*
People's Life Bonds, 64, 64*n*
People's Security Agency (PSA), 88, 88*n*, 93
People's Security Ministry, 88*n*
personal aspirations, 107–109
planning system, market opportunities and,
    84–85
political attitudes, 16, 101–17
    access to information and, 112–14, 116,
        145
    age and, 111
    communication of, 109–12, 116
    currency reform and, 123
    by date of exit, 103–105
    forms of resistance, 112–15
    incarceration and, 111
    national sample, 112, 113*f*
    by occupational status, 111
    perceptions of regime performance,
        103–106, 104*f*, 105*f*
    political stability and, 124

private business activities and, 111
    provincial distribution of, 106*n*, 111
    by social class, 105–106, 115–16
    social surveillance and, 101–102, 115
    survey inferences and, 163
    by time abroad, 106
political conditions, as push factor, 30*t*,
    30–31, 103–104
political economy, 5–15
    of economic reforms, 46, 62–65, 79
    future direction of, 120–25
political freedoms, absence of, 12–13
political offenders, classification as, 28
political police (*bo-wi-bu*), 31, 87
political prison camps (*kwan-li-so*), 13, 82,
    86–87
    abuse in, 97*t*, 97–98
    hard labor in, 89
    human rights issues, 142
    legal process and, 95
    length of imprisonment in, 95, 96*t*
    overview of, 92*t*
    repatriated refugees in, 91
political system, features of, 12–15
postfamine era group, 26, 104–105
postreform group, 16, 26
post-traumatic stress disorder (PTSD), 19,
    36
preference falsification, 101
pregnant women, forced abortions, 28, 29,
    40–41, 96
prereform group, 16, 26
pretrial agent, 94
price levels, economic reforms and, 9, 63
principal-agent relationships, market
    opportunities and, 84–85
prisoners. *See also* incarceration; penal
        system
    abuse of, 82–83, 87, 97*t*, 97–98
    medical experiments on, 41*n*, 97–98
    political, 13
private business activities, 6. *See also*
        marketization from below
    criminalization of, 83–86, 84*f*, 98–99
    engagement in, 59, 59*t*
    household earnings from, 58–62, 60*f*, 62*f*
    income from, 58–62, 59*t*, 60*f*, 62*f*
    political attitudes and, 111
    in postreform era, 66–68, 67*f*
    in prereform era, 45–46, 48–50
    work unit classification and, 58–59, 61,
        70, 72*t*
private lending, 136–37
private sector involvement, from

demographic profile, 20–27, 162–63
on economic reforms, 66, 67f, 68, 69f, 70, 71t, 72t, 77, 78t
on food access, 50–51, 52f, 53f, 55f
food aid perceptions, 56t–57t, 56–58
"four era" periodization, 26
future aspirations, 107–109
household earnings, 58
length of imprisonment, 96t
length of time in South Korea, 27
on marketization from below, 47
occupational status, 22n, 22–24, 23t
perceptions of socialist system, 47
political attitudes, 105f, 105–106, 107f
political communication, 110–11
private business activities, 59t, 59–61, 60f
provincial distribution, 162–63
push factors, 29–31, 30t
resettlement preferences, 107–109, 108f
on social changes, 75–77, 76f
surveys (*See* refugee surveys)
trade with, 8
Soviet Union
dissolution of, 5, 45, 120
refugee surveys, 17, 17n
special economic zones, 135
"speed-battle" mobilization campaigns, 10
state development bank, 130
state-owned enterprises (SOEs), 45, 58–59
economic reforms and, 63, 70, 71t, 74
Sullivan Principles, 145–46
Sunshine Policy (South Korea), 152
Supreme People's Assembly, 122
surveillance
border, 29
social, 101–102, 115
surveys. *See* refugee surveys

taxation, 64, 64n, 132
technical assistance, 133
third countries, on-migration via, 2b, 21, 33, 34–35, 43
time abroad, 26–27, 33, 33t, 43–44, 106
torture, 13, 82, 87, 97t, 97–98
trade
with China, 8
international, 126–27
with South Korea, 8
state control of, 11
trafficking
executions for, 11, 29
fear of, 39, 39t

of women, 19, 33–36, 42, 152
transactions tax, 64, 64n
Transparency International, 130–31
transportation sector, 134–35
treatment effect, 16
trust in society, 115, 123
Tumen River project, 134

unification of Korean peninsula, attitudes toward, 109, 110f, 116
United Nations
Children's Fund (UNICEF), 133
Convention against Torture and Other Cruel, Inhuman or Degrading Treatment or Punishment, 142
Council on Human Rights, 148n
Development Program, 133
Food and Agriculture Organization (FAO), 4n
High Commissioner for Refugees (UNHCR), 28, 147
Human Rights Committee, 148n
Security Council, 130, 144
special rapporteur for human rights, 139
special rapporteur on food and hunger, 143
Working Group on Arbitrary Imprisonment, 142
World Food Program (WFP), 4n, 7, 55, 127, 129, 143n
United States
Agency for International Development (USAID), 55n
diplomatic relations with North Korea, 156
food aid from, 129
policy on refugees, 153–56
political relations with, 13–14
resettlement in, 107–109, 108f, 150, 154–55
Universal Periodic Review, 144

wages, 33–34, 63
well-being
assessment of, 73–75, 75f
perceived pathways to, 75–77, 76f
women. *See* female refugees
work unit classification. *See* occupational status
World Bank, 130–31, 133
World Food Program (WFP), 4n, 7, 55, 127, 129, 143n
World Health Organization, 133
World Trade Organization, 133

## Other Publications from the Peterson Institute for International Economics

### WORKING PAPERS

* = out of print

The Future of World Trade in Textiles and
Apparel*                    William R. Cline
*1987, 2d ed. June 1999*     ISBN 0-88132-110-9
Completing the Uruguay Round: A Results-
Oriented Approach to the GATT Trade
Negotiations*               Jeffrey J. Schott, ed.
*September 1990*             ISBN 0-88132-130-3
Economic Sanctions Reconsidered (2 volumes)
Economic Sanctions Reconsidered:
Supplemental Case Histories
Gary Clyde Hufbauer, Jeffrey J. Schott, and
Kimberly Ann Elliott
*1985, 2d ed. Dec. 1990*   ISBN cloth 0-88132-115-X
                            ISBN paper 0-88132-105-2
Economic Sanctions Reconsidered: History
and Current Policy        Gary Clyde Hufbauer,
Jeffrey J. Schott, and Kimberly Ann Elliott
*December 1990*           ISBN cloth 0-88132-140-0
                            ISBN paper 0-88132-136-2
Pacific Basin Developing Countries: Prospects
for the Future*                Marcus Noland
*January 1991*              ISBN cloth 0-88132-141-9
                            ISBN paper 0-88132-081-1
Currency Convertibility in Eastern Europe*
John Williamson, ed.
*October 1991*              ISBN 0-88132-128-1
International Adjustment and Financing: The
Lessons of 1985-1991*      C. Fred Bergsten, ed.
*January 1992*              ISBN 0-88132-112-5
North American Free Trade: Issues and
Recommendations*     Gary Clyde Hufbauer and
Jeffrey J. Schott
*April 1992*                ISBN 0-88132-120-6
Narrowing the U.S. Current Account Deficit*
Alan J. Lenz
*June 1992*                 ISBN 0-88132-103-6
The Economics of Global Warming
William R. Cline
*June 1992*                 ISBN 0-88132-132-X
US Taxation of International Income:
Blueprint for Reform     Gary Clyde Hufbauer,
assisted by Joanna M. van Rooij
*October 1992*             ISBN 0-88132-134-6
Who's Bashing Whom? Trade Conflict in High-
Technology Industries   Laura D'Andrea Tyson
*November 1992*            ISBN 0-88132-106-0
Korea in the World Economy*        Il SaKong
*January 1993*             ISBN 0-88132-183-4
Pacific Dynamism and the International
Economic System*        C. Fred Bergsten and
Marcus Noland, eds.
*May 1993*                 ISBN 0-88132-196-6
Economic Consequences of Soviet
Disintegration*         John Williamson, ed.
*May 1993*                 ISBN 0-88132-190-7
Reconcilable Differences? United States-Japan
Economic Conflict*      C. Fred Bergsten and
Marcus Noland
*June 1993*                ISBN 0-88132-129-X
Does Foreign Exchange Intervention Work?
Kathryn M. Dominguez and Jeffrey A. Frankel
*September 1993*           ISBN 0-88132-104-4

Sizing Up U.S. Export Disincentives*
J. David Richardson
*September 1993*           ISBN 0-88132-107-9
NAFTA: An Assessment
Gary Clyde Hufbauer and Jeffrey J. Schott, *rev. ed.*
*October 1993*             ISBN 0-88132-199-0
Adjusting to Volatile Energy Prices
Philip K. Verleger, Jr.
*November 1993*            ISBN 0-88132-069-2
The Political Economy of Policy Reform
John Williamson, ed.
*January 1994*             ISBN 0-88132-195-8
Measuring the Costs of Protection in the
United States         Gary Clyde Hufbauer and
Kimberly Ann Elliott
*January 1994*             ISBN 0-88132-108-7
The Dynamics of Korean Economic
Development*                     Cho Soon
*March 1994*               ISBN 0-88132-162-1
Reviving the European Union*
C. Randall Henning, Eduard Hochreiter, and
Gary Clyde Hufbauer, eds.
*April 1994*               ISBN 0-88132-208-3
China in the World Economy
Nicholas R. Lardy
*April 1994*               ISBN 0-88132-200-8
Greening the GATT: Trade, Environment,
and the Future              Daniel C. Esty
*July 1994*                ISBN 0-88132-205-9
Western Hemisphere Economic Integration*
Gary Clyde Hufbauer and Jeffrey J. Schott
*July 1994*                ISBN 0-88132-159-1
Currencies and Politics in the United States,
Germany, and Japan       C. Randall Henning
*September 1994*           ISBN 0-88132-127-3
Estimating Equilibrium Exchange Rates
John Williamson, ed.
*September 1994*           ISBN 0-88132-076-5
Managing the World Economy: Fifty Years
after Bretton Woods      Peter B. Kenen, ed.
*September 1994*           ISBN 0-88132-212-1
Reciprocity and Retaliation in U.S. Trade
Policy                   Thomas O. Bayard and
Kimberly Ann Elliott
*September 1994*           ISBN 0-88132-084-6
The Uruguay Round: An Assessment*
Jeffrey J. Schott, assisted by Johanna Buurman
*November 1994*            ISBN 0-88132-206-7
Measuring the Costs of Protection in Japan*
Yoko Sazanami, Shujiro Urata, and Hiroki Kawai
*January 1995*             ISBN 0-88132-211-3
Foreign Direct Investment in the United States,
3d ed.                   Edward M. Graham and
Paul R. Krugman
*January 1995*             ISBN 0-88132-204-0
The Political Economy of Korea-United States
Cooperation*             C. Fred Bergsten and
Il SaKong, eds.
*February 1995*            ISBN 0-88132-213-X
International Debt Reexamined*
William R. Cline
*February 1995*            ISBN 0-88132-083-8

Reforming the US Corporate Tax
Gary Clyde Hufbauer and Paul L. E. Grieco
*September 2005*          ISBN 0-88132-384-5
The United States as a Debtor Nation
William R. Cline
*September 2005*          ISBN 0-88132-399-3
NAFTA Revisited: Achievements and
Challenges          Gary Clyde Hufbauer and
Jeffrey J. Schott, assisted by Paul L. E. Grieco and
Yee Wong
*October 2005*          ISBN 0-88132-334-9
US National Security and Foreign Direct
Investment          Edward M. Graham and
David M. Marchick
*May 2006*          ISBN 978-0-88132-391-7
Accelerating the Globalization of America: The
Role for Information Technology
Catherine L. Mann, assisted by Jacob Funk
Kirkegaard
*June 2006*          ISBN 978-0-88132-390-0
Delivering on Doha: Farm Trade and the Poor
Kimberly Ann Elliott
*July 2006*          ISBN 978-0-88132-392-4
Case Studies in US Trade Negotiation, Vol. 1:
Making the Rules          Charan Devereaux,
Robert Z. Lawrence, and Michael Watkins
*September 2006*          ISBN 978-0-88132-362-7
Case Studies in US Trade Negotiation, Vol. 2:
Resolving Disputes          Charan Devereaux,
Robert Z. Lawrence, and Michael Watkins
*September 2006*          ISBN 978-0-88132-363-2
C. Fred Bergsten and the World Economy
Michael Mussa, ed.
*December 2006*          ISBN 978-0-88132-397-9
Working Papers, Volume I          Peterson Institute
*December 2006*          ISBN 978-0-88132-388-7
The Arab Economies in a Changing World
Marcus Noland and Howard Pack
*April 2007*          ISBN 978-0-88132-393-1
Working Papers, Volume II          Peterson Institute
*April 2007*          ISBN 978-0-88132-404-4
Global Warming and Agriculture: Impact
Estimates by Country          William R. Cline
*July 2007*          ISBN 978-0-88132-403-7
US Taxation of Foreign Income
Gary Clyde Hufbauer and Ariel Assa
*October 2007*          ISBN 978-0-88132-405-1
Russia's Capitalist Revolution: Why Market
Reform Succeeded and Democracy Failed
Anders Åslund
*October 2007*          ISBN 978-0-88132-409-9
Economic Sanctions Reconsidered, 3d ed.
Gary Clyde Hufbauer, Jeffrey J. Schott, Kimberly
Ann Elliott, and Barbara Oegg
*November 2007*
          ISBN hardcover 978-0-88132-407-5
          ISBN hardcover/CD-ROM 978-0-88132-408-2
Debating China's Exchange Rate Policy
Morris Goldstein and Nicholas R. Lardy, eds.
*April 2008*          ISBN 978-0-88132-415-0
Leveling the Carbon Playing Field:

International Competition and US Climate
Policy Design          Trevor Houser, Rob Bradley, Britt
Childs, Jacob Werksman, and Robert Heilmayr
*May 2008*          ISBN 978-0-88132-420-4
Accountability and Oversight of US Exchange
Rate Policy          C. Randall Henning
*June 2008*          ISBN 978-0-88132-419-8
Challenges of Globalization: Imbalances and
Growth          Anders Åslund and
Marek Dabrowski, eds.
*July 2008*          ISBN 978-0-88132-418-1
China's Rise: Challenges and Opportunities
C. Fred Bergsten, Charles Freeman, Nicholas R.
Lardy, and Derek J. Mitchell
*September 2008*          ISBN 978-0-88132-417-4
Banking on Basel: The Future of International
Financial Regulation          Daniel K. Tarullo
*September 2008*          ISBN 978-0-88132-423-5
US Pension Reform: Lessons from Other
Countries          Martin Neil Baily and
Jacob Funk Kirkegaard
*February 2009*          ISBN 978-0-88132-425-9
How Ukraine Became a Market Economy and
Democracy          Anders Åslund
*March 2009*          ISBN 978-0-88132-427-3
Global Warming and the World Trading
System          Gary Clyde Hufbauer,
Steve Charnovitz, and Jisun Kim
*March 2009*          ISBN 978-0-88132-428-0
The Russia Balance Sheet          Anders Åslund and
Andrew Kuchins
*March 2009*          ISBN 978-0-88132-424-2
The Euro at Ten: The Next Global Currency?
Jean Pisani-Ferry and Adam S. Posen, eds.
*July 2009*          ISBN 978-0-88132-430-3
Financial Globalization, Economic Growth, and
the Crisis of 2007–09          William R. Cline
*May 2010*          ISBN 978-0-88132-4990-0
Russia after the Global Economic Crisis
Anders Åslund, Sergei Guriev, and Andrew
Kuchins, eds.
*June 2010*          ISBN 978-0-88132-497-6
Sovereign Wealth Funds: Threat or Salvation?
Edwin M. Truman
*September 2010*          ISBN 978-0-88132-498-3
The Last Shall Be the First: The East European
Financial Crisis, 2008–10          Anders Åslund
*October 2010*          ISBN 978-0-88132-521-8
Witness to Transformation: Refugee Insights
into North Korea          Stephan Haggard and
Marcus Noland
*January 2011*          ISBN 978-0-88132-438-9

SPECIAL REPORTS

1    Promoting World Recovery: A Statement
     on Global Economic Strategy*
     by 26 Economists from Fourteen Countries
     *December 1982*          ISBN 0-88132-013-7
2    Prospects for Adjustment in Argentina,
     Brazil, and Mexico: Responding to the
     Debt Crisis*          John Williamson, ed.
     *June 1983*          ISBN 0-88132-016-1

WORKS IN PROGRESS

China's Energy Evolution: The Consequences of Powering Growth at Home and Abroad
Daniel H. Rosen and Trevor Houser
Global Identity Theft: Economic and Policy Implications    Catherine L. Mann
Globalized Venture Capital: Implications for US Entrepreneurship and Innovation
Catherine L. Mann
Forging a Grand Bargain: Expanding Trade and Raising Worker Prosperity    Lori G. Kletzer, J. David Richardson, and Howard F. Rosen
Why Reform a Rich Country? Germany and the Future of Capitalism    Adam S. Posen
Global Forces, American Faces: US Economic Globalization at the Grass Roots
J. David Richardson
The Impact of Global Services Outsourcing on American Firms and Workers    J. Bradford Jensen
Policy Reform in Rich Countries
John Williamson, ed.
Banking System Fragility in Emerging Economies    Morris Goldstein and Philip Turner
Aligning NAFTA with Climate Change Objectives    Jeffrey J. Schott, Meera Fickling, and Tanya Lat
Private Rights and Public Problems: The Global Economics of Intellectual Property in the 21st Century    Keith Maskus
The Positive Agenda for Climate Change and Trade    Trevor Houser, Jacob Funk Kirkegaard, and Rob Bradley
Stable Prices, Unstable Currencies: The Weak Link between Exchange Rates and Inflation and What It Means for Economic Policy
Joseph E. Gagnon
How Latvia Came through the Financial Crisis
Anders Åslund and Valdis Dombrovskis
Foreign Direct Investment and Development: Launching a Second Generation of Policy Research, Avoiding the Mistakes of the First, and Reevaluating Policies for Developed and Developing Countries    Theodore H. Moran
Carbon Abatement Costs and Climate Change Finance    William R. Cline

**Australia, New Zealand,
and Papua New Guinea**
D. A. Information Services
648 Whitehorse Road
Mitcham, Victoria 3132, Australia
Tel: 61-3-9210-7777
Fax: 61-3-9210-7788
Email: service@dadirect.com.au
www.dadirect.com.au

**India, Bangladesh, Nepal, and Sri Lanka**
Viva Books Private Limited
Mr. Vinod Vasishtha
4737/23 Ansari Road
Daryaganj, New Delhi 110002
India
Tel: 91-11-4224-2200
Fax: 91-11-4224-2240
Email: viva@vivagroupindia.net
www.vivagroupindia.com

**Mexico, Central America, South America,
and Puerto Rico**
US PubRep, Inc.
311 Dean Drive
Rockville, MD 20851
Tel: 301-838-9276
Fax: 301-838-9278
Email: c.falk@ieee.org

**Asia (*Brunei, Burma, Cambodia, China,
Hong Kong, Indonesia, Korea, Laos, Malaysia,
Philippines, Singapore, Taiwan, Thailand,
and Vietnam*)**
East-West Export Books (EWEB)
University of Hawaii Press
2840 Kolowalu Street
Honolulu, Hawaii 96822-1888
Tel: 808-956-8830
Fax: 808-988-6052
Email: eweb@hawaii.edu

**Canada**
Renouf Bookstore
5369 Canotek Road, Unit 1
Ottawa, Ontario KlJ 9J3, Canada
Tel: 613-745-2665
Fax: 613-745-7660
www.renoufbooks.com

**Japan**
United Publishers Services Ltd.
1-32-5, Higashi-shinagawa
Shinagawa-ku, Tokyo 140-0002
Japan
Tel: 81-3-5479-7251
Fax: 81-3-5479-7307
Email: purchasing@ups.co.jp ˙
*For trade accounts only. Individuals will find
Institute books in leading Tokyo bookstores.*

**Middle East**
MERIC
2 Bahgat Ali Street, El Masry Towers
Tower D, Apt. 24
Zamalek, Cairo
Egypt
Tel. 20-2-7633824
Fax: 20-2-7369355
Email: mahmoud_fouda@mericonline.com
www.mericonline.com

**United Kingdom, Europe
(*including Russia and Turkey*), Africa,
and Israel**
The Eurospan Group
c/o Turpin Distribution
Pegasus Drive
Stratton Business Park
Biggleswade, Bedfordshire
SG18 8TQ
United Kingdom
Tel: 44 (0) 1767-604972
Fax: 44 (0) 1767-601640
Email: eurospan@turpin-distribution.com
www.eurospangroup.com/bookstore

**Visit our website at:
www.piie.com
E-mail orders to:
petersonmail@presswarehouse.com**